Autonomous Mobile Robots in Unknown Outdoor Environments

Autonomous Mobile Robots in Unknown Outdoor Environments

Xiaorui Zhu, Youngshik Kim,
Mark Andrew Minor, and Chunxin Qiu

CRC Press
Taylor & Francis Group
Boca Raton London New York

CRC Press is an imprint of the
Taylor & Francis Group, an **informa** business

Cover photo courtesy of Dadao, Inc.

CRC Press
Taylor & Francis Group
6000 Broken Sound Parkway NW, Suite 300
Boca Raton, FL 33487-2742

First issued in paperback 2020

ISBN 13: 978-0-367-57248-8 (pbk)
ISBN 13: 978-1-4987-4055-5 (hbk)

Visit the Taylor & Francis Web site at
http://www.taylorandfrancis.com

and the CRC Press Web site at
http://www.crcpress.com

Library of Congress Cataloging-in-Publication Data

Names: Zhu, Xiaorui, author. | Kim, Youngshik, author. | Minor, Mark Andrew, author. | Qiu, Chunxin, author.
Title: Autonomous mobile robots in unknown outdoor environments / Xiaorui Zhu, Youngshik Kim, Mark Andrew Minor, Chunxin Qiu.
Description: Boca Raton, FL : CRC Press, Taylor & Francis Group, 2017. | Includes bibliographical references.
Identifiers: LCCN 2017037806 | ISBN 9781498740555 (hb : alk. paper)
Subjects: LCSH: Mobile robots. | Robots--Control systems.
Classification: LCC TJ211.415 .Z49 2017 | DDC 629.8/93--dc23
LC record available at https://lccn.loc.gov/2017037806

Contents

SECTION IV   LOCALIZATION AND MAPPING

Authors

Xiaorui Zhu received BS and MS degrees from Harbin Institute of Technology, Heilongjiang Sheng, China, in 1998 and 2000, respectively, and a PhD degree from the University of Utah, Salt Lake City, Utah, in 2006, all in mechanical engineering. She is currently a professor in the department of automation engineering at Harbin Institute of Technology (Shenzhen), China, where she has been a faculty member since 2007. She has also been the chief scientist and cofounder of several high-tech companies, including DJI International, Inc., and RoboSense, Inc., Shenzhen, China. Her main research interests include mobile robots, unmanned aerial vehicles, autonomous driving, and 3D modeling.

Youngshik Kim received a BS degree from Inha University, Incheon, South Korea, in 1996, and MS and PhD degrees from the University of Utah, Salt Lake City, Utah, in 2003 and 2008, respectively, all in mechanical engineering. He is currently an associate professor in the department of mechanical engineering at Hanbat National University, Daejeon, South Korea. His main research interests include shape memory alloy actuators, bio-inspired robots, sensor fusion, motion control, mobility, and manipulation of compliant robotic systems.

Mark Andrew Minor received a BS degree (1993) in mechanical engineering from the University of Michigan, Ann Arbor, Michigan, and MS (1996) and PhD degrees (2000) in mechanical engineering from Michigan State University, East Lansing, Michigan. He is currently an associate professor with the department of mechanical engineering, University of Utah, Salt Lake City, Utah, where he has been a faculty member since 2000. He is also an adjunct associate professor of computing with the School of Computing, University of Utah. His research interests include the design and control of robotic systems with emphasis on mobile robots, automated ground vehicles, aerial robots, rehabilitative systems, and virtual reality systems.

Chunxin Qiu received a BS degree from Yanshan University, Hebei, China, in 2007, and MS and PhD degrees from Harbin Institute of Technology (Shenzhen), Heilongjiang Sheng, China, in 2010 and 2014, respectively, all in automation engineering. He is currently the CEO of RoboSense, Inc., Shenzhen in China.

INTRODUCTION

1

Introduction

Chapter 1

Introduction

1.1 Outdoor Mobile Robots

In simple terms, a robot is defined as a machine with certain degrees of intelligence. At the preliminary stages, much of the research in this area was focused on robotic arms and manipulators. However, the rapid growth of the automobile industry in the 1980s led to the domination of commercialized manipulators. Since then, the manipulators have become an integral part of the automobile manufacturing industry.

In comparison with the manipulators, mobile robotics is still a relatively young area of research. The great deal of interest in mobile robots is because of their mobility, typical examples of which include unmanned aerial vehicles (UAVs), land rovers, and autonomous driving cars. The most basic part of a mobile robot is the locomotion mechanism, which is quite different from the manipulator's. There are various types of locomotion mechanisms, and each of these poses a different level of challenge in the control of mobile robotic systems.

Autonomy is another significant factor that determines the complexity of mobile robot systems. *Autonomy* refers to the capability of the system to operate in a real-world environment without any external interference for extended periods of time [1]. Previously, it was believed that the final goal of mobile robots was to achieve a full autonomy similar to living systems. But in recent years, the different voices from robotics academia have shifted their focus to semi-autonomy, which is considered to be the most efficient way in which a robot and a human being can take their own advantages and share tasks. Nevertheless, the degree of autonomy is still considered a measure of performance for a mobile robot. Readers may notice that the mobile robots mentioned in this chapter have different levels of autonomy.

Mobile robots have to deal with different environmental conditions. The basic difference between the manipulators and mobile robots is that the latter have to interact with surrounding environments. These can vary from highly structured scenarios to highly unstructured ones, whose terrains could be flat or uneven. Moreover, the environment could be either a small area or a very large one. There are different challenges associated with the system design of mobile robots, and these challenges depend upon the working environment. Among the different types of environments, the outdoor environments are usually the most challenging, e.g., unstructured surroundings, uneven terrains, and a large-scale exploration area. Most things became complicated outdoors. Therefore, mobile robots working outdoors, also called field robotics, have been an active research area for the last decade. Although field robots can work on land, in the air, or under water, this book mainly focuses on field robots on land.

A number of diverse applications have called for mobile robots, especially outdoors. In many outdoor scenarios, people seek help from mobile robots either because of tough or even dangerous working conditions or because of a demand for long-term tedious work. Such real-world applications span from government-driven needs (such as planetary exploration, military applications, and archeological exploration) to industry-driven needs (such as those of forest, farming, and mining industries) to humanistic needs (such as search and rescue).

Planetary exploration was the earliest application of outdoor mobile robots. The typical robotic rover was *Curiosity*, which was launched in 2011. It was designed for exploring Gale Crater on Mars as part of NASA's Mars Science Laboratory [2], Figure 1.1. *Curiosity* had six wheels: two middle wheels went straight, and the corner wheels were omnidirectional. Since the rover might cross rugged terrain,

Figure 1.1 *Curiosity,* **designed for exploring Gale Crater on Mars [2].**

the rocker-bogie design of the chassis was invented to allow the rover to keep all of its wheels even on an uneven surface. Jet Propulsion Laboratory (JPL) stated that this rocker-bogie system had reduced the motion of the main rover body by half compared to other suspension systems. The *Curiosity* was also equipped with an inertial measurement unit (IMU) to support safe traverses. Autonomy of *Curiosity* was kept low because of the special circumstances of space exploration, in which most activities, such as taking pictures, driving, and operating the instruments, would be performed under commands from the flight team.

The forest industry is another field that always has a strong desire to embrace mobile robotic systems. Umea University in Sweden initiated a project called Autonomous Navigation for Forest Machines in 2002 whose long-term goal is to develop an unmanned vehicle that transports timber from the area of felling to the roadside, and that addresses the problems with localization and obstacle avoidance in forest terrain [3]. Moreover, Swedish University of Agriculture Sciences proposed a cleaning mobile robot for improving the growing conditions of the remaining trees in young stands [3]. They required such mobile robots to be capable of operating independently and unattended for several hours in a dynamic and nondeterministic environment. However, there are still many unknown challenges in this area because a forest is a typical unstructured environment. From the perspective of forest industry employees, mobile robots have never been successfully employed in the forest industry. One of the most promising mobile robots was Kelly, a harvesting machine in New Zealand in 2010 [4], Figure 1.2. The locomotion of this system adopted lengthened tracks and could traverse on steep terrain up to 45°.

Figure 1.2   Kelly harvesting machine [4].

Military applications have financed many research teams to create and study mobile robots around the world. For example, DARPA Robot Challenges have lasted a few years to encourage and support advancement of technologies and implementations of real-world mobile robots. The BigDog is a four-legged mobile robot that is probably the most notable outcome in the DARPA robotics program created in 2005 [5], Figure 1.3. That is to say, it is required to traverse on a variety of rough terrains autonomously while keeping a proper speed as a companion of a soldier. Approximately 50 sensors were built onto BigDog to interact with the actuators via the onboard computer in order to accomplish autonomous locomotion control, self-balance control, and autonomous navigation. In 2012, the inventors of BigDog claimed that the militarized Legged Squad Support System variant of BigDog had the capability to hike over tough terrain. At the end of February 2013, Boston Dynamics released video footage of a modified BigDog with an arm that can pick up objects and throw them. The robot relies on its legs and torso to help power the motions of the arm [6].

Archeologists have also preferred mobile robots to assist their traditional and tough works. Harbin Institute of Technology (Shenzhen) developed a modular robotic system in 2009 for recording the internal environment of the underground ancient tombs [7], Figure 1.4. This archeological exploration robot could be assembled as either a manipulator or a mobile robot in order to adapt to different situations in the exploration field. It was allowed to enter tombs through narrow digging holes prepared by regular archeological exploration. The recorded data was used for preservation of antiques inside the ancient tombs as well as for providing valuable

Figure 1.3   BigDog [5].

Figure 1.4   Archeological exploration robot [7].

references to the archeological survey. It was designed with low-level autonomy because of the fragile environments inside the ancient tombs.

Search-and-rescue robots were first tested in real scenarios during the September 11 disaster by iRobot and the University of South Florida [8]. These mobile robots were still prone to get stuck and break in the disaster field, although they demonstrated a certain degree of mobility in order to go into dangerous locations for humans. Many roboticists in Japan have focused on rescue robots for a few decades because earthquakes strike more frequently in Japan than in other countries. For instance, researchers in the Tokyo Institute of Technology have designed different types of snakelike robots to adapt to rough terrain such as Genbu or Souryu [9], Figure 1.5. Genbu is a modular wheeled mobile robot with passive bending joints, whereas Souryu uses tracks with active bending joints.

Figure 1.5   Snakelike robots [9]. (a) Genbu and (b) Souryu.

The unmanned aerial vehicle (UAV) is also a member of the mobile robot family. From large, military-purpose UAVs to consumer-electronics drones, these flying robots have been adopted in a large variety of applications. In 2015, a research project was launched for power network inspection using a robotic copter equipped with advanced sensors [10]. Three-dimensional mapping of the ancient Great Wall heritage using a UAV with a laser scanner was developed by the Harbin Institute of Technology at Shenzhen in 2015 to help record and preserve the cultural heritage [11], Figure 1.6.

The autonomous driving car is another typical field robotic system that has attracted the attention of more and more researchers from both academia and industry in the last decade. The DARPA Urban Challenge, initiated in 2007, is widely known as the competition of autonomous driving cars. Boss, developed by Carnegie Mellon University, was the first winner of this competition with a speed of 22.53 km/h [12], Figure 1.7. Two driverless vans, developed by VisLab at University of Parma in Italy, spent three months traveling to the World Expo of Shanghai from Parma, Italy, an overall traveling distance of around 13,000 km [13], Figure 1.8. Google self-driving cars have traveled over 2,400,000 km as of March, 2016, Figure 1.9 [14].

Some of the aforementioned demands have served as strong motivations to cultivate research in outdoor mobile robotics for more advanced and practical applications. Therefore, different research platforms have also been built commercially including Pioneer 3-AT by Omron Adept MobileRobots, SUMMIT XL STEEL by Robotnik Automation, and Husky by Clearpath Robotics [15–17], Figure 1.10.

In summary, in order to design a complete outdoor mobile robot, we should face the following challenges:

Figure 1.6 **The UAV platform used to build the 3D model of the ancient Great Wall heritage. Courtesy of Harbin Institute of Technology.**

■ Locomotion design to traverse rough natural terrain
■ Precise automatic motion control to move to a specific location or follow a specific path
■ An increase of the level of autonomy via perception of unstructured surroundings and self-localization

Figure 1.7   Boss, the autonomous vehicle that won the 2007 DARPA Urban Challenge [12].

Figure 1.8   The VisLab autonomous vehicle [13].

Figure 1.9   The Google self-driving car [14].

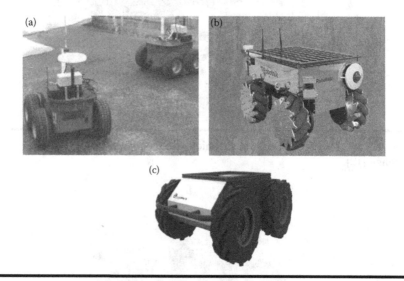

Figure 1.10   Research platforms. (a) Pioneer 3-AT by Omron Adept MobileRobots [16]. (b) SUMMIT XL STEEL by Robotnik Automation [17]. (c) Husky by Clearpath Robotics [15].

Although researchers and scientists have designed various locomotion mechanisms for mobile robots, we have to admit that the most efficient way so far is to use wheels as the mechanism for land locomotion. Wheels can be treated as simplified yet efficient legs, from the perspective of biology inspiration. So the authors of this book designed a compliant, framed, wheeled, modular mobile robot (CFMMR) as a prototype robot, Figure 1.11, which can stand for one category of outdoor mobile robots. Meanwhile, the authors present a general approach to accomplishing precise motion control of the robot, even on rough terrain, to achieve self-localization and mapping of the surroundings.

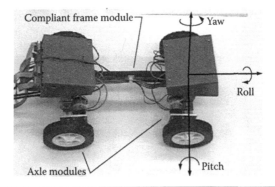

Figure 1.11   CFMMR two-axle scout experimental configuration.

1.2 Overview of the Book

This book discusses many aspects of field robotic systems, such as mechanism design, motion control, localization, and mapping, in which most methodologies were integrated and tested by a prototype wheeled robot, e.g., CFMMR. The involved frameworks and algorithms for designing autonomous mobile robots in unknown outdoor environments are expected to inspire readers to develop more technologies in the field of robotics.

In Chapter 2, the locomotion mechanisms of outdoor mobile robots are discussed. The prototype robot of this book is also presented and analyzed in this chapter in terms of both mobility and maneuverability. In Chapter 3, a general cooperative control and sensing framework is presented. It defines each subsystem and the corresponding requirements of a robot control system including kinematic motion control, dynamic motion control, and a sensory system. Chapters 4 through 7 talk about how to design these subsystems individually to satisfy the requirements mentioned in Chapter 3. In the preceding chapters, the example of a Compliant Framed Wheeled Modular Mobile Robot (CFMMR) provides detailed illustration and experimental verification of related techniques. The methodologies presented after Chapter 7 are more general to field robots. The topic of Chapter 8 is localization and mapping, which can be considered as a higher level of mobile robotic system design. What if a field robot moves around large-scaled environments in which more data and heavier computational load are demanded? A cloud-based architecture is discussed in Chapter 9 to handle self-localization problems caused by long-term consistent navigation.

MECHANISM

Chapter 2

Locomotion Mechanism

2.1 Introduction

The most important feature of a mobile robot is its locomotion. The locomotion mechanism is the basis of development of any autonomous mobile robot system. Whether the locomotion mechanism is simple or complex affects the ways motion control can be designed. A balance between mechanism design and motion control design exists to a certain degree. A simpler mechanism might need more complicated control and vice versa.

When a mobile robot is working outdoors, it may encounter rough off-road terrains or bumps on the roads. This requires that the mechanism of an outdoor mobile robot should be designed to adapt to such nonflat terrains. A variety of design methods have been reported in the literature about field robots, but among these various locomotion designs, legged mechanism, tracked mechanism, and wheeled mechanism are the most popular signs.

From the view of biological inspiration, a legged mechanism is more natural for traversing rough and unstructured terrain because human beings and most animals move in this way. However, a higher degree of freedom and greater mechanical complexity are required in order to achieve movement in the real world. Tracked mechanisms can be found in many outdoor applications such as army tanks, because they have much larger ground contact patches and therefore have great maneuverability and traction over rough and loose terrain. But it is difficult to achieve precise locomotion control because the large amount of skidding during a turn can cause severe and unpredictable slippage on different terrains [18]. Wheeled mechanisms are the most favorable for mobile robots indoors because of their mechanical simplicity and therefore high efficiency. But the question is, how can such advantages be extended to field robots? Variations of these wheeled mechanisms have been developed in the past few years for mobile robots in outdoor environments among which compliant elements are one of the promising mechanisms to allow mobile robots to adapt to rough terrain without much efficiency loss. In fact, efficiency would dramatically decrease if a wheeled mobile robot had to move on very soft or slippery ground. But wheeled field robots are a very broad interdisciplinary subject, and a single book cannot cover all their technical aspects. Hence, issues caused by soft ground are not addressed in this book.

2.2 Compliant Design in Wheeled Mobile Robots

The earliest found reference of compliant vehicles was a system proposed for planetary exploration using compliant members to provide roll and pitch degrees of freedom (DOF) for suspension of the axles [19]. This concept was later extended [20] to the frame of a vehicle composed of helical spring(s) with hydraulic cylinders used to control deflection. In each of these cases, compliance was introduced for accommodating terrain.

Another reference in 1995 introduced compliance for accommodating position measurement error and preventing wheel slip from occurring between independently controlled axle units on a service robot [21]. This robot allowed relative axle yaw that was provided by rotary joints connected to the ends of a frame with limited prismatic compliance. Other flexible robots used actuated articulated joints to provide relative motion between axles, as in the case of the Marsokhod rover [22] and other six-wheeled research rovers with high relative DOF [23]. These actuated kinematic structures provided more direct control of the robot's shape, but it was accomplished at the expense of system complexity.

Compliant design can also be found in some snakelike mobile robots that consist of a serial chain of modules [24]. Inspired by some continuum manipulators, several active-joint articulated snakelike mobile robots have been designed [25,26] so that the serial chain interacts with the ground to propel the robot. Many of these have wheels on the modules for reduced friction or for establishing well-defined kinematics. In some cases, the articulated joints are active and the wheels are passive [27], and in other cases, the wheels are active and articulation is either partially active [28,29] or entirely passive. Active wheels provide direct control over forward velocity and are suitable for traveling over terrain. Active joints allow direct control over robot shape, such as for climbing over very large obstacles, but they are usually slow due to high-torque demands and limited space. Thus, passive compliant joints have evolved for natural terrain adaptation to reduce impact loads damaging to active joints and to facilitate faster travel over rugged terrain. The CFMMR was designed as the prototype of those mobile robots with compliant design while replacing complex and expensive mechanical joints with higher potential for failure with simple and cost-effective compliance. The CFMMR uses passive compliance in a similar spirit to provide independent suspension and advanced steering control between the axles without additional hardware or actuators. The CFMMR is also modular and facilitates numerous configurations and applications. The CFMMR provides similar capability to adapt to terrain, but possesses a minimal locomotion mechanism by which the deflection of the highly compliant frame is controlled by coordinated actuation of the wheels. This mechanism vastly reduces the number of components required to construct a field robotic system, reduces probability of component failure, and allows aspects of modularity to be exploited. Next, in the remaining sections of this chapter, we analyze system kinematics and dynamics using an example of the CFMMR.

2.3 Compliant, Framed, Wheeled, Modular Mobile Robot

2.3.1 Mechanism

The locomotion mechanism of the CFMMR is designed as a reconfigurable and homogeneous modular system such that different configurations can be formed, such as two-axle scouts, a four-axle train, and a four-axle moving platform, Figure 2.1. Reconfigurable modular robotic systems have been of keen interest to researchers during the last two decades, e.g., reconfigurable manipulation [30–33], mobility [25,26,34], or combinations therein [35–40]. Such reconfigurable systems could improve their abilities to overcome obstacles and perform more tasks using

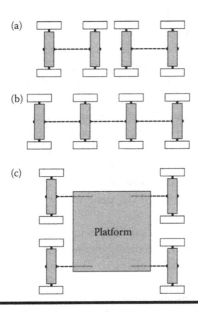

Figure 2.1 Modular configurations. (a) Two-axle scouts, (b) four-axle train, and (c) four-axle array/platform.

a single hardware platform. Moreover, homogeneity could reduce maintenance, increase robustness through redundancy, provide compact and ordered storage, and increase adaptability [25,41]. The CFMMR is an example of applying these concepts on wheeled mobile robots. Hence, various configurations of the CFMMR allow multiple tasks to be achieved. For instance, the two-axle scout configuration is suited to reconnaissance and exploration, whereas the multi-axle train could be tailored to transport payloads for extended distances. The four-axle platform could be utilized to move large objects. As we know, most field robots are required to work in environments with limited resources, such as space exploration, military operations, farming, forestry, and mining. Therefore, the methodology of the locomotion mechanism design of the CFMMR is very inspiring to the ones for resource limited applications.

The two-axle scout is the minimum functional unit that was manufactured, Figure 1.12. This two-axle scout uses a simple structure, i.e., compliant frame elements, to provide suspension and a highly controllable steering capability without adding any additional hardware to the system. To be more exact, a partially compliant frame could provide roll and yaw DOF between the axles. Relative roll provides suspension capability in order to accommodate uneven terrain, and yaw allows the axles to independently change heading for steering. Steering and maneuvering of the system are thus accomplished via coordinated control of the differentially steered axles. Since each axle can be steered independently, the system provides the capability to control the shape of its frame and thus enhance maneuverability in confined environments.

Another feature of the CFMMR is the simplicity of its mechanical design from the perspective of design life and maintenance issues. At the most fundamental level, the axle modules are basic, differentially steered mobile robots; they are rigid structures providing an interface for the frame that support two independently controlled wheels. Other than the wheel drive systems, there are no other moving parts in the axle modules. The compliant frame then provides flexible coupling between the axles to allow them to steer independently and to conform to terrain variations. This alleviates the need for complicated linkages and associated hardware typical of steering and suspension systems. The compliant frame thus significantly reduces complexity and cost of the mechanical structure. Since the only moving parts of the CFMMR are the wheel drive systems, very few components are subject to wear. Thus, the simplicity of the CFMMR design allows straightforward reduction of mechanical failure probability.

Since the CFMMR provides capabilities in steering, mobility, and reconfiguration, modeling of the system needs to be done first to provide a basis for motion control design in the following chapters. The compliance element allows a wide range of steering algorithms to be applied, but it also complicates the kinematic model appreciably and provides significant challenges to motion control algorithms. To simplify the motion control task, steering constraints are established by the ratio of the front and rear axle headings in the following sections. These constraints can provide significant simplification of the kinematics and allow existing unicycle motion control algorithms to be applied. The effect of these simplifications is also illustrated when considering performance metrics such as mobility and maneuverability.

2.3.2 General Kinematic Model

Each axle module in the CFMMR can be treated as a differentially steered, unicycle-type mobile robot, Figure 2.2. Different from unicycle robots that gain stability from additional castor wheels fore and aft of the axle, compliant frame members are used to couple and stabilize multiple axles. Compliant coupling provides suspension to the axles and suits the system to uneven terrain because the axles can deflect to accommodate surface variations. This implies that the kinematic model of the system would be more complicated than traditional rigid mobile robots because coordination of axle behavior must be considered.

Let us begin with the single-axle unit, i.e., the most basic component of the system. Without considering any slips, the orientation angle ϕ_i and forward velocity v_i can be determined by the wheel velocities as follows:

$$
\begin{bmatrix} v_i \\ \dot{\phi}_i \end{bmatrix} = \frac{r_w}{2} \begin{bmatrix} 1 & 1 \\ -\dfrac{1}{d} & \dfrac{1}{d} \end{bmatrix} \begin{bmatrix} \omega_{i,1} \\ \omega_{i,2} \end{bmatrix} \tag{2.1}
$$

where r_w is the wheel radius, $\omega_{i,j}$ is the angular velocity of the jth wheel, and i denotes the axle position in the system. The resulting nonhololomic Cartesian kinematic equations are thus expressed as

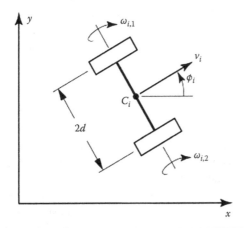

Figure 2.2   Single-axle kinematic model.

$$\dot{x}_i = v_i \cos(\phi_i)$$

$$\dot{y}_i = v_i \sin(\phi_i) \qquad\qquad (2.2)$$

$$\dot{\phi}_i = \omega_i$$

where ω_i is the angular velocity of Axle i about its center point, C_i. Based upon these linear and angular velocities and nonholonomic constraints, each axle imposes displacement boundary conditions on the compliant frame member. Such displacements would produce non-negligible reaction forces acting on the axles because radical steering is always needed to adapt to some rough or uneven terrains commonly encountered in outdoor environments. Hence, different steering strategies associated with frame coupling would greatly affect the kinematic models. In the following sections, we first define several steering strategies that simplify the kinematics of the system, and then we examine frame coupling in these situations.

2.3.2.1 Steering Configurations

According to Figure 2.2, each axle can move in a forward direction with orientation determined by ϕ_i and rotate instantaneously about its center point C_i. This scenario is similar to the pin-slot type of boundary condition described in mechanics of materials [42]. Hence, we could consider one end of the robot to be pinned and the other end to be constrained by a pin-slot such that axle spacing variations resulting from changing axle headings could be analyzed without loss of generality. Then, a straight line, drawn between points C_1 and C_2, can be used to transform the orientation of the robot and the axle deflections relative to this straight line $\overline{C_1 C_2}$.

Three steering configurations shown in Figure 2.3 are selected according to their model reduction characteristics and similarity to existing steering systems where ψ_1 and ψ_2 are relative axle deflections referenced to the horizontally oriented axis $\hat{x}$. To simplify the evaluation of these configurations, the steering ratio a is introduced as the ratio of the relative axle headings ψ_2 and ψ_1 and the angular rates $\dot{\psi}_2$ and $\dot{\psi}_1$, such that

$$\psi_2 = a\psi_1 \quad \dot{\psi}_2 = a\dot{\psi}_1 \qquad\qquad (2.3)$$

In the case of $a = -1$, each axle is steered in equal and opposite directions, which are defined as Type I kinematics, Figure 2.3a. This configuration can most significantly reduce model complexity and traction forces, simplify motion control, and provide good maneuverability. It can reduce the kinematics of the system to that of a simple unicycle defined by a curvature-based path, and it readily accepts such motion control algorithms for full control of robot posture. This steering arrangement is similar to that of an articulated vehicle, but no additional joints or actuators are required.

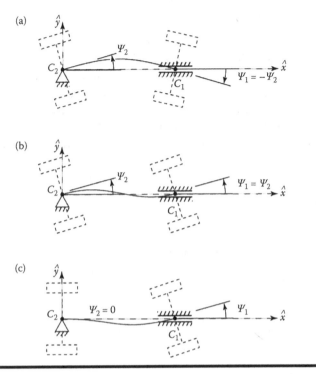

Figure 2.3 Boundary conditions and kinematic steering scenarios. (a) Type I kinematic configuration, (b) Type II kinematic configuration, and (c) Type III kinematic configuration.

In the case of $a = 1$, each axle has equal deflections such that the frame assumes a shape similar to that of a sinusoid. This configuration is defined as Type II kinematics in Figure 2.3b. This model provides simplified kinematics and excellent lateral mobility, but control of orientation is reduced and traction forces are higher. Thus, while this configuration is better for lateral mobility, it provides minimal simplification of motion control where orientation of the robot is considered and ultimately requires large traction forces.

In the case of $a = 0$, the Type III kinematics configuration in Figure 2.3c is similar to Ackerman (automobile) steering since the rear axle is always directed towards the center of the front axle, and each wheel on the robot approximately travels about a common instantaneous center of rotation (ICR) located along a line extended from the rear axle axis. But this varies from the strict Ackerman model since the steering geometry of the CFMMR is produced by steering the entire front axle as opposed to using a complicated linkage to individually steer each front wheel. This model derives some kinematic simplification, but it does not simplify motion control appreciably where strict control of robot posture must be considered. It requires higher traction forces and provides a compromise of maneuverability and lateral mobility.

2.3.2.2 Frame Coupling

As the axles steer, the distance between points C_1 and C_2 would vary to accommodate the new shape of the frame, whereas velocity constraints are imposed on the axles such that the length of $\overline{C_1C_2}$ remains consistent with the frame length under pin-slot boundary conditions. Such a decrease in the length of $\overline{C_1C_2}$ is referred to as *foreshortening* in this book. In order to calculate this shortening effect, we first consider modeling the deflected shape of the frame with an Euler–Bernoulli beam to derive tractable velocity constraint expressions. Then, the pin and pin-slot boundary conditions are imposed to derive a third-order polynomial describing the lateral frame deflection u as a function of the imposed angles ψ_1 and ψ_2

$$u = x^3 \frac{\psi_1 + \psi_2}{L^2} - x^2 \frac{\psi_1 + 2\psi_2}{L} + \psi_2 x \tag{2.4}$$

where L is the undeflected length of frame and x is the position along the frame in the $\hat{x}$ direction. Next, this lateral deflection function can be used to calculate the foreshortening δL[43] as

$$\delta L = \frac{1}{2} \int_0^L \left(\frac{du}{dx} \right)^2 dx = \frac{L}{30} \left(2\psi_2^2 - \psi_1\psi_2 + 2\psi_1^2 \right) \tag{2.5}$$

The foreshortened length of $\overline{C_1C_2}$ is then denoted as L_f:

$$L_f = L - \delta L = L \left(1 - \frac{2\psi_1^2 - \psi_1\psi_2 + 2\psi_2^2}{30} \right) \tag{2.6}$$

The Type I, II, and III kinematics configurations mentioned in the preceding will have different effects of foreshortening on the length of $\overline{C_1C_2}$ because each configuration possesses a different steering frame. Figure 2.4 illustrates foreshortening effects as functions of ψ_1 and compares foreshortening estimates provided by Equation 2.5 with those determined experimentally for a flexible frame characterized by the parameters shown in Table 2.1. Experimental hardware consisted of fixtures maintaining ψ_1 and ψ_2 where one fixture used a linear bearing to allow free axial deflection in order to measure foreshortening. Angular boundary conditions were measured by single turn potentiometers with ±2% linearity that was calibrated by precision fixtures with ±0.2° accuracy across the range of motion. Axial displacements were measured by a Litton RVT K25-3 linear potentiometer with ±4% linearity.

As Figure 2.4 indicates, for $\psi_1 \in [-40°, 40°]$, Equation 2.5 predicts δL within 5.0, 1.7, and 0.2 mm for Types I, II, and III constraints, respectively. Although larger errors are incurred with the Type I constraints, the frame is placed in slight compression, which requires significantly less force than the frame in tension.

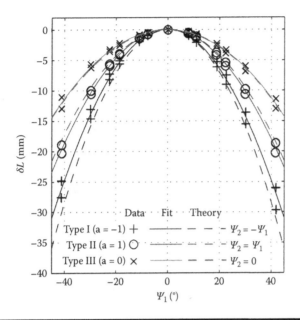

Figure 2.4 Frame foreshortening ($L = 0.350$ m).

Table 2.1 Prototype Parameters

Parameter	Value	Units	Description
r_w	0.073	m	Wheel radius
D	0.172	m	Axle width (half)
L	0.350	m	Frame length
E	2.10×10^{11}	Pa	Frame modulus of elasticity
I	5.47×10^{-13}	m⁴	Frame second moment of area about $\hat{y}$ axis
M	9.53	kg	Robot mass

In contrast, errors theoretically incurred by Equation 2.5 with the Type III constraints are too small, and the beam is in slight tension.

Figure 2.5 shows axial forces produced by deviation from the actual foreshortened length of the frame for three different constraints, respectively. These axial forces have been experimentally determined using the fixture described in the preceding with axial tension and compression forces applied to the linear bearing by a Chattillon Model DPPH100 load cell. Regression lines closely matching experimental data indicate that the stiffness of the frame is significantly higher when in tension (positive displacement) as compared to compression. The dead-band,

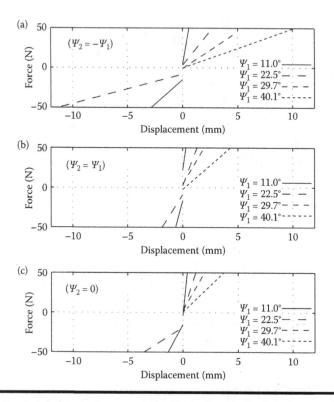

Figure 2.5 Axial frame forces when displacing from foreshortened length. (a) Type I constraints, (b) Type II constraints, and (c) Type III constraints.

near-zero displacement indicates a slight amount of stiction in the linear bearing. According to Figure 2.4, in the case of a heading angle of $\psi_1 = 22.5°$, errors in the theoretical foreshortening calculations are $\begin{bmatrix} -0.82 & -0.20 & 0.39 \end{bmatrix}$ mm, and the produced axial forces would be $\begin{bmatrix} -3.0 & -0.2 & 14.6 \end{bmatrix}$ N, respectively, for the Type I, II, and III constraints according to Figure 2.5. It is observed that a small amount of tension (i.e., positive error) produces significant forces, whereas a small amount of compression produces much smaller forces. This is attributed to the post-buckled configuration of the frame [44]. Moreover, the figures indicate that δL is not negligible for $\psi_1 > 10°$. It is, therefore, concluded that velocity constraints maintaining axle spacing are critical to minimizing traction forces.

To assure that the axles maintain proper spacing, velocity constraints are established for the axles that satisfy Equation 2.5. To determine the velocity constraint, the variation in frame length as a function of time is expressed as

$$\frac{dL_f}{dt} = -\dot{\psi}_1 \frac{L}{30}\left(4\psi_1 - \psi_2\right) - \dot{\psi}_2 \frac{L}{30}\left(4\psi_2 - \psi_1\right) \qquad (2.7)$$

which establishes the general velocity constraint

$$v_1 \cos(\psi_1) - v_2 \cos(\psi_2) = \frac{dL_f}{dt} \qquad (2.8)$$

Combining Equations 2.7 and 2.8, the velocity constraint for Axle 2 is expressed in terms of v_1 as

$$v_2 = \frac{30 v_1 \cos(\psi_1) + (4\psi_1 - \psi_2)L\dot{\psi}_1 + (4\psi_2 - \psi_1)L\dot{\psi}_2}{30 \cos(\psi_2)} \qquad (2.9)$$

Next, this velocity constraint will be expressed entirely as a function of the velocity v_1 and the kinematic state variables.

2.3.2.3 General Kinematics in Polar Coordinates

Figure 2.6 is a diagram of the robot in a general two-axle configuration where ψ_1 and ψ_2 have not yet been specifically constrained or coupled. We strive to control the robot for purposes of posture regulation (position and orientation), path following, or general trajectory tracking by controlling the position of a point on the robot, such as C_1 or O, and the robot orientation described by the angle γ of $\overline{C_1C_2}$. According to Brockett's Theorem [45], a smooth, time-invariant control law cannot be used to provide globally asymptotic stability to continuous nonholonomic systems. However, if we introduce a discontinuous polar coordinate description of the

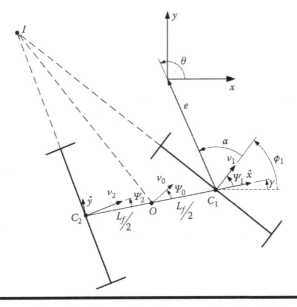

Figure 2.6   General steering kinematics. Frame omitted for clarity.

kinematics, then a smooth, time-invariant control law could be applied [46]. In the polar description, Figure 2.6, choose a point along $\overline{C_1 C_2}$, e.g., C_1 for simplification, and the orientation of its velocity trajectory can be represented by the following variables:

$$
\begin{aligned}
e &= \sqrt{x_1^2 + y_1^2} & \theta &= ATAN2(-y_1, -x_1) \\
\alpha &= \theta - \phi_1 & \gamma &= ATAN2(y_1 - y_2, x_1 - x_2)
\end{aligned}
\tag{2.10}
$$

Hence, the polar kinematic equations are expressed as

$$
\dot{e} = -v_1 \cos \alpha
$$

$$
\dot{\alpha} = -\omega_1 + v_1 \frac{\sin \alpha}{e}
$$

$$
\dot{\theta} = v_1 \frac{\sin \alpha}{e}
\tag{2.11}
$$

$$
\dot{\gamma} = \frac{v_1 \sin \psi_1 - v_2 \sin \psi_2}{L_f}
$$

Apparently, the preceding differential equations become discontinuous when $e = 0$. Considering a curvature-based controller design, the angular velocity of Axle 1 needs to be described as a function of path radius or curvature, r_1 and κ_1, respectively, and forward velocity v_1:

$$
\omega_1 = \dot{\phi}_1 = \frac{v_1}{r_1} = v_1 \kappa_1
\tag{2.12}
$$

Imposing velocity constraint Equation 2.9 in $\dot{\gamma}$ of Equation 2.11 and using the steering ratio a to eliminate ψ_2, the rate of change of robot orientation is then derived as

$$
\dot{\gamma} = -\frac{L \tan(a\psi_1)}{15 L_f} \psi_1 \left(2a^2 - a + 2\right)\dot{\psi}_1 + v_1 \frac{\sin\left(\psi_1(1 - a)\right)}{L_f \cos(a\psi_1)}
\tag{2.13}
$$

where v_1 and κ_1 can be treated as system inputs. ψ_1 can then be expressed as a function of robot orientation γ and other polar coordinates such that

$$
\psi_1 = \theta - \alpha - \gamma.
\tag{2.14}
$$

Hence, combining Equations 2.11, 2.12, and 2.14 can produce

$$\dot{\psi}_1 = v_1 \kappa_1 - \dot{\gamma} \tag{2.15}$$

Then, substitute Equation 2.13 into Equation 2.15, solve for $\dot{\gamma}$, and apply Equation 2.14. The kinematic state equations become purely functions of the polar coordinates with velocity and path curvature inputs v_1 and κ_1 as

$$\dot{e} = -v_1 \cos\alpha$$

$$\dot{\alpha} = -v_1 \left(\kappa_1 - \frac{\sin\alpha}{e} \right)$$

$$\dot{\theta} = v_1 \frac{\sin\alpha}{e} \tag{2.16}$$

$$\dot{\gamma} = v_1 \left(\frac{15}{15 L_f + bL} \right) \left(\frac{bL\kappa_1}{15} + \frac{\sin\left((\theta - \alpha - \gamma)(1-a)\right)}{\cos\left(a(\theta - \alpha - \gamma)\right)} \right)$$

where $b = -\psi_1 \tan(a\psi_1)(2a^2 - a + 2)$ and L_f is determined by Equation 2.6. The actual Axle 1 heading can then be evaluated by

$$\phi_1 = \theta - \alpha = \psi_1 + \gamma \tag{2.17}$$

which prescribes the angular rate to be

$$\dot{\phi}_1 = \omega_1 = \dot{\theta} - \dot{\alpha} = v_1 \kappa_1 \tag{2.18}$$

Given Equation 2.3, the angle of Axle 2 can be described as

$$\phi_2 = \psi_2 + \gamma = a\psi_1 + \gamma \tag{2.19}$$

where ψ_1 can be eliminated by substitution of Equation 2.14 such that only the polar coordinates and γ remain. Then the angle of Axle 2 becomes

$$\phi_2 = a(\theta - \alpha) + \gamma(1-a) \tag{2.20}$$

and the angular rate of Axle 2 is determined by differentiation to be a function of the kinematic variables

$$\dot{\phi}_2 = a(\dot{\theta} - \dot{\alpha}) + \dot{\gamma}(1-a) \tag{2.21}$$

where Equation 2.15 is imposed on Equation 2.9 in conjunction with Equation 2.3 such that the Axle 2 velocity constraint is

$$v_2 = \frac{v_1}{\cos(a\psi_1)}\left(\cos\psi_1 + \frac{L\psi_1}{15}\left(2a^2 - a + 2\right)\left(\kappa_1 - \frac{\dot{\gamma}}{v_1}\right)\right) \qquad (2.22)$$

So far, the forward and angular velocities of Axle 2 can be expressed purely in terms of the state variables by applying Equations 2.14 and 2.16.

Hence, given a motion controller with control inputs v_1 and κ_1 for a system described by Equation 2.16, the velocities for each axle can be determined. While Equation 2.16 provides a generic description of the kinematics, the task of motion control would be complicated due to the complexity of $\dot{\gamma}$ in Equation 2.16.

2.3.3 Simplified Kinematic Models

As the previous section indicates, proper selection of the steering ratio a can significantly reduce the complexity of the kinematic model, which would facilitate motion control in the following chapters.

Type I: Curvature-Based Steering ($\psi_1 = -\psi_2$)
As indicated in Section 2.3.2.1, Type I steering occurs if we constrain $a=-1$. This steering scenario simplifies the kinematics significantly, eliminating the need to consider $\dot{\gamma}$, as described in the next paragraph, and allows standard unicycle motion planners to provide full motion control. This is derived in part from the fact that $\psi_1 = -\psi_2$ imposes a constant moment across the frame, which ideally takes the shape of an arc segment. Geometric properties can then be used to easily describe the postures of the axles.

Observed in Figure 2.7, the motion of Point O (the midpoint of $\overline{C_1 C_2}$) is unique under the Type I steering configuration because it could be determined to be the motion of a simple differentially steered axle, and the orientation γ becomes equivalent to the velocity heading ϕ_O and ultimately orientation α. Thus, the posture of $\overline{C_1 C_2}$ at Point O ultimately possesses kinematics described by Equation 2.2 where v_O and ϕ_O describe the velocity trajectory of the robot. The reason is that the angle α describing the polar orientation of v_0 also describes the robot orientation γ of the segment $\overline{C_1 C_2}$ due to the symmetry of $\psi_1 = -\psi_2$. This provides tremendous simplification of the motion control task since γ is eliminated and polar coordinates θ and α describe the orientation of the robot and the velocity heading, respectively. Hence, the reduced kinematic model of the robot subject to Type I constraints becomes

$$\dot{e} = -v_0 \cos\alpha$$

$$\dot{\alpha} = -v_0\left(\kappa_0 - \frac{\sin\alpha}{e}\right) \qquad (2.23)$$

$$\dot{\theta} = v_0 \frac{\sin\alpha}{e}$$

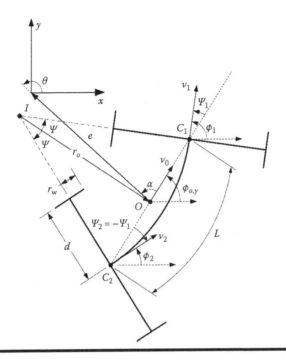

Figure 2.7 Type I steering kinematics.

where the velocity and path curvature of Point O, v_O and κ_O, respectively, are the control inputs.

It is also worth noting that at any instant, O is approximately traveling about an instantaneous center of rotation, indicated as Point I, with a path curvature κ_O and radius r_O

$$r_O = \frac{L}{2\psi}\cos\psi, \quad \kappa_O = \frac{1}{r_O} = \frac{2\psi}{L\cos\psi} \tag{2.24}$$

where $\psi = \psi_1$ represents the relative angle of axles to the segment $\overline{C_1C_2}$. Notice that the curvature κ_O and radius r_O are both functions of actual arc length of the frame L rather than L_f. This phenomenon would greatly simplify the motion control task.

The control inputs v_O and κ_O and the polar coordinates can then be used to determine the desired trajectory of each axle. Based on κ_O, Equation 2.24 determines the relative heading ψ to give the absolute axle headings

$$\phi_1 = \phi_0 + \psi \quad \phi_2 = \phi_0 - \psi \tag{2.25}$$

which can be represented in terms of the polar coordinates since $\phi_0 = \theta - \alpha$. Axle headings and rates are determined by

$$\phi_1 = \theta - \alpha + \psi \quad \phi_2 = \theta - \alpha - \psi \tag{2.26}$$

$$\dot{\phi}_1 = \dot{\theta} - \dot{\alpha} + \dot{\psi} \quad \dot{\phi}_2 = \dot{\theta} - \dot{\alpha} - \dot{\psi} \tag{2.27}$$

where the rate of relative heading change $\dot{\psi}$ is

$$\dot{\psi} = \dot{\kappa} \frac{L \cos^2 \psi}{2(\cos \psi + \psi \sin \psi)} \tag{2.28}$$

as determined by differentiation of Equation 2.24. The velocity magnitude v_O can then be related to that of the axles by

$$v_1 = \frac{v_O}{\cos \psi} - \frac{1}{2} \frac{\mathrm{d}L_f}{\mathrm{d}t} \quad v_2 = \frac{v_O}{\cos \psi} + \frac{1}{2} \frac{\mathrm{d}L_f}{\mathrm{d}t} \tag{2.29}$$

where $\psi = \psi_1 = -\psi_2$. Substituting Equations 2.3 and 2.7 and $a = -1$, the axle velocities are determined by

$$v_{1,2} = \frac{v_O}{\cos \psi} \mp \frac{1}{6} L \psi \dot{\psi} \tag{2.30}$$

Hence, the reduced-order kinematic model obtained in the preceding can fully describe the system posture while allowing easy implementation of curvature-based motion controllers. Even greater simplification can be achieved if velocity constraints are relaxed to neglect foreshortening for small steering angles, which provides

$$v_{1,2} = \frac{v_O}{\cos \psi} \tag{2.31}$$

as was the case in our earlier work [47].

Type II kinematics: $(\psi_1 = \psi_2)$
For the Type II kinematics configuration, a different simplification of the kinematics can be obtained with $\psi_1 = \psi_2$ (i.e., $a = 1$), Figure 2.8. Applying the constraint $a = 1$ to Equation 2.13 results in

$$\dot{\gamma} = -\frac{1}{5} \dot{\psi}_1 \psi_1 \tan(\psi_1) \tag{2.32}$$

This nonzero component is due to the modified velocity that Axle 2 must assume relative to Axle 1 in order to compensate for foreshortening. If the velocity constraints are neglected, foreshortening is an issue and traction forces increase, but

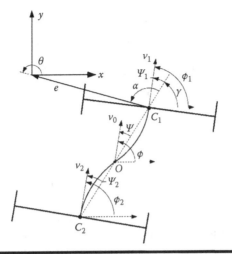

Figure 2.8 Type II steering kinematics.

$\dot{\gamma} = 0$. This nullifies the γ state variable and results in a reduced model similar to Equation 2.23 but referenced to C_1.

Type III kinematics: ($\psi_2 = 0$)
If we impose the constraint $a = 0$, the Type III kinematics configuration is applied with $\psi_2 = 0$ where the rear axle is always directed towards C_1. The kinematic model can be simplified appreciably but not entirely reduced since

$$\dot{\gamma} = v_1 \frac{\sin \psi_1}{L_f} \tag{2.33}$$

Since the γ state variable is not entirely reduced, as in the case of Type I steering, a simple unicycle-type motion-control algorithm will not drive γ to zero.

2.3.4 Mobility and Maneuverability

In order to evaluate the performance of different steering modes, we can develop metrics based upon achievable mobility and maneuverability. Forces imposed by the frame play a critical role in evaluating these capabilities since they directly impact wheel traction forces and achievable steering angles. These capabilities are also affected by the physical interference of components of the robot that may limit steering angles and potentially unstable configurations of the system. In the process of developing these factors and performance metrics, they were evaluated relative to the experimental platform characterized by the parameters shown in Table 2.1.

2.3.4.1 Limiting Factors

Physical Interference: Depending on the proportions of the robot, interference can occur in two extreme scenarios: the wheels on one side of the robot may touch each other, or one of the wheels may contact the frame. Wheel–wheel interference is apt to limit Type I steering, which provides the following equation based upon the geometry shown in Figure 2.7

$$\tan\psi = \frac{2\psi r_w}{L - 2\psi d} \tag{2.34}$$

which must be solved numerically for ψ. Based upon the robot parameters, Table 2.1, the limit is $|\psi_i| \le 36.5°$.

Wheel–frame interference can occur in any of the steering modes if the frame is sufficiently long. Since the deflected shape of the frame and collision point is very difficult to evaluate analytically under these circumstances, this boundary is approximated by the angle of the axle when the leading or trailing edge of the wheel interferes with $C_1 C_2$. This results in the following limit:

$$|\psi_i| \le \arctan\frac{d}{r_w} \tag{2.35}$$

which corresponds to $|\psi_i| \le 67.0°$ for the experimental platform.

Traction Forces: Quasi-static behavior is assumed since dynamic interactions are not considered. Thus, traction forces required to impose boundary conditions on the frame should be evaluated. Assuming foreshortening has been considered in the velocity constraints, boundary condition forces are described by lateral reactions R_i and moments M_i of the frame that result from axle orientations [48]

$$M_1 = \frac{2EI}{L_f}(2\psi_1 + \psi_2) \quad M_2 = -\frac{2EI}{L_f}(\psi_1 + 2\psi_2) \tag{2.36}$$

$$R_1 = -\frac{M_1 + M_2}{L_f} \quad R_2 = -R_1 \tag{2.37}$$

where E is the Young's modulus of elasticity of the frame and I is its cross-sectional moment of inertia of the frame about the bending axis [42]. These forces and moments can then be used to calculate wheel traction forces

$$F_{M,i} = \frac{M_i}{2d}(\hat{x}_i \cos\psi_i + \hat{y}_i \sin\psi_i) \quad F_{R,i} = \frac{R_i}{2}\hat{y} \tag{2.38}$$

where $F_{M,i}$ and $F_{R,i}$ represent the moment and reaction forces on a tire on the ith axle oriented with respect to the frame coordinates, respectively. The net traction force on a tire of the ith axle (− and + representing the left and right wheels, respectively) is then the vector sum $F_{T,i}$

$$F_{T,i} = \pm F_{M,i} + F_{R,i} \tag{2.39}$$

and the maximum traction forces $F_{T,i}^{\max}$ on the ith axle is

$$F_{T,i}^{\max} = \left\| \; |F_{M,i}| + |F_{R,i}| \; \right\|_2 \tag{2.40}$$

The maximum of these axle forces then determines the maximum tire force on the robot as

$$F_T^{\max} = \max\left(F_{T,i}^{\max}, i = 1 \ldots n \right) \tag{2.41}$$

Ultimately, the achievable traction force is limited by the weight of the robot and the wheel-slip characteristics [49]. Assuming that the robot has an evenly distributed mass m, a normal force $mg/4$ will be supported by each wheel. Thus, the maximum traction force can be approximated by

$$F_{\max} = \frac{\mu mg}{4} \tag{2.42}$$

given a coefficient of friction, μ, corresponding to the tire–surface interaction [50,51]. Equations 2.40 and 2.42 can then be solved to determine the ideal maximum steering angle, ψ_1, achievable for a steering ratio, a. Based upon the parameters in Table 2.1, Figure 2.9 illustrates $F_T^{\max}$ as a function of steering ratio for several

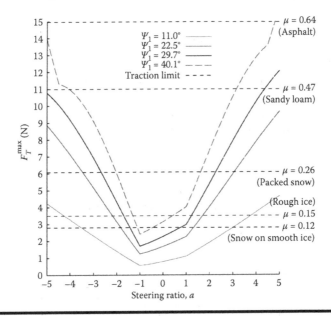

Figure 2.9 Ideal required maximum wheel traction forces and available traction based on typical surfaces [50,51].

relative axle headings. These results indicate that ideally Type I steering requires minimum traction force, followed by Type III and then Type II.

Based upon published tire–surface interactions, these results estimate that all steering modes should function effectively on sandy loam [51] and even snow-covered ice [50]. An important point to remember, though, is that these traction force estimates do not include forces introduced by error in the foreshortening calculations, δL^{err}. If we include these forces, it is evident that the maximum traction forces including foreshortening error F_T^{err} are larger and dependent upon foreshortening predictions, Table 2.2. In situations where $\delta L^{err} > 0$, the frame is in tension and traction forces may increase appreciably, as in the case of the Type III steering, and it is evident that the wheel slip will occur on slippery surfaces. In the case of the Type I and II steering, though, the traction force with foreshortening error is still sufficiently small that the robot should function well on slippery surfaces.

Configuration Instability: Instability could occur in the form of tip-over if the axles are colinear. In the quasi-static case, this occurs when axle orientations satisfy

$$\psi_1 = \pm\frac{\pi}{2} \quad \psi_2 = \pm\frac{\pi}{2}$$

As the physical interference limits indicate, tip-over instability is not a limiting factor in the case study. But it might be a constraint for different mechanisms.

2.3.4.2 Performance Criteria

Maneuverability: The capability to manipulate robot orientation, and thus maneuver the robot around obstacles, can be evaluated by $\dot{\gamma}$, which is generally described by Equation 2.16. Note that this expression is a complex function of steering ratio a, relative axle heading ψ_1, and path curvature κ. In general, ψ_1 is actually determined by the current configuration of the robot as determined by the evolution of the kinematics equation (2.16).

Table 2.2 Ideal Maximum Wheel Traction Force, F_T^{max}, Expected Foreshortening Error, δL^{err}, and Expected Maximum Wheel Traction Forces with Foreshortening Error, F_T^{err}

Steering Mode	$\psi_1 = 11°$			$\psi_1 = 22.5°$		
	$F_T^{max}(N)$	$\delta L^{err}(mm)$	$F_T^{err}(N)$	$F_T^{max}(N)$	$\delta L^{err}(mm)$	$F_T^{err}(N)$
I ($a = -1$)	0.56	−0.18	1.51	1.24	−0.82	2.42
II ($a = 1$)	1.10	0.02	2.29	2.26	−0.02	2.35
III ($a = 0$)	0.79	0.06	6.53	1.68	0.39	8.74

Lateral Mobility: In confined environments, the ability of the robot to move laterally without significant maneuvers is important. This mobility can be quantified by the average relative heading, ψ_{avg}, described by

$$\psi_{avg} = \tfrac{1}{2}\left(\psi_1 + \psi_2\right) \tag{2.43}$$

Scaled Performance Metrics (SPM): Since force is required to deflect the frame, wheel traction and energy are necessary. Objective evaluation of the performance criteria is accomplished by examining the magnitude of $\dot{\gamma}$ and ψ_{avg} per unit of maximum traction force required, represented respectively by $P_{\dot{\gamma}}$ and $P\psi$, as

$$P_{\dot{\gamma}} = \frac{\dot{\gamma}}{F_{T,max}} \qquad P_{\psi} = \frac{\psi_{avg}}{F_{T,max}} \tag{2.44}$$

Evaluation of the SPM was performed based upon the same experimental platform. Larger performance factors are generally desirable for maximizing the use of available wheel traction, but traction requirements, Figure 2.9 and Table 2.2, and kinematic simplifications must be considered.

The SPM plot for maneuverability is shown in Figure 2.10 for a relative steering angle $\psi_1 = 30°$ and several path curvatures, $\kappa = [\,-3, \quad 0, \quad 3]$, as a function of steering ratio, a. For smaller ψ_1, the variation between the curves becomes smaller and less illustrative of the SPM sensitivity to path curvature. Considering the three case studies, note that $P_{\dot{\gamma}}$ is largest for $a = -1$ (Type I) and smallest for $a = 0$ (Type II). The actual maximum of the SPM is at about $a = -2$, but the traction forces are actually much larger and the kinematic simplifications are not significant.

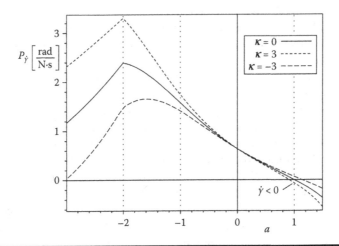

Figure 2.10 The scaled maneuverability performance metric indicates the ability to change robot orientation per unit of traction force. $\psi_1 = 30°$ is shown.

In the case of $\kappa > 0$, note that Figure 2.10 indicates $P_{\dot\gamma} < 0$ at $a = 1$. This indicates potential destabilization since the robot orientation γ is decreasing while axle heading angles ϕ_1 and ϕ_2 are increasing, Figure 2.8. Thus, ψ_1 increases and $\dot\gamma$ becomes even more negative. If $\kappa > 0$ is maintained for sufficient time, $\psi_1 \to 90°$ and Equation 2.22 becomes singular. Prior to this point, though, destabilization can be remedied if $\kappa < 0$ is applied. Similar destabilizing and restabilizing scenarios occur when $\psi < 0$ and $\kappa < 0$ or $\kappa > 0$, respectively.

For robot configuration stability we thus desire ψ_i to remain bounded and to converge to a steady state value proportional to the path curvature. Given $\psi_1 > 0$, this can be achieved by $\dot\gamma > 0$, and $\dot\gamma < 0$ for $\psi_1 < 0$. Thus, we can guarantee configuration stability if

$$a_{\min} < a < a_{\max} \tag{2.45}$$

where $a_{\max} \in [0.91, \ 1.14]$ is derived numerically based upon Figure 2.10 for $\kappa \in [-3, \ 3]$ at $\psi_1 = \pm 30°$. Note that $a_{\max} \to 1$ as ψ_1 approaches zero, but the aforementioned range of $a_{\max}$ is given to indicate the nominal range of $a_{\max}$ that is dependent upon κ. In contrast, we find that $a_{\min}$ is a function of physical limitations (Equation 2.35) and is determined by

$$a_{\min} \approx -\frac{\psi_{\max}}{|\psi_1|} < \frac{67°}{|\psi_1|} \tag{2.46}$$

based on Equations 2.3 and 2.35, which results in $a_{\min} \approx -2.23$ for $\psi_1 = \pm 30°$. This lower limit actually becomes more negative for smaller ψ_1, allowing a greater range of steering ratios, but this provides a conservative static boundary. Steering outside of the range of Equation 2.45 is certainly allowable for short periods, but observing Equation 2.45 is generally desired. Steering near the boundaries of Equation 2.45 is possible, as in Type II steering, but this may lead to stability issues in extreme maneuvers.

The SPM plot for lateral mobility is shown in Figure 2.11 for $\psi_1 = 11°$ and $30°$ as a function of steering ratio a. Type II steering ($a = 1$) provides the best lateral mobility, whereas Type I ($a = -1$) is the worst. $P\psi$ actually is larger for $a > 1$, but stability becomes an issue. When $a < -1$, $P\psi$ becomes negative, indicating behavior counterproductive to lateral mobility. This behavior results from large rear-axle steering maneuvers that are actually better for maneuvering the robot as described in the preceding.

As the SPM indicate, the Type I steering ($a = -1$) is the best for maneuverability, whereas Type II ($a = 1$) is the best for lateral mobility. Type III ($a = 0$) provides a nominal mix of lateral mobility and maneuverability, but this kinematic model cannot be simplified to the same degree as the others, and it introduces significant traction forces in lieu of foreshortening error. The Type I and II kinematics, though, each provide specific performance specialties with reduced kinematic models that vastly simplify motion control to provide control of full-posture regulation with simple unicycle motion controllers.

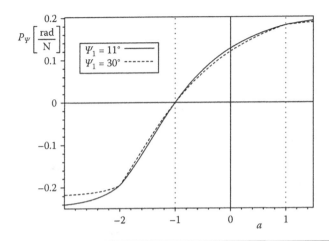

Figure 2.11 Lateral mobility performance metric indicates the ability to translate the robot laterally per unit of traction force without complex maneuvers.

In summary, general kinematics for a two-axle, compliant, frame mobile robot have been characterized by steering ratio a. Based upon three special cases of a, simplified kinematic models have been derived and evaluated. Of these models, only Type I steering guided by Point O provides full control over posture regulation. Types I and III steering guided by C_1 provide full position control with limited control over orientation γ. Type II steering provides control over position, but orientation γ would become unstable given initial conditions requiring aggressive maneuvers. Some experimental evaluations corroborate that the Type I steering requires minimum traction, provides the most accurate posture regulation, and provides maximum maneuverability. Similar methodologies could also be applied and extended to a multi-axle, compliant, frame mobile robot.

2.3.5 Generic Dynamic Model

The kinematic model of the CFMMR in the previous sections has described how the mobile robot moves in response to the motion of each axle module. As we know, however, achievement of any movement of an axle module is related to the corresponding forces and/or torques applied on that module. Especially for a field robot such as CFMMR, interaction with rugged or rocky terrain could introduce additional force/torque elements to the whole robotic system, which protrudes the role of robot dynamics. Hence, we describe the generic dynamic model of CFMMR in this section to provide a basis for the next few chapters.

Since two-axle is the minimum functional unit, we consider a two-axle scout model in Figure 2.12. A fixed global reference frame $G(X,Y)$ is defined, and

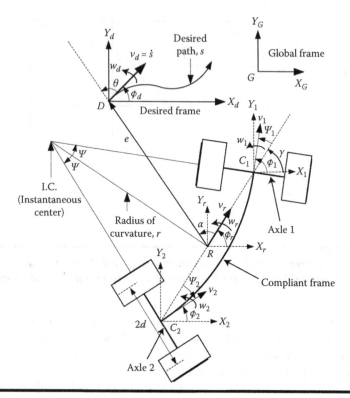

Figure 2.12 The two-axle CFMMR.

moving frames $f_i(x_i, y_i)$ are attached to the points C_i at the midpoint of the ith axle, where $i = 1, 2$. At any instant, the ith axle module is rotating about the instantaneous center (IC), such that the IC's projections onto the x_i axes define point C_i at the midpoint of each axle. A module configuration vector $q_i = \begin{bmatrix} x_i & y_i & \phi_i \end{bmatrix}$ is then attached to this point for each axle. Then, we have the dynamic model as

$$\mathbf{M}_i(q_i)\ddot{q}_i + \mathbf{V}_i(q_i, \dot{q}_i)\dot{q}_i + \mathbf{F}_i(\dot{q}_i) + \mathbf{G}_i(q_i) + \tau_{d,i}$$

$$+ \mathbf{F}_{K,i}(q_i, q_{i\pm1}) = \mathbf{E}_i(q_i)\tau_i - \mathbf{A}_i^T(q_i)\lambda_i \tag{2.47}$$

where $\mathbf{M}_i(q_i) \in R^{3\times3}$ is a symmetric, positive, definite inertia matrix for these ith axle modules; $\mathbf{V}_i(q_i, \dot{q}_i) \in R^{3\times3}$ is the centripetal and Coriolis forces; $\mathbf{F}_i(\dot{q}_i) \in R^{3\times1}$ denotes the friction; $\mathbf{G}_i(q_i) \in R^{3\times1}$ is the gravitational vector; $\tau_{d,i}$ denotes bounded unknown disturbances including unstructured un-modeled dynamics; $\mathbf{E}_i(q_i) \in R^{3\times2}$ is the input transformation matrix; $\tau_i \in R^{2\times1}$ are the input torques; and $\lambda_i \in R^{1\times1}$ is the vector of nonholonomic constraint forces. $\mathbf{A}_i(q_i) \in R^{1\times3}$ is the global matrix associated with the nonholonomic constraints. $\mathbf{F}_{K,i}(q_i, q_{i\pm1}) \in R^{3\times1}$ represents the compliant frame forces, which impose additional physical constraints dependent upon flexible beam interaction. Physical constraints, then, include nonholonomic constraints $\mathbf{A}_i(q_i)\dot{q}_i = \mathbf{0}$ imposed by the wheels, and curvature and velocity constraints imposed by the compliant frame according to Section 2.3.2.

More generally, consider the ith axle of an n-axle CFMMR. Let us define a fixed global reference frame $F(X,Y)$ and any instant, the ith axle module is rotating about the IC such that the IC's projections onto the x_i axes define point C_i at the midpoint of each axle. A module configuration vector $q_i = \begin{bmatrix} X_i & Y_i & \phi_i \end{bmatrix}$ is then attached to this point and oriented with the axle. In order to describe this configuration within the context of the entire system, we assemble each of these module configuration vectors into a system configuration vector $Q = \begin{bmatrix} q_1,\ldots,q_n \end{bmatrix}^T$ where $Q \in R^{3n \times 1}$. It is then possible to assemble a system description of the form

$$\mathbf{M}(Q)\ddot{Q} + \mathbf{V}(Q,\dot{Q})\dot{Q} + \mathbf{F}(\dot{Q}) + \mathbf{G}(Q) + \tau_d + \mathbf{F}_K(Q) = \mathbf{E}(Q)\tau - \mathbf{A}^T(Q)\lambda \quad (2.48)$$

where $\mathbf{M}(Q) \in R^{3n \times 3n}$ is a symmetric, positive, definite inertia matrix assembled from the individual axle module inertia matrices. Assembling individual axle module dynamic characteristics into the system model, $\mathbf{V}(Q,\dot{Q}) \in R^{3n \times 3n}$ represents the centripetal and coriolis forces; $\mathbf{F}(\dot{Q}) \in R^{3n \times 1}$ denotes the friction; $\mathbf{G}(Q) \in R^{3n \times 1}$ is the gravitational vector; τ_d denotes bounded unknown disturbances including unstructured un-modeled dynamics; $\mathbf{E}(Q) \in R^{3n \times 2n}$ is the input transformation matrix; $\tau \in R^{2n \times 1}$ are the input torques; and $\lambda \in R^{n \times 1}$ is the vector of constraint forces. $\mathbf{A}(Q) \in R^{n \times 3n}$ is the global matrix associated with the nonholonomic constraints. Compliant frame forces are described by globally defined stiffness equations that are assembled into $\mathbf{F}_K(Q) \in R^{3n \times 1}$.

MOTION CONTROL

Chapter 3

Cooperative Motion Control and Sensing Architecture

3.1 Introduction

The motion control of wheeled mobile robots has received appreciable attention where rigid, axle-wheeled mobile robots are predominant platforms. In earlier stages, most research was based on the kinematic model of a wheeled mobile robot where the input was velocity. However, tracking the velocity commands with an actual robot and rejecting the resulting drift was not trivial. Thus, the uniform dynamic controllers derived in [52,53] were based on the kinematic and dynamic model of the robot such that the robot can be controlled using wheel torque commands. As we mentioned in Chapter 2, a mobile robot working on the fields such as CFMMR is different from other types of mobile robots in mechanism, which correspondingly results in different motion-control issues. For instance, motion control of the CFMMR is different in two aspects. First, the physical constraints, especially the axle velocity and curvature constraints imposed by the frame, are not typical in rigid-body, wheeled mobile robots that are the focus of the uniform dynamic controllers. Second, the interaction forces between the axles are highly nonlinear functions of relative axle postures. Thus, coordinating relative axle postures is a critical concern that should not be considered by the uniform dynamic controllers. In contrast, the motion-control architecture discussed in this chapter is more suitable for coordinating motion of the axles in lieu of interaction constraints, which could frequently appear in field robotic systems.

Coordination is a common issue in cooperative mobile robotics, and has been studied with a variety of techniques [54–59]. Some of them only focus on motion planning and coordination issues without sensor architecture involved [54,58]. Some consider only motion planning and sensor architecture, ignoring robot dynamics [54,57]. Others focus only on dynamic motion control and coordinated force control without considering motion planning and sensor issues [55,56,59]. A number of cooperative wheeled mobile robots have been investigated in recent decades. The most well-known cooperative wheeled mobile robot was the snakelike robot Genbu, which used entirely passive joints to allow cooperation amongst wheel axles for adaptation to uneven terrain. However, motion control of Genbu focused only on simple posture alignment and functional ability [60]. No one considered general navigation issues and accurate motion control combining motion planning, dynamic motion control, and sensor fusion. There was no general solution to resolve all three aspects. In reality, motion planning, dynamic control, and sensor architecture issues, however, all affect the efficiency of cooperative motion control.

Burdick and his students proposed controllability and motion-planning issues for multi-model systems, including over-constrained wheeled vehicles where conventional nonholonomic motion planning and control theories did not apply [61]. They developed a power-dissipation method (PDM) and talked about the conditions of kinematic reducibility for such systems. Then the solutions of PDM were shown to be the solutions of kinematic reducibility. The PDM technique was provided to simplify motion-control analysis from the full Lagrangian mechanical framework. As they stated, however, the full Lagrangian framework still played an important role in analyzing mechanical systems in general. Therefore, this chapter provides a motion control and sensing architecture based on the general full Lagrangian analysis to accommodate the conventional nonholonomic control theories onto the cooperative nonholonomic system. As mentioned in Chapter 2, the CFMMR uses compliant frame members to couple rigid axle modules with independently controlled wheels. Wheel commands are used to deform the frame for advanced steering capability. Frame compliance also allows the robot to twist its shape and adapt to rugged terrain. Hence, we use the CFMMR as the example platform in the rest of this chapter to illustrate motion control and sensing issues in cooperative mobile robotic systems.

In this chapter, we discuss a cooperative sensing and control architecture in order for the system to be scalable, distributed, and cooperative. This architecture is applicable to any cooperative mobile robotic system, whereas the specific algorithms in the modules may need to be customized for a particular application. Furthermore, given the modular structure of the architecture, it is easy to customize specific components to satisfy the navigation requirements of the robot and to allow a team to design the components in parallel for faster implementation. The architecture, Figure 3.1, consists of kinematic (K) control, dynamic (D) control, and sensing (S) system components. In this architecture, each axle module is treated individually as an autonomous mobile robot unit. Thus, identical algorithms can be

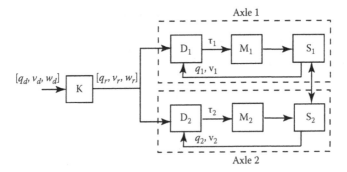

Figure 3.1 Distributed sensing and control configurations where K represents kinematic motion control, D represents dynamic motion control, S represents the sensory system, and M represents each module of the robot.

applied to each unit of the system, which provides a naturally distributed computational burden. Compliant coupling complicates this task, however, since each axle imposes boundary conditions on its neighboring compliant frame elements and resulting interaction forces are created.

In order to reduce interaction forces in lieu of nonholonomic constraints, axle cooperation is managed via centralized kinematic control. Based on ideal kinematics, the kinematic controller considers frame boundary conditions and provides bounded posture and velocity commands such that the system follows a reference trajectory or regulates to a final posture asymptotically. The distributed dynamic controllers then track these reference commands such that physical constraints are satisfied during movement of the robot in lieu of disturbances. Since off-tracking between neighboring axles can increase interaction forces, the distributed sensing system includes a relative position sensor within a tiered fusion algorithm to provide accurate posture and velocity estimates.

3.2 Motion Control and Sensing Strategy

Given a two-axle CFMMR, the control objective is to solve multiple navigation tasks using a general approach. These tasks include posture regulation, path following, and trajectory tracking.

Let us analyze the target system first. Compared to the traditional unicycle-type wheeled mobile robot, the CFMMR also has physical constraints imposed by the frame in addition to nonholonomic constraints. The frame also complicates the dynamics by introducing highly nonlinear compliance. Resulting forces are quite dependent on the ability of the measurement system to predict relative axle posture, and thus the data fusion and instrumentation systems must be modified to improve relative position sensing.

Towards the control objective, the motion control and sensing architecture is presented, Figure 3.1. In order to characterize the performance of this architecture, the tracking errors due to the kinematic motion controller, dynamic motion controller, and sensing algorithms are defined as

$$q_r - q_d = e_k$$

$$q_s - q_r = e_d \qquad (3.1)$$

$$q - q_s = e_s$$

Refer to Figure 2.12; q_d is the desired trajectory according to the virtual desired frame D, $q_d = [x_d, y_d, \phi_d]$; q_r is the reference trajectory created by the kinematic controller that the dynamic motion controller refers to, $q_r = [x_r, y_r, \phi_r]$; q_s is the trajectory estimated from the sensory system; and q is the actual trajectory of the axles. We then desire to minimize the total tracking error e_{tot}, which is expressed as

$$e_{tot} = q - q_d = e_k + e_d + e_s \qquad (3.2)$$

The norm of the total tracking error, $\|e_{tot}\|$, is then

$$\|e_{tot}\| = \|e_k + e_d + e_s\| \le \|e_k\| + \|e_d\| + \|e_s\| \qquad (3.3)$$

Thus, to minimize the total tracking error, each component error should be minimized

$$\min(\|e_k\| + \|e_d\| + \|e_s\|) = \min(\|e_k\|) + \min(\|e_d\|) + \min(\|e_s\|) \qquad (3.4)$$

In the following sections, the kinematic motion controller, dynamic motion controller, and sensory system should be designed to minimize $\|e_k\|$, $\|e_d\|$, and $\|e_s\|$, respectively, in lieu of physical constraints due to the cooperative configuration, i.e., the compliant frame on CFMMR.

3.3 Kinematic Motion Controller

According to the control architecture mentioned in Section 3.1, the kinematic motion controller considers physical constraints and provides the reference velocity inputs to the dynamic motion controllers. As shown in Figure 2.12, suppose that a desired trajectory, $q_d = [x_d, y_d, \phi_d]$, is produced by the desired linear and angular velocities, v_d and ω_d, such that the path has curvature κ_d. The kinematic motion controller is designed such that

1. The robot is asymptotically driven to the desired trajectory using the reference velocity inputs v_r and ω_r such that $\|e_k\| = 0$.
2. The path of the robot produced by the reference velocity inputs v_r and ω_r will not violate physical constraints at any point of the path. Then, the compliant frame curvature is limited to a certain value related to the physically feasible configurations. Since the compliant frame forces $\mathbf{F}_{K,i}$ are a function of the two axle postures $(q_i, q_{i\pm1})$, they are bounded for all the robot configurations during the navigation given the kinematic motion controller.
3. The kinematic motion controller should be based on ideal kinematics, e.g., no feedback signal should be introduced from the actual robot since this perturbs convergence of the kinematic controller.
4. The compliant frame should be subjected to pure bending $(\psi = \psi_1 = -\psi_2)$, Figure 2.12. This minimizes disturbance forces acting on the dynamic controller [62] and improves performance of the sensory system [63].

As mentioned in Chapter 2, polar coordinates (e, θ, α) are used to describe the reference configuration q_r, and the reference velocity inputs are designed according to requirements (1) and (2) as

$$v_r = u_1(e, \theta, \alpha)$$
$$\omega_r = u_2(e, \theta, \alpha)$$

(3.5)

The controlled system then becomes

$$\dot{e} = f_1(e, \theta, \alpha, v_r, \omega_r) = f_1'(e, \theta, \alpha)$$

$$\dot{\theta} = f_2(e, \theta, \alpha, v_r, \omega_r) = f_2'(e, \theta, \alpha)$$

(3.6)

$$\dot{\alpha} = f_3(e, \theta, \alpha, v_r, \omega_r) = f_3'(e, \theta, \alpha)$$

where the polar configuration of the robot goes to the equilibrium point $(e = \theta = \alpha = 0)$ as time goes to infinity, i.e., $\|e_k\| = 0$.

If the velocity inputs have small perturbations $\hat{v}_r = v_r + \delta v_r$ and $\hat{\omega}_r = \omega_r + \delta \omega_r$ where $\delta v_r \neq 0$ and $\delta \omega_r \neq 0$, which happens if (3) is violated, then requirement (1) cannot be guaranteed. Under the perturbed velocity input, the controlled system becomes

$$\dot{\tilde{e}} = f_1'(\tilde{e}, \tilde{\theta}, \tilde{\alpha}) + g_1(\tilde{e}, \tilde{\theta}, \tilde{\alpha}, \delta v_r, \delta \omega_r)$$

$$\dot{\tilde{\theta}} = f_2'(\tilde{e}, \tilde{\theta}, \tilde{\alpha}) + g_2(\tilde{e}, \tilde{\theta}, \tilde{\alpha}, \delta v_r, \delta \omega_r)$$

(3.7)

$$\dot{\tilde{\alpha}} = f_3'(\tilde{e}, \tilde{\theta}, \tilde{\alpha}) + g_3(\tilde{e}, \tilde{\theta}, \tilde{\alpha}, \delta v_r, \delta \omega_r)$$

where

$$g_1(\tilde{e},\tilde{\theta},\tilde{\alpha},0,0) = 0$$

$$g_2(\tilde{e},\tilde{\theta},\tilde{\alpha},0,0) = 0 \tag{3.8}$$

$$g_3(\tilde{e},\tilde{\theta},\tilde{\alpha},0,0) = 0$$

Then, for $\delta v_r \neq 0$ and $\delta \omega_r \neq 0$, the new equilibrium point is nonzero, which violates requirement (1). The requirement (3) is therefore proven.

In order to satisfy the above requirements, a centralized kinematic motion controller is presented as [64]

$$v_r = \frac{\begin{Bmatrix} k_1 e\sqrt{\zeta - \cos 2\theta}\, \tanh(e - r\sqrt{2}\sqrt{\zeta - \cos 2\theta}) \\ + v_d e \cos\theta\sqrt{\zeta - \cos 2\theta} + v_d r\sqrt{2}\sin 2\theta\left(\sin\theta + \kappa_d e\right) \end{Bmatrix}}{e\sqrt{\zeta - \cos 2\theta} + r\sqrt{2}\sin 2\theta \sin\alpha} \tag{3.9}$$

$$\omega_r = k_2 \tanh(\theta + \alpha) + \frac{2}{e}\left(v_r \sin\alpha - v_d \sin\theta\right) - v_d \kappa_d$$

where r is the radius of a circular *path manifold*. $\zeta = 1 + \varepsilon$ and ε is a sufficiently small perturbation. Refer to [64] for detailed derivation of this controller.

Since the above kinematic motion controller is centralized, the cascade connection was developed to provide commands to each axle [65]. To satisfy the pure bending requirement (4), ψ may be solved numerically using the expression for the path radius of point R,

$$\frac{1}{r} = \frac{2\psi}{L\cos\psi}, \tag{3.10}$$

where L is the frame length. Hence, the linear and angular velocities of each axle, $v_{r,i}$ and $\omega_{r,i}$, are obtained by

$$v_{r,i} = \frac{v_r}{\cos\psi} + \frac{(-1)^i}{6}L\psi\dot{\psi} \qquad \begin{cases} i = 1 \text{ for front axle} \\ \\ i = 2 \text{ for rear axle} \end{cases} \tag{3.11}$$

$$\omega_{r,i} = \omega_r + (-1)^{i-1}\dot{\psi}.$$

which satisfies physical constraints imposed by the frame.

In the centralized kinematic controller, the velocity $(v_r, \cdot\omega_r)$ of the middle point of the front and rear axle units, R, was introduced as the auxiliary centralized states. These centralized states were then passed between the axle units using the cascade connection mentioned above. The limitation of the centralized kinematic controller is that scalability of the aforementioned controller to multi-axle configurations is not trivial [63], which is discussed in Chapter 4.

3.4 Dynamic Motion Controller

Likewise, the dynamic motion controller provides wheel torque commands to the robot based upon the reference trajectory from the kinematic motion controller $(q_{r,i}, v_{r,i}, \omega_{r,i})$. The dynamic motion controller is designed such that

1. Dynamic motion control is distributed for scalability and reduced axle-level computational burden.
2. Model-based, frame-interaction force estimates are included in the controller such that frame force disturbances on e_d are reduced.
3. Each axle follows the individual reference trajectories from the kinematic motion controller robustly using wheel torque commands. When the CFMMR works on rough terrain or even more complicated environments, the compliant frame forces might not be estimated accurately enough. So the dynamic motion controller should be robust and adaptive to the uncertainties caused by the complex interaction forces and the other dynamic disturbances. The trajectory-tracking error should be uniformly bounded based on the bounded compliant frame forces, i.e., $\|e_d\| \le \varepsilon_d, \varepsilon_d > 0$.

In order to satisfy all three requirements, a distributed motion controller is given by [64,66]

$$\tau_i = -(\mathbf{S}_i^T \mathbf{E}_i)^{-1} K_i \mathbf{e}_{c,i} \|\xi_i\|^2 \tag{3.12}$$

Here

$$\xi_i^T = \left\{ \|\mathbf{v}_i\| \|\mathbf{v}_i\|, \|\mathbf{v}_i\|, \|\mathbf{v}_{r,i}\|, \|\dot{\mathbf{v}}_{r,i}\|, 1, \|\mathbf{F}_{K,i}(q_{s,i}, q_{s,i\pm1})\| \right\} \tag{3.13}$$

$$\mathbf{e}_{c,i} = \mathbf{v}_i - \mathbf{v}_{c,i} \tag{3.14}$$

$$\mathbf{v}_{c,i} = \begin{bmatrix} v_{r,i} \cos e_{\phi,i} + k_{X,i} e_{X,i} \\ \omega_{r,i} + k_{Y,i} v_{r,i} e_{Y,i} + k_{\phi,i} v_{r,i} \sin e_{\phi,i} \end{bmatrix} \tag{3.15}$$

$$\begin{bmatrix} e_{X,i} & e_{Y,i} & e_{\phi,i} \end{bmatrix}^T = \mathbf{R}_{\phi,i} (q_{r,i} - q_{s,i}) \tag{3.16}$$

$$\mathbf{R}_{\phi,i} = \begin{bmatrix} \cos\phi_{s,i} & \sin\phi_{s,i} & 0 \\ -\sin\phi_{s,i} & \cos\phi_{s,i} & 0 \\ 0 & 0 & 1 \end{bmatrix} \tag{3.17}$$

$$\mathbf{E}_i = \frac{1}{r_w} \begin{bmatrix} \cos\phi_{s,i} & \sin\phi_{s,i} & -d \\ \cos\phi_{s,i} & \sin\phi_{s,i} & d \end{bmatrix}^T \tag{3.18}$$

$$\mathbf{S}_i^T = \begin{bmatrix} \cos\phi_{s,i} & \sin\phi_{s,i} & 0 \\ 0 & 0 & 1 \end{bmatrix} \tag{3.19}$$

where ξ_i is a known, positive definite vector. $K_i = \begin{bmatrix} K_{1,i} & 0 \\ 0 & K_{2,i} \end{bmatrix}$ is the matrix control gain, and $K_{1,i}$, $K_{2,i}$, $k_{X,i}$, $k_{Y,i}$, and $k_{\phi,i}$ are positive constants. $\mathbf{v}_i = [v_{s,i} \quad \omega_{s,i}]^T$ is the estimated axle velocity vector obtained from the sensory system. The r_w and d are wheel radius and half axle length, respectively, Figure 2.12. $\mathbf{F}_{K,i}$ is the estimated frame force vector [66]. For the detailed derivation of these equations, refer to Chapter 6.

3.5 Sensory System

The sensor system provides posture and velocity feedback to the dynamic motion controllers according to the architecture, Figure 3.2. The sensor system is designed such that

1. Independent sensors are distributed on each axle.
2. Cooperative sensors provide relative posture estimates between neighboring axles.
3. Sensor data (either independent or cooperative) is fused to minimize posture-estimate error, Figure 3.2, i.e., $\|e_s\| \leq \varepsilon_s, \varepsilon_s > 0$.
4. Sensor fusion is distributed for scalability and reduced axle-level computational burden.

Traditional independent sensors (odometry, inertial measurements, and even GPS) fused with common model-based extended Kalman filters provide axle posture estimates that are prone to drift and uncertainty. Such estimates are insufficient for managing cooperation amongst robots where interaction forces

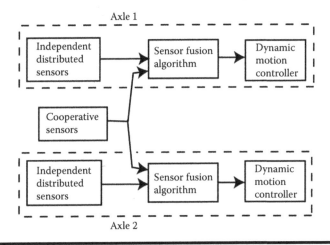

Figure 3.2 Sensor fusion algorithm block diagram.

may occur. In the case of the CFMMR, frame compliance could cause large inter-action forces due to drift in relative axle-posture estimates. Thus, requirement (2) specifies that cooperative sensors be provided to bound relative posture-estimate error.

A sensory system incorporating relative position sensors (RPS) is presented to satisfy the above requirements [66,67]. The cooperative RPS consists of a series of strain gauges placed at known locations along the length of the compliant frame in order to provide a strain polynomial. The relative posture $(x_{RPS}, y_{RPS}, \phi_{RPS})$ of one axle to the other is calculated by piecewise integration of dx, dy, and $d\phi$. Assuming a sufficiently small step size, dL, the dx, dy, and $d\phi$ can be calculated as

$$d\phi = dL / \rho$$

$$dx = \rho \sin(d\phi) \tag{3.20}$$

$$dy = \rho(1 - \cos(d\phi))$$

where the frame radius of curvature ρ is obtained directly from the strain polynomial.

The EKF is used as the first tier of the sensor fusion algorithm in order to provide axle-level posture estimates based upon independent sensors. Since these estimates will drift and provide poor relative axle-posture estimates, the covariance intersection (CI) filter is used for second-tier data fusion to combine EKF and RPS data to bound relative posture estimates. Identical implementations of these fusion algorithms operate on each axle module. Readers can refer to Chapter 5 for more detail of the sensory system design.

Chapter 4

Kinematic Motion Control

4.1 Introduction

Within the motion control and sensing architecture discussed in Chapter 3 [68], a kinematic controller provides velocity commands that act as reference inputs for a dynamic controller responsible for rejecting disturbances and tracking the kinematic reference trajectory. The dynamic controller then produces force/torque commands to drive the actual robot. So the kinematic motion control deals with the study of motion without considering forces required to create the motion. In this chapter, we discuss how to design the corresponding kinematic motion-control algorithms considering the physical constraints of compliantly coupled multi-robot systems such as the CFMMR, Figure 4.1.

In other words, the CFMMR can be used as the motivating example of multi-robot coordination. The control algorithm is thus derived based upon the physical limitations of the CFMMR, where the steering and maneuvering of the system are accomplished via coordinated control of the axles. Homogeneity of the CFMMR allows it to be reconfigured for different applications, such as the multi-axle, snake-like robot shown in Figure 4.1b. However, the compliant frame accentuates the general issues of path curvature and velocity constraints in mobile robots.

General physical constraints in a wheeled mobile robot [69] can be established as path curvature and velocity limitations based upon actuator limitations, mechanical design features, and terrain features. As we mentioned in the last two chapters, limited actuators of real robots can produce only finite speeds; wheel traction forces are limited by tire-ground interactions; and achievable path curvature is limited by physical design and dynamic effects. Most kinematic motion controllers ignore these physical effects, though, and focus solely on control and planning considering nonholonomic constraints. It is important to include physical considerations in the kinematic motion controller since these commands are typically used as inputs to

(a)

(b)

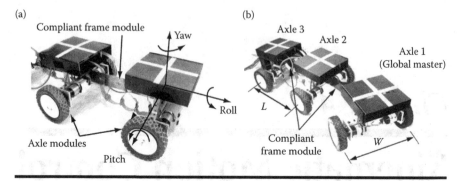

Figure 4.1 Compliant framed modular mobile robot platforms; $L=w=0.366$ m, wheel radius $=0.073$ m. (a) Two-axle CFMMR and (b) Multi-axle CFMMR.

the dynamic controller of the physical system. The mobility and maneuverability of a multi-robot system are also critically impacted by the interactions among coupled modules as well as by the general physical constraints of each module. In order to resolve interactions and physical constraints, motion control of the system must be coordinated.

Traditionally, the primary motion-control tasks of posture regulation, path following, and trajectory tracking have been treated separately. As a result, discontinuous or switching motion algorithms [70–73] have been applied to solve these motion-control tasks, which may produce large errors or lead to slow convergence. In this chapter, we present a single smooth time-invariant control law capable of all three motion-control tasks while considering physical constraints. The path manifold–based controller [69] is thus presented to simultaneously solve the primary motion-control problems for unicycle-type wheeled mobile robots subject to physical constraints (Figure 4.2). The path manifold–based controller can also be applied directly to two-axle robots whose kinematics can be reduced equivalently to a unicycle-type model. Due to finite-time forward smooth path convergence,

Figure 4.2 Unicycle-type wheeled mobile robot; $W=0.22$ m, $L=0.18$ m, $H=0.2$ m.

the designed controller can provide this capability given particular regions of initial conditions and paths and trajectories with constrained velocity and curvature.

We then present a distributed master-slave control structure for the multi-axle CFMMR train to provide simplicity and uniform extendibility to the controller. In this control structure, the first axle of the robot, Axle 1, Figure 4.1, guides motion of the robot as a global master. The other axles then become local masters and/or slaves depending on their relative positions in the train. Axle i ($i \geq 2$) is a slave relative to Axle $i-1$, whereas it is the master of Axle $i+1$. A slave then tracks its master while complying with kinematic and dynamic constraints.

Since the kinematics of the global master module is described only by a unicycle-type model, controllers derived for unicycle-type robots can be applied as the global master controller. In this book, the path manifold–based controller is used since it can solve motion-control problems while satisfying path curvature and velocity constraints. An axle's slave controller is then determined to accommodate foreshortening and orientation of the compliant frame while following its master. Given a global master controller that resolves physical constraints on path curvature and velocity, the Axle i controller is designed to satisfy physical constraints as well.

4.2 Control of Unicycle-Type Robots

Kinematic control of mobile robotic systems has received a great deal of attention since the end of last century and many motion-control schemes have been presented to consider their nonholonomic constraints. Traditionally, Cartesian coordinates have been used to model and control mobile robots [74–77], but these efforts have resulted in discontinuous or time-varying control laws. This is because a smooth, time-invariant control law cannot be realized to stabilize nonholonomic robots in Cartesian coordinates, as proven in [45]. Discontinuous velocity trajectories are not easily reproduced on real robots. Time-varying control schemes are generally slow and show oscillatory behaviors, as shown in [70]. Faster convergence can be achieved using a non-smooth, time-varying controller [78], but it is difficult to ensure bounded velocity and curvature commands since these schemes are based upon conversion to a chained form.

It is important to note that Brockett's theorem [45] requires a system to be continuous in a neighborhood of the equilibrium point. Thus, by introducing discontinuity in the equilibrium point with a polar coordinate system, Brockett's theorem cannot be applied, and a smooth, time-invariant control law is allowed. Similarly, circles can be used for discontinuous coordinate transformation [79]. The polar representation was introduced by Badreddin and Mansour [80] to provide local asymptotic stability in posture regulation using time-invariant control. Aicardi et al. [71] and Astolfi [81] subsequently applied polar coordinates to derive smooth and globally stabilizing state-feedback control laws. Singularity occurs at the origin in the polar coordinate system. Singularity issues can be avoided by appropriately selecting initial conditions or intermediate points [81], or by applying a simple state-feedback control law to make the closed loop system nonsingular [80,81]. Thus, the polar representation has been commonly adopted for posture regulation.

Path curvature is generally an issue for mobile robots, given steering restrictions determined by mechanical design and traction limitations. As shown in Figure 4.3, it is assumed that permissible steering paths are restricted. Thus, arcs or circles are frequently used to construct curvature constrained paths between two given points in motion planning [82,83]. Actuators likewise possess limited capabilities, and realizable wheel velocity is restricted. Furthermore, excessive velocity commands may cause wheel slip, large path curvature, or excessive traction forces. In some motion-control research [84–86], velocity and curvature constraints have been considered simply using saturation or by designing control gains. In contrast, appreciable motion planning algorithms have been presented to generate feasible reference paths for hazard or obstacle avoidance considering physical constraints on acceleration, velocity, or path curvature [87–91]. Most notably, though, we consider these constraints in closed-loop kinematic controls as opposed to path planning. This helps to assure that the robot does not violate physical constraints while converging to its reference, as opposed to the latter that focuses on assuring that the path itself is mindful of constraints.

In order to satisfy velocity and curvature limitations while performing all three motion-control tasks, we first embed curvature constraints in the controller using a path manifold. The path manifold is a geometric tool that defines the shape of the path that the robot follows while converging to its target or trajectory. The path manifold also provides nonsingular uniform coordinates to solve the primary motion-control problems. In this case, a circular path manifold with radius-satisfying curvature constraints is used. The robot is driven to the path manifold using a Lyapunov-based control design similar to the sliding-mode

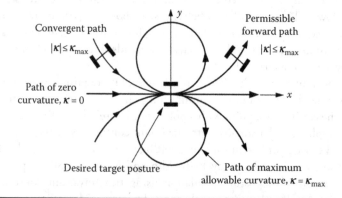

Figure 4.3 **Permissible forward paths and convergent paths of a mobile robot with respect to the path curvature.**

control algorithms [92,93]. However, the resulting path manifold–based controller is smooth and continuous without the switching characteristic of the sliding mode control.

Once the robot reaches a neighborhood of the path manifold in finite time, velocity and curvature limitations are satisfied for posture regulation and for sufficiently constrained path and trajectory properties. However, transient controller commands during convergence to the path manifold critically depend upon initial conditions and path/trajectory properties. Thus, controller parameters are optimized to maximize the region of allowable initial conditions while satisfying curvature and velocity constraints for posture regulation. Initial conditions in immediate proximity to the target are limited by curvature constraints, but this can be easily resolved by providing intermediate target configurations within allowable regions. Controller dynamics are then extended to accommodate the actual initial conditions of the robot. We then demonstrate that this time-invariant controller provides smooth bounded commands for all three motion-control tasks given allowable initial conditions and constrained path/trajectory properties.

4.2.1 Kinematic Model

In this section, the general kinematics of a unicycle-type robot are derived in the polar representation. To consider the primary motion-control tasks simultaneously, the reference posture is denoted using the reference frame R, Figure 4.4.

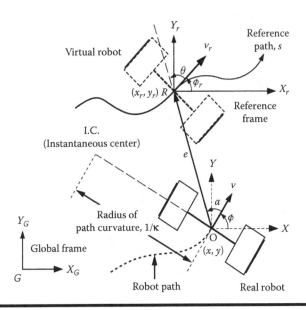

Figure 4.4 **Kinematics of a unicycle-type mobile robot for kinematic motion control.**

The reference posture is described using a virtual robot that inherits kinematics of the real robot such that it provides reference paths or trajectories that the robot can follow. We first consider the unicycle-type kinematic models of robot posture and reference posture described by Cartesian variables, $[x, y, \phi]$ and $[x_r, y_r, \phi_r]$, respectively:

$$\dot{x} = v \cos\phi, \quad \dot{y} = v \sin\phi, \quad \dot{x}_r = v_r \cos\phi_r, \quad \dot{y}_r = v_r \sin\phi_r \qquad (4.1)$$

where x and y are the Cartesian coordinates of a moving coordinate frame attached to the point O. A reference position (x_r, y_r) is attached to the moving frame R to describe its location relative to the global frame G. The variable v represents the velocity of the coordinate frame O moving in a heading ϕ relative to the global frame G. The subscript r denotes the reference frame. Thus, v_r and ϕ_r are the reference velocity and the reference-heading angle of the coordinate frame R, respectively. In this book, we focus on forward motion along paths, i.e., $v_r \geq 0$. Furthermore, backward motion can easily be realized by using coordinate transformation.

Using the polar representation relative to posture O, the kinematics can be written in error coordinates. The error states in polar representation are defined as

$$e = \sqrt{(x - x_r)^2 + (y - y_r)^2}$$

$$\theta = ATAN2\left(-(y - y_r), -(x - x_r)\right) - \phi_r \qquad (4.2)$$

$$\alpha = \theta - \phi + \phi_r$$

To derive error-state equations in polar coordinates, we differentiate Equation 4.2:

$$\dot{e} = \frac{(x_r - x)(\dot{x}_r - \dot{x}) + (y_r - y)(\dot{y}_r - \dot{y})}{e}$$

$$\dot{\theta} = \frac{(\dot{y}_r - \dot{y})(x_r - x) - (y_r - y)(\dot{x}_r - \dot{x})}{(x_r - x)^2 \sec^2(\theta + \phi_r)} - \dot{\phi}_r \qquad (4.3)$$

$$\dot{\alpha} = \dot{\theta} - \dot{\phi} + \dot{\phi}_r$$

Substituting Equations 4.1 and 4.2 into Equation 4.3 and applying trigonometric identities, the error-state equations are then obtained:

$$\dot{e} = -v \cos\alpha + v_r \cos\theta$$

$$\dot{\theta} = v \frac{\sin\alpha}{e} - v_r \frac{\sin\theta}{e} - \dot{\phi}_r \qquad (4.4)$$

$$\dot{\alpha} = v \frac{\sin\alpha}{e} - v_r \frac{\sin\theta}{e} - \dot{\phi}$$

where the angular velocity of point O can be described as a function of the path curvature, κ, and the linear velocity, v, such that $\dot{\phi} = v\kappa$. Likewise, the reference angular velocity is expressed as $\dot{\phi}_r = v_r \kappa_r$.

The path-following and trajectory-tracking problems can be solved by applying traditional nonlinear techniques to Equation 4.4. However, traditional tracking controllers lack the ability to stabilize the robot to the desired posture when the reference coordinates are fixed (i.e., posture regulation). For this reason, posture regulation and reference tracking have traditionally been considered as different problems. Note that the reference frame R represents a virtual reference posture such that it may describe the primary motion-control tasks simultaneously. For posture regulation, the frame R is fixed in the global frame G. For path following, the frame R moves along a predefined geometric path consisting of the locus of positions and orientations. Arbitrary but bounded velocities can thus be chosen for the reference. Further, for trajectory tracking, both trajectories of the frame R and the desired path are identically parameterized by time such that velocities are specified at each position. Thus, by simply modifying reference velocity expressions, the trajectory-tracking controller may easily solve all primary motion-control tasks.

4.2.2 Path Manifold

The path manifold is used as a geometric tool to specify path shape in nonsingular uniform coordinates during convergence to a desired posture or trajectory. In this section a circular path manifold is defined to satisfy curvature constraints. The path manifold is then applied to the kinematic equations to derive velocity expressions that assure stabilization along the manifold. To realize a circular path manifold, Figure 4.5, position and angle conditions are derived first. Position error in the coordinate frame of the reference is determined by

$$\hat{x}_e = \hat{x}_r - \hat{x} = r \sin 2\theta, \quad \hat{y}_e = \hat{y}_r - \hat{y} = r - r \cos 2\theta \qquad (4.5)$$

where r is the radius of the circular path manifold. Applying Equation 4.5 to the error definition (Equation 4.2), the position e is defined as, $e = \sqrt{(r \sin 2\theta)^2 + (r - r \cos 2\theta)^2} = r\sqrt{2}\sqrt{1 - \cos 2\theta}$ where requirements for θ can be deduced from Figure 4.5. Note that the velocity vector $\mathbf{v}$ and reference velocity vector $\mathbf{v}_r$ are tangent to Circles I and II. The position error vector $\mathbf{e}$ bisects the angle between $\mathbf{v}$ and $\mathbf{v}_r$ such that the angle α is equal and opposite of θ on the manifold. Denoting $\eta = \sqrt{1 - \cos 2\theta} \geq 0$, the circular path manifold is thus

$$e = \sqrt{2}r\eta, \quad \alpha = -\theta \qquad (4.6)$$

Several features of the circular path manifold are noted. First, since the path manifold is tangential to the $\hat{X}_r$ axis, this results in $\theta = \alpha = 0$ at the reference origin. Second,

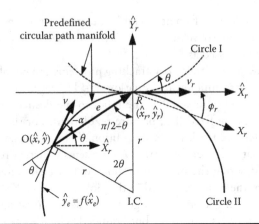

Figure 4.5 **Curvature based approach using a circular path manifold.**

we have $r \geq r_{min} = 1/\kappa_{max}$ to consider the curvature constraint $|\kappa| \leq \kappa_{max}$. In particular, we choose $r = 1/\kappa_{max}$ here to demonstrate steering capability using maximum curvature. Finally, the circular path manifold selected depends upon initial orientation, $\theta(0)$: Circle I for $0 \leq \theta(0) \leq \pi$ and Circle II for $-\pi \leq \theta(0) < 0$, Figure 4.5. Note that Circles I and II are symmetric with respect to the x-axis. Thus, paths generated by Circles I and II are also symmetric with respect to the x-axis.

We now show that velocities can be calculated to assure convergence of the error-state equations (Equation 4.4) along the path manifold. In order to determine generalized velocity expressions, derivatives of Equation 4.6 are first expressed as

$$\begin{aligned} \dot{e} &= 2r\dot{\theta}U\cos(\theta) \\ \dot{\alpha} &= -\dot{\theta} \end{aligned} \quad ; \quad U = \begin{cases} 1, & \text{if } 0 \leq \theta(0) \leq \pi \\ -1, & \text{if } -\pi \leq \theta(0) < 0 \end{cases} \qquad (4.7)$$

where U is determined based upon the initial condition of the robot and $\dot{\theta}$ has the opposite sign of U such that $\dot{\theta}U = -|\dot{\theta}|$. Applying Equation 4.6 to Equation 4.4, we then obtain the system equations along the circular path manifold

$$\dot{e} = (-v + v_r)\cos\theta$$

$$\dot{\theta} = -\frac{(v + v_r)}{2r}U - \dot{\phi}_r \qquad (4.8)$$

$$\dot{\alpha} = -\frac{(v + v_r)}{2r}U - \dot{\phi}$$

where path following and trajectory tracking are also considered given v_r and $\dot{\phi}_r$. Velocity expressions are then evaluated to make Equation 4.8 equivalent to Equation 4.7

$$v = v_r + 2r\,|\dot{\theta}\,|$$

$$\dot{\phi} = 2\dot{\theta} + \dot{\phi}_r$$

(4.9)

which provides stabilization along the path manifold. Thus, these velocities drive the robot to the origin along a circular path such that $(e,\,\theta,\,\alpha)$ converge to zero. Once at the origin, Equation 4.9 gives $v = v_r$ and $\dot{\phi} = \dot{\phi}_r$ such that $\dot{e} = \dot{\theta} = \dot{\alpha} = 0$. The origin of the error coordinates is thus an equilibrium point for trajectory tracking and path following as well as posture regulation. Also note that the singularity observed in Equation 4.4 is not present in Equation 4.8 given the path manifold.

4.2.3 Control Law

We now derive a smooth, time-invariant motion controller that will drive the robot to the path manifold, which then steers the error coordinates to their origin. As a result, the robot is asymptotically driven to an arbitrarily small neighborhood of the desired posture, path, or trajectory. Control parameters are then tuned to assure that physical constraints are satisfied. In the case of the CFMMR [69], we can establish curvature and velocity constraints based upon actuator limitations, mechanical design, and terrain features limiting robot dynamic motion by $|v| \leq v_{max}$, $|\dot{\phi}| \leq \dot{\phi}_{max}$, and $|\kappa| \leq \kappa_{max}$ where $\kappa_{max} = 3$ m^{-1}, $v_{max} = 0.5$ m/s, and $\dot{\phi}_{max} = 1.5$ rad/s.

4.2.3.1 Lyapunov-Based Control Design

Lyapunov-based techniques are used to derive the foundation of our motion controller, as indicated in Theorem 1, to drive the robot to the path manifold. Corollaries 1 and 2 then prove that the controller drives the robot along the path manifold to the origin of the error coordinates. Unacceptable potential singularities exist, however. Based on Theorem 1, the final velocity controller is thus presented in Equation 4.27 with slight modifications to remove unacceptable singularities and to introduce the perturbed path manifold to allow α and θ to be well defined at the equilibrium point. Theorem 2 proves convergence to the perturbed path manifold in posture regulation. The equilibrium point of the perturbed path manifold is presented in Theorem 3, and local stability is proven in Corollary 3. Asymptotic stability of the error coordinates is examined in Corollary 4. Finally, regions of attraction are discussed.

The discontinuity at the origin of the polar coordinates allows a time-invariant controller to be derived, and Brockett's obstruction does not apply [71]. Due to the singularity, Lyapunov-based techniques are valid everywhere except for the origin, but linearization at the origin can be used to verify stability. Thus, for practical purposes, a stabilizing control law can be derived using Lyapunov functions [71,81].

Similar to sliding mode control techniques, a state feedback control law is derived to steer the system to the path manifold (Equation 4.6) where $z_1 = 0$ and $z_2 = 0$ by denoting

$$z_1 = e - \sqrt{2}r\eta$$

$$z_2 = \theta + \alpha$$

(4.10)

Note that $z_1 \geq -\sqrt{2}r\eta$ since $e \geq 0$. Once the robot reaches the path manifold, the path manifold guarantees stabilization of the robot to the origin of the error coordinates.

Theorem 1. The following control law provides asymptotic convergence of the states in $M = \left\{ (e, \theta, \alpha) \in R^3 \middle| e > 0 \text{ and } \alpha \neq -\tan^{-1}\left(\dfrac{e\sqrt{1 - \cos 2\theta}}{r\sqrt{2}\sin(2\theta)} \right) \right\}$ to the path manifold, which drives z_1 and z_2 to zero

$$v = \frac{k_1\eta(z_1 + \sqrt{2}r\eta)\tanh z_1 + v_r\eta(z_1 + \sqrt{2}r\eta)\cos\theta + v_r r\sqrt{2}\sin 2\theta\left(\sin\theta + \kappa_r(z_1 + \sqrt{2}r\eta)\right)}{\eta(z_1 + \sqrt{2}r\eta)\cos(z_2 - \theta) + r\sqrt{2}\sin 2\theta\sin(z_2 - \theta)}$$

(4.11)

$$\dot{\phi} = \kappa v = k_2 \tanh z_2 + 2\dot{\theta} + \dot{\phi}_r$$

(4.12)

Proof: First, define quadratic Lyapunov candidate functions

$$V = V_1 + V_2 ; \quad V_1 \equiv \frac{1}{2}z_1^2, V_2 \equiv \frac{1}{2}z_2^2$$

(4.13)

Applying Equations 4.11 and 4.12, the time derivatives of V_1 and V_2 are then negative definite

$$\dot{V_1} = z_1\dot{z_1} = z_1\left(v_r\cos\theta - v\cos(z_2 - \theta) - \frac{r\sqrt{2}\sin 2\theta}{\eta}\dot{\theta} \right)$$

$$= -k_1 z_1 \tanh(z_1) \leq 0$$

(4.14)

$$\dot{V_2} = z_2\dot{z_2} = z_2(2\dot{\theta} + \dot{\phi}_r - \dot{\phi}) = -k_2 z_2 \tanh(z_2) \leq 0$$

(4.15)

where k_1 and k_2 are positive control gains that determine maximum convergence rates. Thus, $\dot{V} = \dot{V_1} + \dot{V_2}$ is negative definite, which proves that the states asymptotically approach the path manifold where $z_1 = 0$ and $z_2 = 0$.

Note that the presented control law is nonsingular if the denominator of Equation 4.11 is nonzero since the numerator is bounded. Applying

$\eta = \sqrt{1 - \cos 2\theta}$ to the denominator of Equation 4.11 and rewriting in error coordinates, we have

$$den(v) = e \cos(\alpha)\sqrt{1 - \cos 2\theta} + r\sqrt{2} \sin(2\theta) \sin(\alpha) \neq 0 \qquad (4.16)$$

Solving Equation 4.16 for α, we then have

$$\alpha \neq -\tan^{-1}\left(\frac{e\sqrt{1 - \cos 2\theta}}{r\sqrt{2} \sin(2\theta)}\right) \qquad (4.17)$$

Thus, v is nonsingular if Equation 4.17 is provided. The control law v is modified subsequently to resolve this singularity issue, and initial conditions are further discussed.

Notice that tanh functions are implemented to make the Lyapunov function derivatives negative definite and to guarantee smooth bounded control inputs for arbitrarily large initial conditions. This resolves the common problem of excessive velocity commands given large initial conditions. While this is similar in spirit to [86], their controller only provides posture regulation, whereas we provide all three primary motion-control tasks.

Corollary 1. The control law equations (4.11 and 4.12) stabilizes the closed loop system to the origin of the polar error coordinate system along the path manifold.
Proof: Let $\alpha = (z_3 - 1)\theta$ where $z_3 \in R^1$; we have,

$$z_2 = z_3\theta \qquad (4.18)$$

Differentiating Equation 4.18 and substituting into Equation 4.15, we have

$$\dot{V}_2 = z_2(\dot{z}_3\theta + z_3\dot{\theta}) = \theta^2 z_3\dot{z}_3 + z_3^2\theta\dot{\theta} = -k_2 z_2 \tanh(z_2) \leq 0 \qquad (4.19)$$

In order to provide a unique equilibrium point, we define

$$S = \left\{ e > 0, \quad \theta \in [-\pi, \pi], \alpha \in [-\pi, \pi], \alpha \neq -\tan^{-1}\left(\frac{e\sqrt{1 - \cos 2\theta}}{r\sqrt{2} \sin(2\theta)}\right) \right\} \subset M$$

Then, define Lyapunov functions to show the stabilization of θ to zero in S

$$V_3 = \frac{1}{2}z_3^2, \quad V_4 = \frac{1}{2}\theta^2 \qquad (4.20)$$

First, consider Case (i) where $\theta \neq 0$ in S where $t \geq 0$. According to Equations 4.15 through 4.19, the variables z_3, $\dot{z}_3$, and $\dot{\theta}$ are bounded since z_2 and θ are bounded. Note that z_2 asymptotically converges to zero by Theorem 1 for any θ and α for

$t \geq 0$, and by Equation 4.18 $z_3=0$, if and only if $z_2=0$ for all $\theta \neq 0$. In order for Equation 4.19 to be true for any nonzero θ, z_2, and z_3, it must be true that $\dot{V}_3 = z_3 \dot{z}_3 < 0$ and $\dot{V}_4 = \theta \dot{\theta} < 0$. Further, since $z_2 \to 0$ as $t \to \infty$, it is easily verified that $\dot{V}_3 \to 0^-$ and $\dot{V}_4 \to 0^-$ such that θ and z_3 asymptotically approach zero.

Now consider two other cases where $\theta=0$. In Case (ii) where z_3 is bounded (i.e., $|z_3| < \infty$), it must be true from Equation 4.18 that $z_2=0$ and boundedness of $\dot{z}_3$ is shown by Equation 4.19. As a result, we have $\theta^2 z_3 \dot{z}_3 = 0$. Thus, Equation 4.19 becomes $z_3^2 \theta \dot{\theta} = -k_2 z_2 \tanh(z_2)$, which can be rewritten as

$$\dot{V}_4 = \theta \dot{\theta} = \frac{-k_2 z_2 \tanh(z_2)}{z_3^2} = \frac{-k_2 \theta^2 \tanh(z_2)}{z_2} \tag{4.21}$$

Applying $z_2=0$ and $\theta=0$ to Equation 4.21, by L'Hopital's rule, we have

$$\dot{V}_4\Big|_{\substack{\theta=0 \\ z_2=0}} = -k_2 \theta^2\Big|_{\theta=0} \cdot \lim_{z_2 \to 0} \frac{\tanh(z_2)}{z_2} = -k_2 \theta^2\Big|_{\theta=0} = 0 \tag{4.22}$$

Further, in Case (iii) consider $\theta=0$ and unbounded z_3 (i.e., $z_3=\pm\infty$). It is verified that $\theta^2 z_3 \dot{z}_3$ and $z_3^2 \theta \dot{\theta}$ must be bounded to satisfy Equation 4.19. As a result, in conjunction with Case (ii), $\dot{V}_4 = \theta \dot{\theta} = 0$ must always be true when $\theta=0$.

Summarizing the aforementioned cases, it is shown that $\dot{V}_4 < 0$ for $\theta \neq 0$ and $\dot{V}_4 = 0$ for $\theta=0$. This proves that θ asymptotically converges to zero as $t \to \infty$. Further, since $z_1 \to 0$ and $z_2 \to 0$ as $t \to \infty$ (by Theorem 1), we thus have $e \to \sqrt{2}r\eta \to 0$ and $\alpha \to -\theta \to 0$ as $t \to \infty$ per Equation 4.10.

The closed loop system, Equation 4.4 with Equations 4.11 and 4.12, is then analyzed near the origin based upon linearization in Corollary 2.

Corollary 2. The origin of the closed loop system is locally exponentially stable by the control law equations (4.11 and 4.12).

Proof: The controller (Equation 4.12) drives $\alpha \to -\theta$ by Theorem 1 such that the system (Equation 4.4) becomes

$$\dot{e} = (-v + v_r)\cos\theta$$
$$\dot{\theta} = -\dot{\alpha} = -(v + v_r)\frac{\sin\theta}{e} - \dot{\phi}_r \tag{4.23}$$

The following must be true near the equilibrium point per Equation 4.23,

$$v \to v_r, \quad e \to -\frac{2v_r}{\dot{\phi}_r}\sin\theta \tag{4.24}$$

Applying Equation 4.24 to the control law equations (4.11 and 4.12), and linearizing near the origin, we have

$$v = k_1 e + v_r$$

$$\dot{\phi} = k_2(\theta + \alpha) + 2k_1\alpha + \dot{\phi}_r \tag{4.25}$$

Further, applying Equation 4.25 to Equation 4.4 and linearizing, we then have

$$\dot{e} = -k_1 e$$

$$\dot{\theta} = k_1\alpha = -k_1\theta \tag{4.26}$$

$$\dot{\alpha} = -k_2\theta - (k_1 + k_2)\alpha = -k_1\alpha$$

which proves that the control law provides local exponential stability if $k_1 > 0$.

While the above shows theoretically that ideal convergence is achieved, it must be noted that α and θ are arbitrarily defined at $e=0$. To assure that they are well defined at the equilibrium of the system, we modify the path manifold by introducing an arbitrarily small $\varepsilon > 0$

$$\eta = \sqrt{1 + \varepsilon - \cos 2\theta} \tag{4.27}$$

which produces a perturbation on the controller (Equation 4.11) that will be discussed in the following Theorems and Corollaries.

Further, note that a singularity occurs at $[\alpha, \theta] = [\pi/2, \pi/2]$ in the control law (Equation 4.11). Thus, we also modify Equation 4.11 to resolve this problem by eliminating $\cos(z_2 - \theta) = \cos(\alpha)$ in the denominator of Equation 4.11, which leads to

$$\dot{V}_1 = z_1\dot{z}_1 = -k_1 z_1 \tanh z_1 + z_1 v(1 - \cos\alpha) \tag{4.28}$$

Note that Equation 4.28 is identical to Equation 4.14 as α converges to zero. The final control law, v, is then

$$v = \frac{k_1\eta(z_1 + \sqrt{2}r\eta)\tanh z_1 + v_r\eta(z_1 + \sqrt{2}r\eta)\cos\theta + v_r r\sqrt{2}\sin 2\theta\left(\sin\theta + \kappa_r(z_1 + \sqrt{2}r\eta)\right)}{\eta(z_1 + \sqrt{2}r\eta) + r\sqrt{2}\sin 2\theta\sin(z_2 - \theta)} \tag{4.29}$$

These modifications provide an arbitrarily small perturbation, which is analyzed next. The controller equations (4.11 and 4.29) produces almost similar outputs and they become identical for small α and as the robot approaches the path manifold. Now, we analyze how these modifications affect the closed loop system. We first consider posture regulation since closed form analysis can be shown.

Theorem 2. The control law equations (4.12 and 4.29) converges the states defined in $D = \{(e, \theta, \alpha) \in R^3 \mid e \geq \sqrt{2}r\eta \text{ (i.e., } z_1 \geq 0), |\theta| \leq \pi, |\alpha| \leq \pi\}$ to a perturbed path manifold in posture regulation.

Proof: The perturbed path manifold is defined by introducing $\varepsilon > 0$ in Equation 4.27

$$e = r\sqrt{2}\sqrt{1+\varepsilon - \cos(2\theta)}, \quad \theta = -\alpha \tag{4.30}$$

Applying arbitrarily small ε, the perturbed path manifold (Equation 4.30) is arbitrarily close to the path manifold (Equation 4.6). It is important to note that $z_2 = \theta + \alpha$ is not affected by the modified path manifold. Thus, considering the same Lyapunov function for V_2 in Equation 4.13, the control law (Equation 4.12) satisfies Equation 4.15, which maintains asymptotic convergence of z_2 to zero, as shown in Theorem 1. We now provide a state equation for z_1 to discuss convergence to the perturbed path manifold. By differentiating $z_1 = e - \sqrt{2}r\eta$, we have

$$\dot{z}_1 = -k_1 \tanh(z_1) + f(v,\alpha) \tag{4.31}$$

where $f = f(v,\alpha) = (1-\cos\alpha)v$ and $0 \le f \le 2v_{max}$ given $0 \le v \le v_{max}$. Note that nonvanishing f perturbs the equilibrium point of z_1 to a finite value that depends on the relative magnitude of $-k_1 \tanh(z_1)$ in Equation 4.31, which is discussed further in the next theorem.

Considering posture regulation ($v_r = 0$, $\dot{\phi}_r = v_r\kappa_r = 0$), Equation 4.29 can be simplified

$$v = \frac{k_1\eta(z_1 + \sqrt{2}r\eta)\tanh z_1}{\eta(z_1 + \sqrt{2}r\eta) + r\sqrt{2}\sin 2\theta \sin(z_2 - \theta)} \tag{4.32}$$

Note that $e = z_1 + \sqrt{2}r\eta > 0$ in M. In order to show convergence of z_1, it is important to note that z_1 and θ are coupled such that their convergence must be considered simultaneously. By applying Equation 4.32 to Equation 4.31 and the θ state equation in Equation 4.4, and noting $z_2 \to 0$, we have

$$\dot{z}_1 = -\tanh(z_1)\cos(\theta)F \tag{4.33}$$

$$\dot{\theta} = -\sin(\theta)\tanh(z_1)G \tag{4.34}$$

where

$$F = \frac{k_1(\eta z_1 + \varepsilon r\sqrt{2})}{\eta z_1 + \varepsilon r\sqrt{2} + 2\sqrt{2}r(1-\cos\theta)\sin^2\theta}$$

$$\tag{4.35}$$

$$G = \frac{k_1\eta}{\eta z_1 + \varepsilon r\sqrt{2} + 2\sqrt{2}r(1-\cos\theta)\sin^2\theta}$$

It should be noted that the controller is applied in D where $z_1 \ge 0$, or $e \ge \sqrt{2}r\eta$, to satisfy the curvature constraint $|\kappa| \le \kappa_{max}$, which excludes the inside of the path manifold. In particular, asymptotic convergence can guarantee that the robot stays in D given proper initial conditions (i.e., $z_1(0) \geq 0$). Further, since $\varepsilon > 0$ and $\eta > 0$, we can easily verify that the denominator in Equations 4.32 through 4.34 is always positive for $z_1 \geq 0$ such that we have $v \geq 0$, $F > 0$, and $G > 0$, which is useful in Lyapunov analysis and guarantees only forward motion.

Finally, we can easily show that the derivative of V_4 is negative definite for $z_1 > 0$ and zero for $z_1 = 0$ by using the Lyapunov function V_4 in Equation 4.20, which shows that

$$\dot{V}_4 = \theta\dot{\theta} = -\tanh(z_1)(\theta\sin\theta)G \tag{4.36}$$

indicating that θ can only decrease while z_1 is finite in D. At the same time, the derivative of V_1 is negative definite for $|\theta| < \pi/2$ and zero for $z_1 = 0$

$$\dot{V}_1 = z_1\dot{z}_1 = -(\cos\theta)(z_1\tanh z_1)F \tag{4.37}$$

which indicates that z_1 asymptotically converges to zero if $|\theta| < \pi/2$. Further, Equation 4.36 indicates that θ will decay such that $|\theta| < \pi/2$ can easily be achieved given $z_1 > 0$. Thus, in a worst-case situation ($\pi/2 \leq |\theta(0)| \leq \pi$), Equations 4.37 and 4.36 indicate that z_1 increases while θ simultaneously decreases. As soon as $|\theta|$ becomes less than $\pi/2$, z_1 and θ both asymptotically decrease until $z_1 = 0$ is achieved. Thus, convergence to the perturbed path manifold is proven in posture regulation.

In the general case where $v_r \neq 0$, the closed loop state equations for z_1 and θ are difficult to analyze analytically. Thus, we first numerically establish a unique equilibrium point to show the effect of perturbations on the system. We then use linearization to show local convergence to the path manifold near the equilibrium point.

Theorem 3. Using Equations 4.12 and 4.29, an equilibrium point $(z_1{}^*, \theta^*)$ is created in D that can be made arbitrarily close to the origin of the error coordinates by tuning ε.

Proof: Again, note that the controller (Equation 4.12) converges z_2 to zero by Theorem 1. We can thus rewrite Equation 4.29 by

$$v = \frac{k_1\eta(z_1 + \sqrt{2}r\eta)\tanh z_1 + v_r g}{h} \tag{4.38}$$

where

$$h = \eta z_1 + \varepsilon r\sqrt{2} + 2\sqrt{2}r(1 - \cos\theta)\sin^2\theta$$

$$g = \eta(z_1 + \sqrt{2}r\eta)\cos\theta + r\sqrt{2}\sin 2\theta\left(\sin\theta + \kappa_r(z_1 + \sqrt{2}r\eta)\right) \tag{4.39}$$

Expressing e in terms of z_1 by applying the coordinate transformation $e = z_1 + \sqrt{2}r\eta$ to Equations 4.4 and 4.31, and assuming z_2 has already converged to 0, the state equations for z_1 and θ then become

$$\dot{z}_1 = -k_1 \tanh(z_1) + (1 - \cos\theta)v = -\tanh(z_1)\cos(\theta)F + v_r(1 - \cos\theta)\frac{g}{h}$$

$$\dot{\theta} = -\dot{\alpha} = -(v + v_r)\frac{\sin\theta}{z_1 + \sqrt{2}r\eta} - \dot{\phi}_r = -\sin(\theta)\tanh(z_1)G - v_r\left(\frac{g}{h} + 1\right)\frac{\sin\theta}{z_1 + \sqrt{2}r\eta} - \dot{\phi}_r$$

$$(4.40)$$

Note that an equilibrium point cannot be solved analytically due to nonlinearity in the closed system (Equations 4.40 and 4.38). These state equations are thus solved numerically to find the equilibrium point $(z_1{}^*, \theta^*)$ as shown in Table 4.1. Three references are shown to illustrate the effect of reference speed and ε. References (A) and (B) are used to demonstrate the general case where $v_r \neq 0$. It should be noted that $z_1{}^*$ remains in a small neighborhood of the origin in spite of a large variation of reference velocities and ε. Reference (C) illustrates that posture regulation produces $z_1{}^*=0$, as mentioned in Theorem 2. In contrast, θ^* varies proportionally to ε and κ_r. Most importantly, $z_1{}^*$ and θ^* are unique in D and can be made arbitrarily small by decreasing ε. Increasing k_1 can also attenuate the perturbations, but k_1 need to be sufficiently small to satisfy v_{max}.

Note that we have $v=v_r$ and $\dot{\phi}=\dot{\phi}_r$ (i.e., $\kappa=\kappa_r$) at the equilibrium point since $g/h=1$ in Equations 4.40 and 4.38 as designed. Also note that in path following and trajectory tracking, κ_r is explicitly defined by a reference. In contrast, in posture regulation where a reference is a fixed point ($v_r=0$ and $\dot{\phi}_r = 0$), κ_r is arbitrarily

Table 4.1 Numerical Solution of the Equilibrium Point for (z_1, θ) with $k_1=1$ and Reference (A) $[v_r \text{ (m/s)}, \kappa_r \text{ (m}^{-1})] = [0.5\ v_{max}, 0.33\ \kappa_{max}]$, (B) $[0.75\ v_{max}, 0.75\ \kappa_{max}]$, and (C) $[0, 0.33\ \kappa_{max}]$ Where $v_{max}=0.5$, $\kappa_{max}=3$

Ref.	ε	$z_1{}^*$ (m)	θ^* (rad)	λ_1	λ_2
(A)	1×10^{-1}	7.91×10^{-4}	-0.0796	0.996	3.14
(A)	1×10^{-6}	7.78×10^{-9}	-2.50×10^{-4}	1	999.9
(A)	1×10^{-12}	0	-9.16×10^{-11}	1	1.06×10^6
(B)	1×10^{-1}	0.0173	-0.305	0.892	2.81
(B)	1×10^{-6}	1.21×10^{-7}	-8.02×10^{-4}	1	1.05×10^3
(B)	1×10^{-12}	1.42×10^{-15}	8.72×10^{-8}	1	1.75×10^6
(C)	1×10^{-1}	0	-0.0791	0.996	0
(C)	1×10^{-6}	0	-2.50×10^{-4}	1	0
(C)	1×10^{-12}	0	-5.82×10^{-10}	1	0

defined. In this chapter, we have $\kappa \rightarrow \kappa_r$ such that κ has a finite value according to a trajectory path generated by the control law given an initial condition.

Corollary 3. The perturbed equilibrium point is locally exponentially stable for $v_r \neq 0$ and asymptotically stable for $v_r = 0$.

Proof: Local stability can be determined by linearizing Equation 4.40 at the equilibrium point such that

$$\dot{z}_1 \approx -\lambda_1 (z_1 - z_1^*), \quad \dot{\theta} \approx -\lambda_2 (\theta - \theta^*) \tag{4.41}$$

where eigenvalues $-\lambda_1$ and $-\lambda_2$ are

$$\lambda_1 = \lim_{\substack{\theta \rightarrow \theta^* \\ z_1 \rightarrow z_1^*}} \left(\cos(\theta) F \right)$$

$$\lambda_2 = \lim_{\substack{\theta \rightarrow \theta^* \\ z_1 \rightarrow z_1^*}} \left(\tanh(z_1) G + v_r \left(\frac{g}{h} + 1 \right) \frac{1}{z_1 + \sqrt{2} r \eta} \right) \tag{4.42}$$

It is important to note that λ_1 is always positive, and that λ_2 is positive for $v_r \neq 0$, which proves local exponential stability for path following and trajectory tracking. Also, note that λ_1 converges to k_1 and λ_2 increases proportional to $1/\eta$ as ε decreases for $v_r \neq 0$, which are both illustrated in Table 4.1 for $k_1 = 1$.

For $v_r = 0$, we have $z_1^* = 0$ as indicated in Table 4.1 such that $\lambda_2 = 0$ by Equation 4.42, which is insufficient to show asymptotic stability. However, Theorem 2 proves via Lyapunov analysis that θ asymptotically decreases until $z_1 = 0$. Since $z_1 = 0$ is a unique equilibrium point for Equations 4.33 and 4.34, θ is then in equilibrium on the path manifold, which proves local asymptotic stability in posture regulation. As a result, the states converge to the perturbed path manifold where $z_1 = 0$, $z_2 = 0$, and $\theta = \theta^*$.

Given convergence to the perturbed path manifold, we now estimate the resulting equilibrium point $(e^*, \theta^*, \alpha^*)$. Corollary 1 is then extended to show asymptotic stability of the new equilibrium point.

Corollary 4. The system is asymptotically stabilized to a new equilibrium point $(e^*, \theta^*, \alpha^*)$ that can be made arbitrarily close to the origin by applying the control law equations (4.12 and 4.29).

Proof: As shown in Theorems 2 and 3, and Corollary 3, the equilibrium point of the closed loop system $(e^*, \theta^*, \alpha^*)$ is on the perturbed path manifold (Equation 4.30)

$$e^* = r\sqrt{2}\sqrt{1 + \varepsilon - \cos(2\theta^*)}, \theta^* = -\alpha^* \tag{4.43}$$

which avoids the singularity issue at the origin. Using Equation 4.24, we have

$$e^* = -\frac{2v_r}{\dot{\phi}_r} \sin \theta^* \tag{4.44}$$

Solving Equations 4.43 and 4.44 simultaneously and linearizing, we then have

$$e^* = \frac{r\sqrt{2\varepsilon}}{\sqrt{1-(r\kappa_r)^2}}, \quad \alpha^* = -\theta^* = \frac{r\kappa_r\sqrt{\varepsilon}}{\sqrt{2(1-(r\kappa_r)^2)}} \qquad (4.45)$$

where $|r\kappa_r| < 1$ since $r = 1/\kappa_{max}$ and $|\kappa_r| < \kappa_{max}$. This result shows that the equilibrium point of the closed loop system is perturbed into an arbitrarily small neighborhood of the origin given arbitrarily small ε.

Let $\hat{\theta} = \theta - \theta^*$ and $\hat{\alpha} = \alpha - \alpha^*$ to prove asymptotic convergence of the states to $(e^*, \theta^*, \alpha^*)$. We then have $z_2 = \theta + \alpha = (\theta + \alpha) - (\theta^* + \alpha^*) = \hat{\theta} + \hat{\alpha}$ and $\hat{\alpha} = (\hat{z}_3 - 1)\hat{\theta}$ such that $z_2 = \hat{z}_3, \hat{\theta}$. Thus, Corollary 1 is applied to prove that $\hat{\theta}$ and $\hat{\alpha}$ asymptotically converge to zero (i.e., $\theta \to \theta^*$ and $\alpha \to \alpha^*(=-\theta^*)$). We then have $e \to e^*$ per Equations 4.10 and 4.27 since $z_1 \to 0$. Finally, these results prove that the controller asymptotically stabilizes the system to the equilibrium point arbitrarily close to the origin without singularity.

In path following and trajectory tracking, the reference must be smooth and satisfy the physical limitations of the robot (i.e., $v_r < v_{max}$ and $\kappa_r < \kappa_{max}$) such that the robot has sufficient authority to compensate for error. For a slower moving reference, the robot has greater ability to catch up to the reference, and the range of initial conditions allowing convergence is greater. In contrast, a faster moving reference results in a smaller set of allowable initial conditions. Given the nonlinearity of the system, we illustrate this point using phase portraits for two sets of reference velocities, Figure 4.6. Regions of attraction indicate initial conditions that provide convergence to the equilibrium point $(e^*, \theta^*, \alpha^*)$. Note that the region of attraction becomes smaller for higher reference speeds and larger for slower references. If an initial condition does not satisfy the region of attraction, trajectory tracking or path following can be achieved by slowing the reference. This allows the region of attraction to expand to include the initial condition. The robot can then converge sufficiently close to the trajectory such that it can resume its normal pace. Given that a trajectory or reference path typically starts close to the robot initial condition, this is generally not a problem, and the controller can easily provide path following and trajectory tracking.

To summarize, by applying the controller equations (4.29 and 4.12) to the system (Equation 4.4), we have $(e, \theta, \alpha) \to (e^*, \theta^*, \alpha^*)(\approx (0,0,0)$, for sufficiently small ε), $(\dot{e}, \dot{\theta}, \dot{\alpha}) \to (0,0,0)$, $v \to v_r$, and $\dot{\phi} \to \dot{\phi}_r$, (i.e., $\kappa \to \kappa_r$) as $t \to \infty$, which assures tracking, regulation, and path-following capability. The ability of particular initial conditions and control gains k_1 and k_2 to satisfy velocity and path curvature constraints are discussed in following subsections.

4.2.3.2 Dependence on Initial Conditions

Due to fundamental path geometry constraints, allowable initial conditions must be considered to assure that curvature bounds are satisfied during convergence

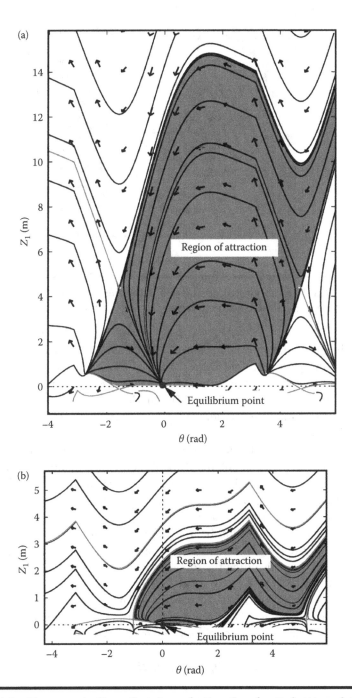

Figure 4.6 Phase portraits and region of attraction for Ref. (A) and (B) with
$\varepsilon = 1 \times 10^{-6}$, $k_1 = 1$, $v_{max} = 0.5$ m/s, $\kappa_{max} = 3$ m^{-1}. (a) Ref. (A): $v_r = 0.5$ v_{max}, $\kappa_r = 0.33$ κ_{max}
and (b) Ref. (B): $v_r = 0.75$ v_{max}, $\kappa_r = 0.75$ κ_{max}.

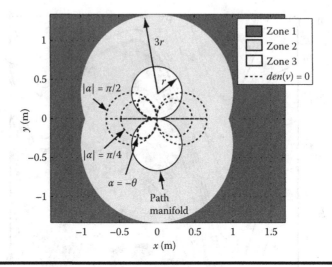

Figure 4.7 **Limitation on initial positions of a mobile robot in the error coordinates based upon maximum path curvature, $r = 1/\kappa_{max} = 0.34\,m$.**

to the path manifold. Initial conditions are divided into three zones, Figure 4.7, based upon the path manifold using $r = 1/\kappa_{max}$. Zone 3 is the interior of the circle defined by κ_{max}, and the path must violate curvature constraints in order to asymptotically converge to the path manifold. Note that the robot cannot compensate for distance errors for $z_1(0) = 0$ in posture regulation where $v_r = 0$ since we have $v = 0$ per Equation 4.29. Thus, $z_1(0) > 0$ is necessary to ensure forward motion and satisfy the curvature constraint of the actual robot during convergence to the path manifold. In Zone 2, the curvature constraint is violated for certain initial orientations due to limited steering space. Zone 2 is estimated by considering maximum path curvature here. To be guaranteed to satisfy curvature constraints for any initial orientation, the robot must start in Zone 1. However, Zone 1 could be much larger depending upon initial orientation. Further, the issue of initial conditions found in Zones 2 and 3 can be resolved easily by commanding the robot to move into Zone 1 using intermediate goal postures.

It must also be noted that large velocity commands are provided when the denominator of Equation 4.29 becomes zero. By using coordinate transformation (Equation 4.10), the denominator of Equation 4.29 is written

$$den(v) = \eta e + r\sqrt{2}\,\sin(2\theta)\sin(\alpha) \tag{4.46}$$

Considering the worst case where $den(v) = 0$, we can solve for e as a function of α and θ, in order to determine where this singularity can occur

$$e = -\frac{r\sqrt{2}\sin(2\theta)\sin(\alpha)}{\eta} = -\frac{r\sqrt{2}\sin(2\theta)\sin(\alpha)}{\sqrt{1+\varepsilon-\cos(2\theta)}} \tag{4.47}$$

Dashed lines in Figure 4.7 based on Equation 4.47 provide locus where singularity will occur for specific values of α. The locus was generated by plotting e as a function of θ where $\varepsilon = 1 \times 10^{-6}$. Note that e is largest at $|\alpha| = \pi/2$ and when $\theta \approx 0$ or $\pm\pi$. Further, e decreases and goes to zero as the magnitude of α does the same and when θ approaches $\pm\pi/2$. There is also a very small region at $\theta = 0$ or $\pm\pi$ where $e = 0$ due to ε in the denominator of Equation 4.47. It is important to note that these loci are contained well inside of Zone 2, where initial conditions are known to possibly cause difficulty. Most importantly, though, the controller (Equation 4.12) quickly forces $\alpha = -\theta$ (i.e., $z_2 = 0$), which causes the locus to contract entirely into Zone 3 as shown in Figure 4.7 where they are not a threat. Thus, this singularity issue is essentially resolved by the controller driving the system to the path manifold.

4.2.3.3 Boundedness by Design of k_1 and k_2

Control gains k_1 and k_2 must be designed to assure boundedness of v and $\dot{\phi}$ during convergence to the path manifold. Once the robot reaches the path manifold (Equation 4.6), the control law equations (4.29 and 4.12) then converge to the velocities (Equation 4.9) such that both curvature and velocity are bounded. It is assumed in this analysis that allowable initial conditions have been specified.

Implementing a fixed k_1 in the controller, it is observed in the workspace analysis that the maximum velocity increases as e decreases. This phenomenon is not desirable considering physical limitations of performing tight steering maneuvers at higher velocities. Furthermore, since the velocity and curvature expressions are highly nonlinear, simple closed form expressions of k_1 and k_2 for bounded control inputs are not easily found.

Optimization techniques based upon worst-case analyses are used to determine k_1 and k_2 in order to provide bounded curvature and velocities. Workspace mapping is thus conducted to find the worst cases where maximum velocity and curvature commands are produced, respectively, given e applying constant k_1 and k_2. Worst cases for k_1 and k_2 are observed at $(\theta, \alpha) \approx (0.2557, -1.6047)$ and $\theta(0) = \alpha(0) = \pi$, where respective maximum velocity is commanded and large orientation correction is required. Table 4.2 shows a selected optimized set of k_1 and the posture of the robot when maximum velocity occurs as a function of e. These optimization results illustrate that k_1 lies in approximately $0.2 \le k_1 \le 0.5$ and is proportional to the inverse of e. Thus, k_1 is determined as a function of states

$$k_1 = (k_{1\max} - k_{1\min})\left(1 - \tanh\left(\frac{g_1}{e}\right)\right) + k_{1\min} \tag{4.48}$$

Table 4.2 Optimized Values of k_1 for Increasing e

e (m)	θ (rad)	α (rad)	k_1
0.84	0.3092	−1.6096	0.2029
1	0.2567	−1.6048	0.2652
3	0.2136	−1.6019	0.3919
10	0.2557	−1.6047	0.4671
30	0.2556	−1.6047	0.4890
100	0.2556	−1.6047	0.4890
300	0.2556	−1.6047	0.4989
Note: Robot posture at maximum velocity is indicated.			

where $g_1 = 1.3$, $k_{1max} = 0.5$, and $k_{1min} = 0.2$ are selected such that k_1 correlates to the optimized results in Table 4.2. The value of k_{1min} determines the minimum convergence rate of e, and g_1 establishes a boundary beyond which k_{1max} will dominate.

Gain k_2 is a parameter governing the angular velocity and curvature commands. Similar to k_1, the parameter k_2 is optimized based upon worst-case conditions, Table 4.3. These results show that k_2 is significantly dependent upon e. An expression for k_2 is then determined as a function of states, e and α, and initial error distance, $e(0)$, in order to match this data and provide bounded curvature such that

$$k_2 = 0.3 \tanh\left(\frac{1}{e(0)}\right) \tanh\left(\frac{1}{2|\alpha|}\right) + 0.3 \tanh\left(\frac{1}{e}\right) \qquad (4.49)$$

These gains improve boundedness as shown in Figure 4.8b and d compared to the cases where constant gains are applied, Figure 4.8a and c. Also, note that k_1 and k_2 are always positive, and the previously discussed stability proof still applies.

Table 4.3 Optimal k_2 as a Function of e with $\theta = \alpha = \pi$ (rad)

e (m)	k_2
1	0.2938
3	0.1971
5	0.1635
10	0.1192
30	0.0601
50	0.0385
100	0.0195
300	0.0054

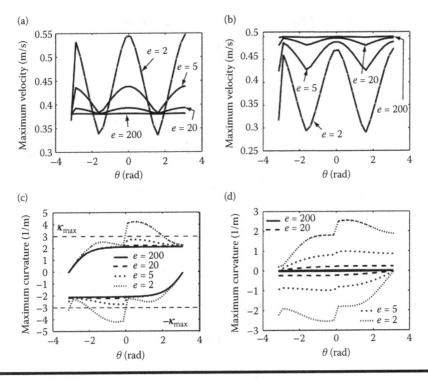

Figure 4.8 Velocity and path curvature profiles; (a) and (c) before optimization with $k_1=0.38$ and $k_2=0.8$; (b) and (d) after optimization with $k_1=$ Equation 4.48 and $k_2=$ Equation 4.49.

4.2.3.4 Dynamic Extension

Initial values of v and κ specified by Equations 4.29 and 4.12 rarely match those of the robot. These problems may be resolved by extending the controller dynamics in a cascade fashion per Bacciotti Theorem 19.2 [94] by introducing new states

$$\dot{v} = -k_v(v - v_D) + \dot{v}_D \ ; \ k_v > 0, \ k_c > 0$$

$$\dot{\kappa} = -k_c(\kappa - \kappa_D) + \dot{\kappa}_D \tag{4.50}$$

where v and κ are the extended velocity and curvature states used to command the robot, and v_D and κ_D are the desired control velocity and curvature established by Equations 4.29 and 4.12. Since the dynamic extensions add additional servo-loops to the original system (Equation 4.4), the eigenvalues k_v and k_c of the dynamic extension should be faster than those of the original system. Since k_1 and k_2 are both small (recall $k_1 \leq 0.5$ and $k_2 \leq 0.3$), we simply use $k_v = k_c = 1$.

4.2.4 Controller Implementation and Evaluation

4.2.4.1 Methods and Procedures

We evaluate the path-manifold–based controller in simulation and experiment. Simulations are used to validate the controller's capability to satisfy curvature and velocity constraints from a wide variety of initial postures. Posture regulation, path following, and trajectory tracking are evaluated in simulation. Zones of valid initial conditions are more precisely defined via workspace sweeps.

Experimental results are shown to demonstrate application of the controller to an actual robot considering physical constraints. Both posture regulation and path following are considered in experiment. A high traction carpet surface is used to illustrate performance under ideal circumstances. Both simulation and experimental results are based upon the ideal unicycle kinematic model (4.4). In experiments, the controller equations (4.12 and 4.29) combined with Equation 4.50 are first applied to the two-axle CFMMR, Figure 4.1a, using MATLAB with Real-Time Workshop and a dSPACE tethered to the robot for rapid control prototyping and controller evaluation. The complex kinematics of the two-axle CFMMR, Figure 4.9, is reduced to Equation 4.4 in unicycle-equivalent coordinates O by applying curvature based steering where $\psi = \psi_1 = -\psi_2$ as established in Chapter 2. The steering angle ψ may also be solved numerically by

$$\kappa = \frac{1}{r} = \frac{2\psi}{L \cos \psi} \tag{4.51}$$

given the frame length, L, and curvature command, κ. The linear and angular velocities of each axle v_i and $\dot{\phi}_i$ and wheel angular velocities $\dot{q}_{i,j}$ can then be found using v and $\dot{\phi}$ of the center posture O

$$v_i = \frac{v}{\cos \psi} + \frac{(-1)^i}{6} L \psi \dot{\psi}$$

$$\dot{\phi}_i = \dot{\phi} + (-1)^{i-1} \dot{\psi} \quad ; \quad \begin{cases} i = 1 \text{ for front axle} \\ i = 2 \text{ for rear axle} \\ j = 1 \text{ for right wheel} \\ j = 2 \text{ for left wheel} \end{cases} \tag{4.52}$$

$$\dot{q}_{i,j} = \frac{v_i + (-1)^{j-1} \dot{\phi}_i d}{r_w}$$

The controller is also applied to the untethered unicycle-type mobile robot, Figure 4.2, with an Arduino Due using C/C++ based Arduino programming language to demonstrate microcontroller implementation. More technical details on microcontroller implementation, such as sampling times and wheel servo controllers, can be found in [95,96].

Since we focus on ideal kinematic motion-control algorithms that can produce references for the dynamic controller, robot dynamics and disturbances are

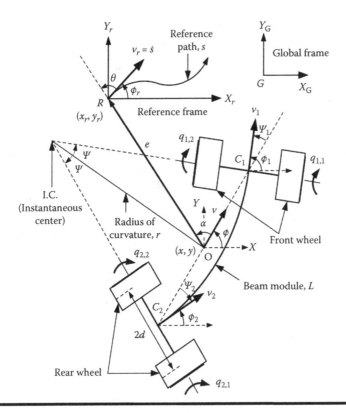

Figure 4.9   General kinematics of the CFMMR.

not considered here. Traditional servo-type wheel controllers based upon filtered wheel encoder odometry are used to drive the robot. In a worst-case scenario, wheel odometry is fed directly to the kinematic controller instead of using ideal kinematic models. Final robot positions are obtained relative to grid work suspended above the robot to illustrate actual performance independently of wheel odometry. Measurements are taken with a tape measure, and the estimated accuracy of these measurements is ±1 mm. These experiments ultimately demonstrate that the kinematic controller is also robust to disturbances and can also be used in traditional servo loop configurations.

Since reference paths and trajectory generation are not the focus of this book, we implement typical simple paths with constant curvature [83]. In path following, the reference path is $v_r = v_{des} \tanh(0.1/e)$, $\kappa_r = \kappa_{des}$, where v_{des} and κ_{des} represent desired path-segment velocity and curvature, respectively. In trajectory tracking, the reference trajectory is $\dot{x}_r = v_{des} \cos(\phi_r(t))$, $\dot{y}_r = v_{des} \sin(\phi_r(t))$, and $\dot{\phi}_r(t) = \kappa_{des} v_{des}$ where $x_r(0) = y_r(0) = 0$ m.

4.2.4.2 Results and Discussion

Figure 4.10 shows the posture regulation response of the controller given different initial orientations with the same initial error distance of $e(0)=2\,\text{m}$. Paths, states, velocities, and curvatures of Point O are shown in Figure 4.10a–d, respectively. These results confirm that the paths have smooth bounded curvature and require only forward motion as designed. In the worst case, curvature is 2.9 m^{-1} and velocity is 0.37 m/s, which is less than $\kappa_{max}=3$ m^{-1} and $v_{max}=0.5$ m/s, respectively. For symmetric positive and negative initial orientations, curvature profiles and robot paths are symmetric with respect to the x-axis, whereas velocity profiles are identical. Further, the error states approach a small neighborhood of the origin in finite time and converge to the perturbed equilibrium point asymptotically. Note that in all cases z_1 and z_2 converge faster than the error states as designed, Figure 4.10 b and c. This verifies that the robot approaches the perturbed path manifold first and then error states are stabilized along the path manifold, which is proven in theorems and corollaries in Section 4.2.3.1.

Path following demonstrates similar smooth paths and convergence of error states. Boundedness of path curvature and velocity are demonstrated in Figure 4.11 for a circular reference path with a 1 m radius. Velocity and curvature profiles vary according to their initial orientation angles similar to posture regulation. In both posture regulation and path following, larger velocity and path curvature are commanded for large initial orientation errors. Likewise, maximum velocity is detected at $\alpha(0)=-\pi$ while maximum curvature is observed at $\alpha(0)=-3\pi/4$.

Figure 4.12 illustrates that velocities and curvatures are bounded even with the most awkward initial posture of $\alpha(0)=\pi$ regardless of the magnitude of $e(0)$. Variations in curvature are considerable, though, as $e(0)$ increases. Thus, Figure 4.12 is nondimensionalized based upon data shown in Table 4.4. As designed, the maximum velocity approaches 0.5 m/s with larger $e(0)$ and is maintained for a longer period. For smaller $e(0)$, the maximum velocity decreases ~25% and is maintained for a shorter period, which is desirable for such tight maneuvers.

The nondimensional curvatures, Figure 4.12b, are nearly identical until dimensionless time, $t/t_{final}=0.3$, after which they approach different steady state values according to radii of their approaching paths. This phenomenon is caused by the controller directing the path to asymptotically converge to the path manifold. For larger $e(0)$, maximum curvature decreases and resulting paths become longer and require more space. As a result, for large $e(0)$ it would be pertinent to use the controller to track paths optimized for a particular workspace. The point here is that regardless of initial conditions, bounds on velocity and curvature are well established even in the most awkward initial conditions.

Table 4.5 presents final postures in posture regulation as a function of ε for two different initial positions to compare numerical simulation and analytic estimates. These results verify several important controller properties: (1) the control law equations (4.12 and 4.29) asymptotically converge z_1 and z_2 to zero independently

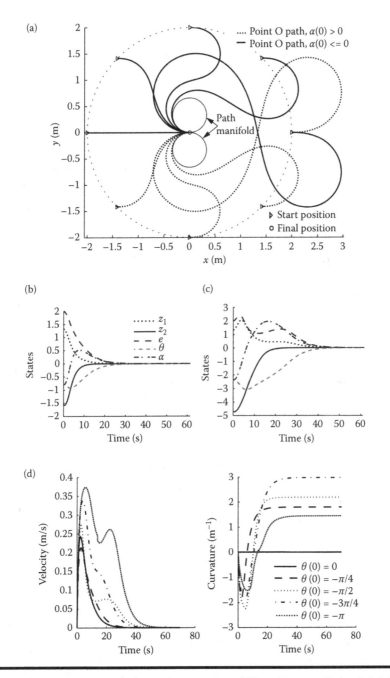

Figure 4.10 Posture regulation, IC: $e(0)=2\,$m, $\theta(0)=\alpha(0)=\pm n\pi/4$ $(n=0,1,2,3,4)$. (a) Trajectory paths of posture regulation, (b) posture regulation, $\theta(0)=-\pi/4$, (c) posture regulation, $\theta(0)=-3\pi/4$, and (d) control inputs for posture regulation.

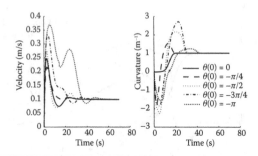

Figure 4.11 Control inputs for path following, IC: e(0)=2 m, $\theta(0)=\alpha(0)=\pm n\pi/4$ (n=0,1,2,3,4), reference path: $x^2+(y-1)^2=1$, $v_{des}=0.1$ m/s, $\kappa_{des}=1$ m^{-1}.

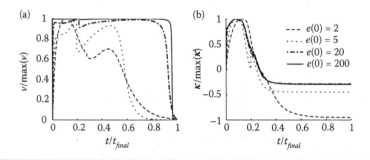

Figure 4.12 Posture regulation: control inputs for a difficult steering case of $\theta(0)=\alpha(0)=\pi$ with increasing e(0). (a) Non-dimensional velocity and (b) non-dimensional curvature.

Table 4.4 Simulation Results of Posture Regulation: $\theta(0)=\alpha(0)=\pi$

e (m)	Runtime, t_{final} (s)	max(v) (m/s)	max(κ) (m^{-1})
2	50	0.3735	1.5218
5	100	0.4811	0.7987
20	290	0.4960	0.2040
200	2700	0.4996	0.02

of ε as indicated in Theorem 3; (2) the equilibrium point $(e^*, \theta^*, \alpha^*)$ changes as a function of ε; and (3) simulated final postures are identical to the equilibrium point (Equation 4.45) estimated by solving the closed loop system in Corollary 4. Based upon analytical, numerical, and simulation results shown in Tables 4.1 and 4.5, $\varepsilon=1 \times 10^{-6}$ is sufficiently small for the CFMMR such that this value is implemented in experiment.

The long and circuitous paths that result from awkward initial conditions can easily be eliminated by allowing backward motion. As indicated in Section 4.2.1,

Table 4.5 Final Posture Errors as a Function of ε in Posture Regulation Simulation with IC (A) [e(0), θ(0), α(0)] = [1 m, $\pi/4$ rad, $\pi/4$ rad] and (B) = [2 m, $\pi/4$ rad, $\pi/4$ rad], Simulation Time, t_f = 200 s, Integration Tolerance = 1 × 10^{-12}

IC	ε	Simulation					Analytic Estimation by Using Equation 4.45	
		z_1	z_2	$\kappa(t_f)$ (m^{-1})	e^* (m)	$\theta^*(=-\alpha^*)$ (rad)	e^* (m)	$\theta^*(=-\alpha^*)$ (rad)
(A)	1×10^{-12}	1.18×10^{-12}	0	−2.28	7.26×10^{-7}	8.27×10^{-7}	7.26×10^{-7}	8.27×10^{-7}
(A)	1×10^{-6}	2.15×10^{-14}	0	−2.28	7.26×10^{-4}	8.27×10^{-4}	7.26×10^{-4}	8.27×10^{-4}
(A)	1×10^{-1}	2.03×10^{-14}	0	−2.17	0.216	0.237	0.216	0.235
(B)	1×10^{-12}	3.56×10^{-14}	0	−1.69	5.71×10^{-7}	4.84×10^{-7}	5.71×10^{-7}	4.84×10^{-7}
(B)	1×10^{-6}	7.94×10^{-14}	0	−1.69	5.71×10^{-4}	4.84×10^{-4}	5.71×10^{-4}	4.84×10^{-4}
(B)	1×10^{-1}	3.49×10^{-14}	0	−1.59	0.176	0.141	0.176	0.140

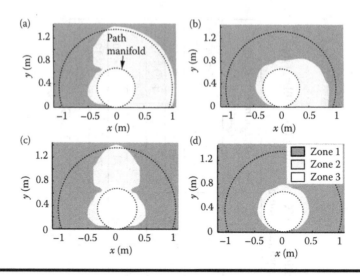

Figure 4.13 Workspace analysis of initial conditions; (a, b) only forward motion, (c, d) forward motion for $|\theta(0)| \leq \pi/2$ and backward motion for $\pi/2 < |\theta(0)| \leq \pi$. (a, c) $\phi(0) = 0$ and (b, d) $\phi(0) = \theta(0)$.

backward motion is generated by using coordinate transformation in Quadrants 1 and 4 (e.g., when $x(0) > 0$). A workspace sweep with forward and backward motion indicates the allowable initial conditions, Zones 1 and 2, as discussed in Section 4.2.3.2. Due to symmetry, only the zones for $y \geq 0$ are shown. Forward motion results are shown in Figure 4.13a and b, whereas Figure 4.13c and d indicate results when backward motion is allowed.

In both forward and backward motion, results indicate that Zone 1 is actually much larger than initially estimated. Initial conditions again play a role in determining how large these zones are. If the robot is always initially pointed towards the origin where $\phi(0) = \theta(0)$, allowable initial conditions increase since Zone 2 is significantly reduced, as illustrated in Figure 4.13b and d. If backward motion is allowed, Zone 2 is almost eliminated and Zone 1 is nearly maximized, Figure 4.13d. Thus, the actual range of allowable initial conditions is much larger than initially estimated in Figure 4.7. Due to the fact that the controller asymptotically converges to the path manifold, any initial conditions in Zone 3 will violate curvature constraints. If the robot starts within Zone 3, it is necessary to pick an intermediate goal point in Zone 1.

Allowable initial conditions that satisfy velocity and curvature constraints are more complex when considering trajectory tracking with a moving reference frame. A workspace mapping is used to illustrate how initial conditions are affected by a reference, Figure 4.14. Linear and circular references were used with the same initial heading angle, $\phi(0) = 0$ rad. These results verify that for a slower moving reference with smaller path curvature, the robot has greater ability to catch up to

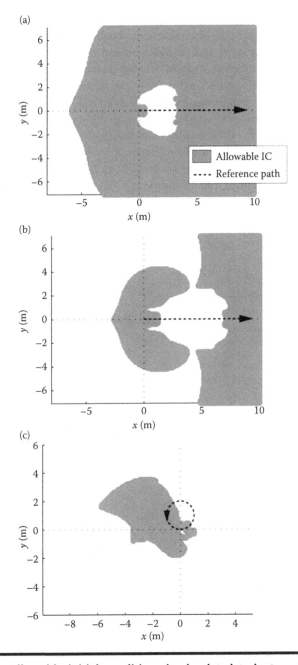

Figure 4.14 **Allowable initial conditions in simulated trajectory tracking with** $\phi(0)=0$ **rad,** $v_{max}=0.5$ **m/s, and** $\kappa_{max}=3$ **m**$^{-1}$**. (a) Linear reference with** $v_r=0.2\,v_{max}$ **and** $\kappa_r=0$**, (b) linear reference with** $v_r=0.5\,v_{max}$ **and** $\kappa_r=0$**, and (c) circular reference with** $v_r=0.5\,v_{max}$ **and** $\kappa_r=0.33\,\kappa_{max}$**.**

the reference and the range of initial conditions allowing convergence is greater as discussed in Section 4.2.3.1. Note that a reasonable neighborhood of the origin (where the trajectories start) and positions behind the target are allowable initial conditions, which is sufficient for most existing tracking problems.

Trajectory tracking simulations are shown in Figures 4.15 and 4.16 for a linear trajectory with initial conditions in Zone 1. Points (Q1, Q2, Q3) and (P1, P2, P3) are selected to show performance with both well-defined and awkward initial conditions, respectively. These results show that paths, states, and control inputs are smooth and that the robot tracks reference trajectories well. These results verify trajectory tracking capability of the control design (Theorem 3, and Corollaries 3 and 4). For the well-defined initial conditions (Q1, Q2, Q3), control inputs are well

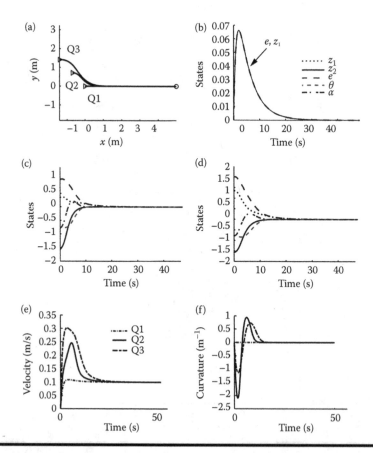

Figure 4.15 Trajectory tracking for a linear reference path with $\nu_{des}=0.1$ m/s using well defined initial conditions [e(0), θ(0), α(0)], **Q1**=[~0,0,0], **Q2**=[1 m, $-\pi/4$ rad, $-\pi/4$ rad], **Q3**=[2 m, $-\pi/4$ rad, $-\pi/4$ rad]. **(a) Path, (b) Q1, (c) Q2, (d) Q3, (e) control input, v, and (f) control input, κ.**

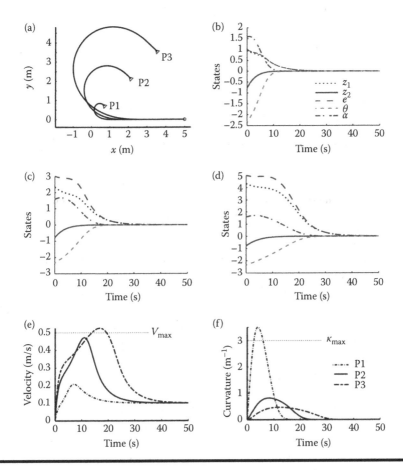

Figure 4.16 **Trajectory tracking for a linear reference path with $v_{des}=0.1$ m/s with awkward initial conditions at fixed orientations ($\theta(0)=-3\pi/4$ rad, $\alpha(0)=\pi/2$ rad): P1 ($e(0)=1$ m), P2 ($e(0)=3$ m), P3 ($e(0)=5$ m). (a) Path, (b) P1, (c) P2, (d) P3, (e) control input, v, and (f) control input, κ.**

bounded as designed. However, control inputs may exceed desired maximum limits for awkward initial conditions (P1 and P3) as expected, Figure 4.13.

To resolve initial condition problems found in trajectory tracking, reference trajectories may be designed to move slowly until the robot approaches a small neighborhood of the reference. As a result, initial trajectories during this approach phase become similar to those of posture regulation where initial conditions in Zone 1 are required to assure bounded control inputs. The approach phase can be included in the trajectory tracking algorithm by simply modifying the reference trajectory to $\dot{x}_r = v_{des}\tanh(t/30)\cos(\phi_r(t))$, $\dot{y}_r = v_{des}\tanh(t/30)\sin(\phi_r(t))$. Thus, this trajectory tracking algorithm provides bounded control inputs in P1, P2, and P3, as shown in Figure 4.17. Since we have already discussed how to avoid the

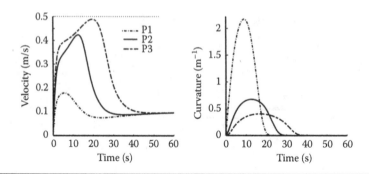

Figure 4.17 Trajectory tracking by modifying the reference trajectory with the same initial conditions (P1, P2, P3) used in Figure 4.16.

initial conditions outside of Zone 1, initial condition problems can be resolved for the primary motion-control tasks.

Experimental results in Figure 4.18 were obtained by using wheel odometry on a high-traction carpeted surface and correspond well to simulation results. Table 4.6 shows final posture errors on carpet and sand, which was obtained by using wheel odometry and actual measurements. Velocity and curvature are bounded as designed. As expected, better performance is also obtained on a higher traction surface (carpet) compared to lower traction surface (sand), according to actual measurements. Whereas odometry data provide consistently small error, actual final position errors increase on lower traction surfaces. These results confirm that larger wheel slip occurs on the lower traction sand surface such that larger odometry errors cause larger actual errors, Figure 4.19. Further, Tests 2 and 3 were conducted by using the path manifold–based controller equations (4.12 and 4.29), whereas Tests 4 and 5 were obtained by using a different kinematic controller with the same initial conditions as reported in [62]. These results show that the path manifold–based controller decreases actual distance errors, e, by ~28% on carpet, and ~44% on sand, respectively. The improved error is attributed to reduced wheel slip and traction forces. Thus, the path manifold–based controller provides better performance and efficient motion control. Further, the path manifold–based controller is robust near the origin, whereas traditional methods needed to switch controllers to guarantee bounded commands near the origin.

Experimental results, Figure 4.20, show actual trajectory paths obtained from posture regulation of the unicycle-type robot with an inexpensive microcontroller. The robot was stabilized to several different final postures, P_i, starting from the given initial posture, $P_0 (x_0, y_0, \phi_0) = (0\,\text{m}, 0\,\text{m}, 90°)$. Finite-time smooth path convergence is achieved for all scenarios as designed. Physical constraints are also well satisfied. Final posture errors critically depends on initial and surface conditions as discussed above. In particular, final distance errors, $e(t_f) = ~1.1\,\text{cm}$, are measured applying the final posture, $P_4 (2\,\text{m}, 0\,\text{m}, 90°)$. These experimental results verify

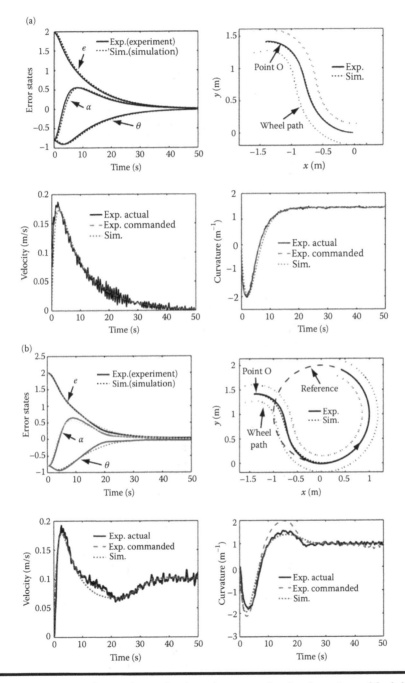

Figure 4.18 Experimental results based upon wheel odometry with initial $(e, \theta, \alpha) = (2, -\pi/4, -\pi/4)$. (a) Posture regulation and (b) path followings: reference path $x^2 + (y-1)^2 = 1$, $v_{des} = 0.1$ m/s, $\kappa_{des} = 1$ m^{-1}.

Table 4.6 Final Posture Errors for the CFMMR in Posture Regulation with Initial $(e, \theta, \alpha) = (1.9, 40°, 40°)$ based upon Wheel Odometry and Actual Measurement

No.	Surface	Wheel Odometry					Actual Measurement		
		$e \pm \sigma_e$ (cm)	$\theta \pm \sigma\theta$ (°)	$\alpha \pm \sigma\alpha$ (°)	Max(v) (m/s)	Max(κ) (m⁻¹)	$e \pm \sigma_e$ (cm)	$\theta \pm \sigma\theta$ (°)	$\alpha \pm \sigma\alpha$ (°)
1	Simulation	0.0	0.0	0.0	0.19	1.1	–	–	–
2	Carpet	2.4 ± 0.7	0.4 ± 0.2	−0.4 ± 0.2	0.16	1.7	7.7 ± 1.6	133.0 ± 3.7	133.0 ± 3.7
3	Sand	1.0 ± 0.6	−2.7 ± 4.0	−2.8 ± 4.2	0.15	2.5	13.9 ± 4.6	−34.8 ± 17.9	20.2 ± 11.1
4	Carpet	–	–	–	–	–	10.7 ± 0.7	139.6 ± 1.0	148.5 ± 1.0
5	Sand	–	–	–	–	–	24.8 ± 9.7	134.7 ± 4.3	145.6 ± 6.2

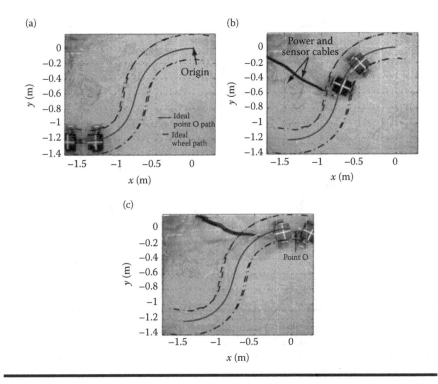

Figure 4.19 Sequential snapshots of experiment for posture regulation on sand, initial $(e, \theta, \alpha) = (1.9, 40°, 40°)$. (a) Initial posture at $t=0$ s, (b) posture at $t=12$ s, and (c) final posture at $t=60$ s.

a microcontroller with relatively limited capabilities can be used to solve motion control problems without loss of control performance.

The control algorithms presented here respect physical constraints for a wide variety of initial conditions while performing posture regulation, path following, and trajectory tracking. It is also important to note that all error states in experiment converge to zero asymptotically, which means that the robot converges to the origin or tracks the reference along smooth path trajectories. These results verify that our control algorithm performs efficiently for both posture regulation and path following, especially considering that the dynamics of the robot were ignored. For posture regulation and path following, the linear velocity and the path curvature are well bounded by v_{max} and κ_{max}, respectively, although more noise is apparent due to wheel backlash and servo-loop dynamics. Ultimately, our kinematic controller can be used to provide an ideal reference input to a robust dynamic controller to reduce errors in experiment. Most importantly, though, it must be noted that the kinematic motion controller presented in this chapter provides curvature and velocity commands satisfying physical constraints even with nonideal sensor systems and basic servo-type dynamic controllers.

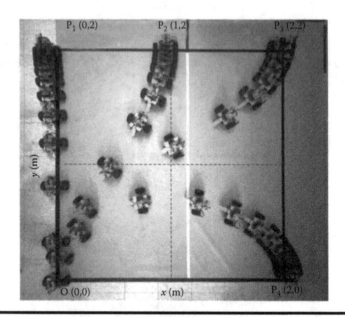

Figure 4.20 **Posture regulation using the unicycle-type robot with a microcontroller. The robot is stabilized applying the initial posture, O $(x_0, y_0, \phi_0) = (0\,\text{m}, 0\,\text{m}, 90°)$ and several different final postures; $P_1(0, 2, 90°)$, $P_2(1, 2, 90°)$, $P_3(2, 2, 90°)$, and $P_4(2, 0, -90°)$.**

4.3 Control of Multi-Axle Robots

In this section, we discuss the kinematic motion control of cooperative multi-robot systems while considering the physical constraints of the system. A distributed master-slave control law is thus presented to provide velocity and curvature commands that can satisfy the physical constraints of the multi-axle CFMMR. A steering command is also designed to minimize traction forces in creeping locomotion or to minimize the required workspace in sidewinding.

Most multi-robots in the literature have adopted noncompliant or articulated elements for modularity. Some snakelike robots use multiple wheeled modules to imitate snake locomotion. These snakelike robots typically use active or passive wheels connected through active or passive articulated joints. The CFMMR can represent active-wheeled passive-joint robots. Control of these robots has been either feed-forward using path planning based upon sinusoidal functions or by a remote human operator. In this section, we provide distributed closed-loop kinematic motion-control algorithms for coordinating compliant snakelike robots considering physical constraints.

Serially connected truck-trailer systems can also be treated as active-wheeled and passive-joint systems similar in spirit to the CFMMR. Motion planning for these systems can be traced to the 1990s, where the focus was shipping and baggage handling [97]. These systems used a tractor in order to pull trailers with fixed geometric properties and only passive behavior. These systems allowed the kinematic equations to be converted to chained form [75] and easily controlled via sequences of discrete maneuvers. Similar to the CFMMR, some fire trucks provide an additional steering input on the rear axle of the trailer to improve maneuverability, but since geometric properties of the fire truck are fixed, chained form can still be used for planning. In compliantly coupled systems such as the CFMMR, such conversion is not possible due to varying geometric properties of the system. In contrast to aforementioned feed-forward motion-planning research, we focus on closed-loop, drift-free motion control in this book.

In path following for multi-body autonomous robots as well as for articulated vehicles such as n-trailers, traditional approaches focused on convergence of an ideal center point of the vehicle to a path (e.g., an intermediate joint or a midpoint of either the front or rear axle). However, this method caused off-tracking errors in the other parts of the robot [98]. Altafini [99] alternatively considered multi-axle distance errors for n-trailers rather than a single distance error. However, since only one steering input is allowed in passive steering mechanisms, this effort still produces off-tracking. In contrast, snakelike robots with active steering mechanisms can provide ideal tracking, whereas they require complex controls. In this section, we present closed-loop, kinematic motion control of active-wheeled, passive-joint robots and address an issue of the path convergence.

In the master-slave control structure, the first axle of the robot guides the motion of the robot as a global master. The other axles as local slaves then track their masters while complying with kinematic and dynamic constraints. The leader-follower technique used by many researchers to provide motion planning for multiple mobile robots [100,101] is also similar to the master-slave structure. Again, the significant difference is that the axle modules of the CFMMR are compliantly coupled. In typical research [100,101], robots are not physically connected and relative distances and steering angles amongst robots can vary significantly so long as collision is avoided. In the CFMMR and other snakelike robots, geometric constraints are critical and must be incorporated into the slave controllers. We thus present distributed motion-control algorithms that consider these constraints. Our distributed control resolves computational burden and reduces complexity of the controller, which has also been examined in light of leader-follower techniques [101].

The leader-follower technique has also been used for multi-robot manipulation. Applications include mobile manipulators [102,103] and mobile robots [104,105] with partial compliance for carrying a payload. In [55], holonomic wheels were used for simple geometric relations among robots, and the motion of the leader was easily tracked by the followers. In [103], compliance was provided by actively controlling a complicated linkage system. More similar to the CFMMR, nonholonomic wheels were used in most of the aforementioned research. Most of these researchers strive to minimize coupling interactions by introducing compliance in their system while maneuvering their payload, whereas we minimize compliant forces considering physical limitations and coupling interactions as the robot maneuvers. While most of the aforementioned research used open-loop control, closed-loop kinematic control was presented for some mobile manipulators [102,103]. In these manipulators, upper-level trajectory planning was used to provide a reference trajectory for each mobile base. A lower-level kinematic controller was then applied to track this trajectory. A proportional controller [103] and a time-varying stabilizing controller [102] were applied as lower-level controllers.

In our distributed master-slave control structure, a kinematic controller is applied to solve typical motion-control problems. In our algorithm, any controller derived for unicycle-type robots could be applied as the global master controller, but it is important that the controller considers physical limitations. As mentioned in previous sections, many motion-control schemes have been proposed in past decades to consider the nonholonomic constraints of unicycle-type robots. However, velocity saturation has traditionally been used to consider physical limitations such that their approaches are limited to posture regulation, and bounded path curvature cannot be guaranteed. Note the path manifold–based control law derived in Section 4.2.3 can solve motion-control problems of wheeled mobile robots while satisfying the physical constraints characterized by velocity and curvature limits. The path manifold–based controller is therefore adopted for the global master controller to respect physical constraints.

A slave then follows a master while considering kinematic and physical constraints. Two steering algorithms are also presented to specify steering angles in the slave controller such that control of axle and frame modules is coordinated. Basic creeping-like steering is presented to minimize the required wheel-traction forces in motion control and ultimately to converge the robot configuration to a path executed by the master controller. Extended creeping-like and sidewinding-like steering algorithms are then presented to demonstrate posture regulation for a final posture aligned along a straight line. The extended-creeping controller adds an approach segment to the basic-creeping controller such that it provides additional full posture regulation capability with minimal forces, but larger workspaces are required. The sidewinding controller also provides full posture regulation capability, but smaller workspaces are required and traction forces are higher. Most importantly, we focus on closed-loop kinematic motion control to coordinate compliantly coupled axle motion in snakelike configuration and provide reference commands for a dynamic controller, whereas other researchers focused on dynamic control to minimize compliance effects.

4.3.1 Kinematic Model

We establish the kinematic model of the *n*-axle CFMMR considering the compliant frame and nonholonomic constraints simultaneously. Figure 4.21 shows the general steering kinematics of the *n*-axle CFMMR. Table 4.7 then summarizes

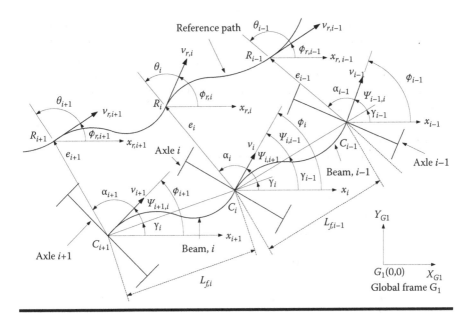

Figure 4.21 General steering kinematics of a multiple-axle robot.

Table 4.7 Notations for Robot Kinematics

Variable	Description
e_i, θ_i, α_i	Axle i distance and orientation errors
v_i	Forward Axle i velocity
$\psi_{i-1,i}$	Axle $i-1$ steering angle relative to Axle i
$\psi_{i,i-1}$	Axle i steering angle relative to Axle $i-1$
x_i, y_i	Axle i position
ϕ_i	Axle i heading angle
$L_{f,i-1}$	Foreshortened $i-1$th frame length
γ_{i-1}	Relative $i-1$th frame orientation

notations that describe Axle i and Beam $i-1$. Using polar representation based upon a unicycle-type model [69], Axle i $(i=1,...,n)$ kinematics are

$$\dot{e}_i = -v_i \cos \alpha_i + v_{r,i} \cos \theta_i$$

$$\dot{\theta}_i = v_i \frac{\sin \alpha_i}{e_i} - v_{r,i} \frac{\sin \theta_i}{e_i} - \dot{\phi}_{r,i} \qquad (4.53)$$

$$\dot{\alpha}_i = v_i \frac{\sin \alpha_i}{e_i} - v_{r,i} \frac{\sin \theta_i}{e_i} - \dot{\phi}_i$$

Using notations presented in Figure 4.21, the subscript i denotes Axle i such that v_i represents the velocity of the coordinate frame C_i moving in a heading, ϕ_i, relative to the fixed global frame G_i. In this section, we focus on forward motion along paths without cusps for simplicity and smooth regulation. The subscript r denotes the reference frame that represents the reference posture. Thus, $v_{r,i}$ and $\phi_{r,i}$ are the reference velocity and the heading angle of the reference coordinate frame R_i, respectively. The angular velocity can be described as a function of the path curvature κ and the linear velocity v such that we have $\dot{\phi}_i = v_i \kappa_i$ and $\dot{\phi}_{r,i} = v_{r,i} \kappa_{r,i}$, respectively. The error states in polar representation are defined as

$$
e_i = \sqrt{(x_i - x_{r,i})^2 + (y_i - y_{r,i})^2}
$$
$$
\theta_i = ATAN2\left(-(y_i - y_{r,i}), -(x_i - x_{r,i})\right) - \phi_{r,i} \tag{4.54}
$$
$$
\alpha_i = \theta_i - \phi_i + \phi_{r,i}
$$

where x_i and y_i are the Cartesian coordinates of a moving coordinate frame attached to the point, C_i. A reference position $(x_{r,i}, y_{r,i})$ is attached to the moving frame, R_i. The reference frame is considered as a virtual robot that inherits the kinematics of the real robot in order to produce realistic reference trajectories.

In order to describe relative postures between front and rear axles of each beam module, a relative beam orientation, γ, is introduced as a new state variable in addition to (e, θ, α). Thus, we define γ_{i-1} $(i=2,\ldots,n)$ between Axle $i-1$ and Axle i by

$$
\gamma_{i-1} = ATAN2(y_{i-1} - y_i, x_{i-1} - x_i) \tag{4.55}
$$

Observing velocity relations shown in Figure 4.21, a state equation for γ_{i-1} is

$$
\dot{\gamma}_{i-1} = \frac{v_{i-1} \sin \psi_{i-1,i} - v_i \sin \psi_{i,i-1}}{L_{f,i-1}} \tag{4.56}
$$

where $\psi_{i-1,i}$ is the steering angle of Axle $i-1$ relative to Axle i, $\psi_{i,i-1}$ is vice versa, and $L_{f,i-1}$ represents the shortened beam length between Axle $i-1$ and Axle i, $\overline{C_{i-1}C_i}$ due to bending of the beam. Applying the foreshortening concept [43] commonly used to model elastic beams with geometric nonlinearities, we have

$$
L_{f,i-1} = L\left(1 - \frac{2\psi_{i-1,i}^2 - \psi_{i-1,i}\psi_{i,i-1} + 2\psi_{i,i-1}^2}{30}\right) \tag{4.57}
$$

where L is the undeformed beam length. Further, considering heading and steering angles of Axle i and $i-1$th beam modules in Figure 4.21, we have

$$\psi_{i-1,i} = \phi_{i-1} - \gamma_{i-1} = \theta_{i-1} + \phi_{r,i-1} - \alpha_{i-1} - \gamma_{i-1}$$

$$\alpha_i = \theta_i - \phi_i + \phi_{r,i} = \theta_i + \phi_{r,i} - \psi_{i,i-1} - \gamma_{i-1} \qquad (4.58)$$

$$\phi_i = \gamma_{i-1} + \psi_{i,i-1}$$

Referring to Equations 4.53 and 4.56, and applying Equation 4.58, the kinematic state equations of the entire system can be expressed symbolically

$$\dot{\mathbf{q}}_i = \mathbf{F}_i(\mathbf{q}_i) + \mathbf{G}_i(\mathbf{q}_i, \mathbf{u}_i); \quad i = 1, \dots, n \qquad (4.59)$$

where states and control inputs are denoted respectively by $\mathbf{q}_i = [e_i, \theta_i, \alpha_i, \gamma_{i-1}]^T$, $\mathbf{u}_i = [\kappa_i, v_i, \psi_{i,i-1}]^T$, and $\gamma_0 = \kappa_0 = v_0 = \psi_{10} = 0$. Functions $\mathbf{F}_i$ and $\mathbf{G}_i$ are highly nonlinear as described in Equations 4.53 and 4.56.

4.3.2 Control Law

A distributed control law is presented to solve the primary motion-control tasks of the CFMMR considering physical constraints. The Axle 1 master controller is presented. Slave axle controllers will then be presented to coordinate axle motion considering velocity constraints imposed by the frame.

4.3.2.1 Global Master Controller on Axle 1

In the master-slave control scheme, Axle 1 is steered independently of the other modules as a global master. Axle 1 can thus be described only by the well-understood unicycle-type kinematic model (Equation 4.4 or 4.53). Previously, the path manifold–based controller equations (4.12 and 4.29) was derived to respect physical constraints of a unicycle-type robot. In this algorithm, a circular path manifold guides the robot to a trajectory or posture along a curved path satisfying curvature constraints. This path manifold–based controller is thus used to guide the motion of the global master and is now expressed for Axle 1 by

$$v_1 = \frac{v_{r1}e_1\eta_1\cos\theta_1 + v_{r1}r\sqrt{2}\left(\sin\theta_1 + \kappa_{r1}e_1\right)\sin 2\theta_1 + k_1e_1\eta_1\tanh(e_1 - r\eta_1\sqrt{2})}{e_1\eta_1 + r\sqrt{2}\sin 2\theta_1\sin\alpha_1}$$

$$(4.60)$$

$$\kappa_1 = \frac{k_2\tanh(\theta_1 + \alpha_1) + 2\dot{\theta}_1 + \dot{\phi}_{r1}}{v_1}$$

Note $\eta_1 = \sqrt{1 - \cos 2\theta_1 + \varepsilon}$, ε is an arbitrarily small perturbation, and r is the radius of the circular path manifold as described in Section 4.2.2. As a result, Axle 1 converges to the origin or reference trajectory asymptotically along the path manifold such that $v_1 \to v_{r1}$, $\dot{\phi}_1 \to \dot{\phi}_{r1}$ (i.e., $\kappa_1 \to \kappa_{r1}$), and $(e_1, \theta_1, \alpha_1) \to (0,0,0)$ as $t \to \infty$ by

Theorems 2 and 3, and Corollary 3 in Section 4.2.3.1. Also note that the physical constraints of the CFMMR [69] were previously established as $\kappa_{max}=3$ m^{-1}, $v_{max}=0.5$ m/s, and $\dot{\phi}_{max}=1.5$ rad/s such that we choose $r=1/\kappa_{max}=0.33$ m. Control gains (Equations 4.48 and 4.49) are then written by $k_1=0.3[1-\tanh(1.3/e_1)]+0.2$, and $k_2=0.3\ \tanh(|\alpha_1|/2)/(e_1(0)+\varepsilon)+0.3\ \tanh(1/e_1)$, which were tuned to assure bounded velocity and curvature during convergence to the path manifold. We also apply dynamic extensions (Equation 4.50) to match initial values of robot and the control inputs, v and κ specified by Equation 4.60. More details on the derivation and proof of this control law can be found in in Section 4.2.3.

4.3.2.2 Slave Controllers on Axle i (i=2,...,n)

A general slave controller is derived such that Axle i tracks Axle $i-1$, which all ultimately track the master axle trajectory. The slave controller provides velocity commands for Axle i based upon the motion of Axle $i-1$, geometric constraints imposed by the compliant frames and steering commands. We thus extend the velocity constraints introduced in [62] using generalized coordinates for the n-axle CFMMR.

Axle and frame motion must satisfy boundary conditions imposed by the coupling. Based upon the frame foreshortening (Equation 4.57) and orientation (Equation 4.58), relative forward and angular velocities of the frame are described by

$$\dot{L}_{f,i-1} = \frac{L}{30}\left[\dot{\psi}_{i-1,i}(\psi_{i,i-1}-4\psi_{i-1,i})+\dot{\psi}_{i,i-1}(\psi_{i-1,i}-4\psi_{i,i-1})\right]$$

$$\dot{\phi}_i - \dot{\phi}_{i-1} = \dot{\psi}_{i,i-1}-\dot{\psi}_{i-1,i}$$

(4.61)

Considering boundary conditions, we have

$$v_{i-1}\cos\psi_{i-1,i} - v_i\cos\psi_{i,i-1} = \dot{L}_{f,i-1}.$$

(4.62)

Using Equations 4.61 and 4.62, we can easily determine axle i velocities v_i, and $\dot{\phi}_i$ as functions of v_{i-1}, $\dot{\phi}_{i-1}$, and steering angles. The slave controller thus specifies v_i and κ_i, for each axle

$$v_i = \frac{\left[30v_{i-1}\cos(\psi_{i-1,i})+(4\psi_{i-1,i}-\psi_{i,i-1})L\dot{\psi}_{i-1,i}+(4\psi_{i,i-1}-\psi_{i-1,i})L\dot{\psi}_{i,i-1}\right]}{30\cos(\psi_{i,i-1})}$$

(4.63)

$$\kappa_i = \frac{\dot{\phi}_i}{v_i} = \frac{\dot{\phi}_{i-1}+\dot{\psi}_{i,i-1}-\dot{\psi}_{i-1,i}}{v_i}$$

based upon steering commands $\psi_{i,i-1}$ that are derived in Section 4.3.3 to further minimize traction forces and assure stability.

4.3.3 Steering Algorithm

This subsection presents two steering algorithms to coordinate slave axles in particular robot configuration shapes that can minimize traction forces and assure stability while tracking the master trajectory. Note that the steering command specifies frame deflection and orientation, as shown in Equations 4.56 through 4.58. Thus, we can realize robot configuration shapes by specifying steering commands $\psi_{i,i-1}$ in the slave controller (Equation 4.63). The basic creeping-like steering algorithm is first presented in Section 4.3.3.1 to provide efficient master-tracking ability while minimizing required wheel-traction forces. Toward this goal, we evaluate traction forces considering frame deflection and minimize them. Extended creeping-like and sidewinding-like steering algorithms are then presented in Section 4.3.3.2 to demonstrate posture regulation for a final posture aligned along a straight line. The extended-creeping controller adds an approach segment to the basic-creeping controller such that it provides additional full posture regulation capability with minimal forces, but larger workspaces are required. The sidewinding controller also provides full posture regulation capability, but smaller workspaces are required and traction forces are higher.

4.3.3.1 Basic Creeping-Like Steering Algorithm

Basic creeping-like steering is presented similar to creeping locomotion of a snake to provide efficient master tracking ability while minimizing wheel traction forces. The steering command, $\psi_{i,i-1}$, coordinates steering angles of subsequent axle modules, which critically impacts traction forces. Since allowable steering commands are physically limited by available wheel traction forces, we first evaluate traction forces imposed by the frame. We then present a steering command that minimizes maximum required traction forces. As a result, the basic creeping-like steering algorithm is then realized by applying this steering command to the slave controller (Equation 4.63). Further, we show that the robot configuration converges to a constant curvature path or tracks a path described by equilibrium steering angles in this algorithm.

4.3.3.1.1 Traction Forces

We now formulate wheel-traction forces as a function of steering angles. Given the negligible dynamics of the frame, the traction forces required to impose boundary conditions on the frame can be evaluated considering frame reaction forces and deflection in a quasi-static equilibrium. Figure 4.22 shows free body diagrams and boundary conditions for the frame and axle modules in a quasi-static equilibrium. Lateral reaction forces R and moments M of the frame can be determined as a function of steering angles applying boundary conditions illustrated in Figure 4.22a to the theory of elasticity

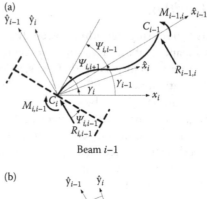

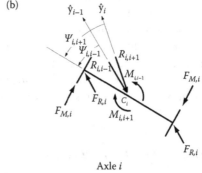

Figure 4.22 Reaction forces and moments exerted on Beam *i*−1 and Axle *i* module.

$$
\begin{bmatrix} M_{i-1,i} \\ M_{i,i-1} \end{bmatrix} = \frac{2EI}{L} \begin{bmatrix} 2 & 1 \\ -1 & -2 \end{bmatrix} \begin{bmatrix} \psi_{i-1,i} \\ \psi_{i,i-1} \end{bmatrix}
$$

(4.64)

$$
R_{i-1,i} = -R_{i,i-1} = \frac{M_{i,i-1} - M_{i-1,i}}{L}
$$

where the robot parameters are as follows; the modulus of elasticity, $E = 2.10 \times 10^{11}$ Pa, the second moment of area about the bending axis, $I = 1.5 \times 10^{-12}$ m^4, the frame length, $L = 0.366$ m, and the half length of the axle, $d = 0.183$ m. These forces and moments are then used to calculate the moment and reaction forces on a tire on Axle *i*, $F_{M,i}$ and $F_{R,i}$ ($i = 1, \ldots, n$). Applying force and moment equilibrium at Axle *i*, Figure 4.22b, we then have

$$
\mathbf{F}_{M,i} = \frac{M_{i,i+1} - M_{i,i-1}}{2d} \left(\hat{\mathbf{x}}_{i-1} \cos \psi_{i,i-1} + \hat{\mathbf{y}}_{i-1} \sin \psi_{i,i-1} \right)
$$

$$
\mathbf{F}_{R,i} = 0.5 \left[R_{i,i+1} \sin(\psi_{i,i-1} - \psi_{i,i+1}) \right] \hat{\mathbf{x}}_{i-1} + 0.5 \left[R_{i,i-1} + R_{i,i+1} \cos(\psi_{i,i-1} - \psi_{i,i+1}) \right] \hat{\mathbf{y}}_{i-1}
$$

(4.65)

where boundary conditions are $M_{1,0}=M_{n,n+1}=R_{1,0}=R_{n,n+1}=0$, $\psi_{10}=\psi_{12}$, $\hat{\mathbf{x}}_0=\hat{\mathbf{x}}_1$, and $\hat{\mathbf{y}}_0=\hat{\mathbf{y}}_1$. Note that coupling interactions in the n-axle robot are more complicated when compared to the two-axle robot as shown by reaction forces (Equation 4.65). Further, a traction force acting on a tire is a result of these reaction forces, $F_{T,i}=F_{R,i}\pm F_{M,i}$. Considering the net traction forces on each axle, ideally required maximum wheel-traction forces are then

$$F_T^{max} = \max(\| \mathbf{F}_{R,i} \pm \mathbf{F}_{M,i} \|_2; \quad i=1,\ldots,n) \tag{4.66}$$

where $-$ and $+$ represent the left and right wheels, respectively.

4.3.3.1.2 Steering Ratios for Minimum Traction Forces

In Chapter 2, a steering ratio was applied as a simple metric that defined a steering shape of a two-axle CFMMR during motion. Similarly, the steering ratio, a_{i-1}, is introduced here to describe the steering command, $\psi_{i,i-1}$, as a function of the steering angle, $\psi_{i-1,i}$,

$$\psi_{i,i-1} = a_{i-1}\psi_{i-1,i} \tag{4.67}$$

Again, it is important to note that a steering algorithm is realized by applying this steering command to the slave controller (Equation 4.63). In the two-axle CFMMR, applying $i=1, 2$ to Equations 4.64 through 4.66, F_T^{max} becomes a function of ψ_{12} and $\psi_{21}(=a\psi_{12})$ such that the steering ratio can easily be determined to minimize F_T^{max} given the steering angle ψ_{12}. Thus, as presented in Chapter 2, steering by $a=-1$ minimized required traction forces and provided efficient maneuverability and steering.

Now, steering ratios are determined to minimize traction forces in a n-axle CFMMR. Note that F_T^{max} is piecewise continuous and $F_{T,i}^{max}$ is a function of two adjacent steering angles, $\psi_{i-1,i}$ and $\psi_{i,i+1}$, and the steering command $\psi_{i,i-1}$ per Equations 4.64 through 4.66. Thus, in contrast to the two-axle robot, it is difficult to find these steering ratios analytically. However, applying optimization techniques, we can easily establish steering ratios that provide minimum F_T^{max} in a given steering workspace, as shown in Figure 4.23. The resulting optimal steering ratios, a^*, are almost consistently distributed with the approximate mean value of -1. In particular, $a^*=-1$ when axle modules have the same steering angle, $\psi_{i,i+1}=\psi_{i-1,i}$, which is the case of the robot aligned with a constant curvature path. In Figure 4.23, a_1 is discontinuous at $\psi_{12}=0$ since a_{i-1} is poorly defined when $\psi_{i-1,i}=0$ and $\psi_{i,i-1}\neq0$ per Equation 4.67. Traction forces are quite small at small steering angles, however, and it is more important to note that for large steering angles where forces can become large, we still have $a^* \approx -1$. Thus, for simplicity, it is assumed that $a^* \approx -1$ for all steering angles. The effect of this decision can be evaluated by applying $a_{i-1}=-1$ to moments and forces (Equations 4.64 and 4.65), such that

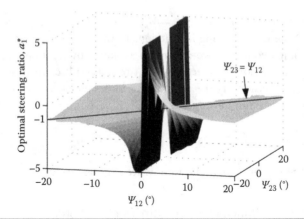

Figure 4.23 Optimal steering ratio, a_1* as a function of steering angles.

$$M_{i-1,i} = M_{i,i-1} = \frac{2EI}{L}\psi_{i-1,i}, \ R_{i,i-1} = R_{i-1,i} = 0, \ \mathbf{F}_{R,i} = \mathbf{0},$$

(4.68)

$$\mathbf{F}_{M,i} = \mathbf{0} \text{ except for } \|\mathbf{F}_{M,1}\|_2 = \frac{EI}{Ld}|\psi_{1,2}| \text{ and } \|\mathbf{F}_{M,n}\|_2 = \frac{EI}{Ld}|\psi_{n-1,n}|$$

Note that traction forces are acting only on the first and last axles when $a=-1$. As a result, the maximum traction force (Equation 4.66) is expressed by

$$F_T^{\max}(a = -1) = \max(\|\mathbf{F}_{M,1}\|_2, 0, \ldots, 0, \|\mathbf{F}_{M,n}\|_2) = \frac{EI}{Ld}\max(|\psi_{1,2}|, |\psi_{n-1,n}|) \quad (4.69)$$

The steering angle limit, $|\psi| \leq 0.637$ rad (i.e., 36.5°) is determined considering wheel–wheel and wheel–frame interferences. Per Equation 4.69, we then have $F_T^{\max} < 3.35$ N when $a=-1$.

In order to further evaluate the effect of setting $a=-1$ in an n-axle CFMMR, we show $F_T^{\max}$ as a function of a steering ratio using several different steering angles, Figure 4.24. The absolute minimum $F_T^{\max}$ when $\psi_{i,i+1} = \psi_{i-1,i}$ is shown in Figure 4.24a, whereas Figure 4.24b shows the general cases when $\psi_{i,i+1} \neq \psi_{i-1,i}$, which is more likely in general navigation. It is important to note that in both cases, the traction forces have similar minimum magnitude near $a=-1$, which are well within the traction afforded by most surfaces [50]. Our previous point that the steering ratio is not critical at small steering angles can be validated by comparing $\psi_{23} = 0 \neq \psi_{12}$ to the ideal case ($\psi_{23} = \psi_{12} = 11°$), Figure 4.24b, where it is observed that the traction forces are virtually equal near $a=-1$. Finally, it is also worth noting that the n-axle robot requires higher traction forces than the two-axle robot as a increases.

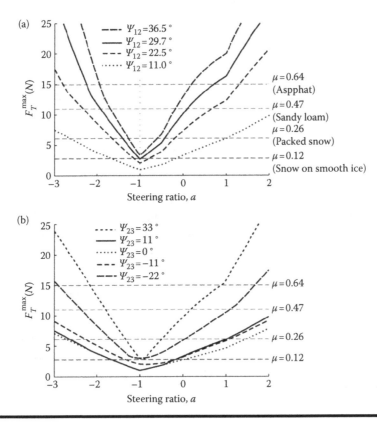

Figure 4.24 Available traction on typical surfaces and maximum wheel traction forces on the CFMMR when $a_i=a$. (a) $\psi_{i,i+1}=\psi_{i-1,i}$ for the *n*-axle CFMMR and (b) $\psi_{12}=11.0°$, $\psi_{i,i+1}\neq\psi_{i-1,i}$ for the 3-axle CFMMR.

4.3.3.1.3 Creeping Motion Analysis

In the previous section, basic creeping-like steering is created by applying $a_{i-1}=-1$ (i.e., $\psi_{i,i-1}=-\psi_{i-1,i}$) to the slave controller. In this section, we analyze creeping motion. As we show, a steering equation is derived to show stability towards an equilibrium point. Further, we show that creeping motion causes the robot configuration to converge to an arced shape where the relative axle steering angles, $\psi_{i-1,i}$, converge to values proportional to the path curvature of the master axle.

Now, we derive the steering equation using the steering ratio and controller presented in the previous sections. For convenience, we substitute $i=2$ into equations derived for Axle i. Thus, applying $a_1=-1$ to the slave controller (Equation 4.63) and the kinematic equations (4.56 through 4.58), we have

$$v_2 = v_1 + \frac{L\dot{\psi}_{12}\psi_{12}}{3\cos(\psi_{12})}, \quad \dot{\gamma}_1 = \frac{(v_1 + v_2)\sin\psi_{12}}{L_{f1}}, \quad L_{f1} = L\left(1 - \frac{\psi_{12}^2}{6}\right), \quad \text{and } \dot{\psi}_{12} = \dot{\phi}_1 - \dot{\gamma}_1$$

(4.70)

Applying the first and second equations in Equation 4.70 to the fourth equation, we then have,

$$\dot{\psi}_{12} = \dot{\phi}_1 - \frac{6v_1\sin\psi_{12} + L\dot{\psi}_{12}\psi_{12}\tan(\psi_{12})}{3L_{f1}}$$

(4.71)

Solving Equation 4.71 for $\dot{\psi}_{12}$, a state equation for ψ_{12} is formed that is a function of v_1, $\dot{\phi}_1$ and ψ_{12}. Since $\dot{\phi}_1 = v_1\kappa_1$, the steering equation, $\dot{\psi}_{12}$, can ultimately be expressed as a function of the master axle path curvature and velocity (v_1 and κ_1, respectively), as commanded by the master axle controller (Equation 4.60)

$$\dot{\psi}_{12} = \frac{3\dot{\phi}_1 L_{f1} - 6v_1\sin\psi_{12}}{3L_{f1} + L\psi_{12}\tan(\psi_{12})} = \frac{3v_1(\kappa_1 L_{f1} - 2\sin\psi_{12})}{3L_{f1} + L\psi_{12}\tan(\psi_{12})}$$

(4.72)

This steering equation is used to find an equilibrium point and prove stability. Note that the denominator of Equation 4.72 and v_1 are always positive here. For simple notation, we denote a positive definite term, $h = 3v_1/(3L_{f1} + L\psi_{12}\tan(\psi_{12})) > 0$, and the rest, $f = \kappa_1 L_{f1} - 2\sin\psi_{12}$, in Equation 4.72 such that we have

$$\dot{\psi}_{12} = h(\psi_{12}, v_1) f(\psi_{12}, \kappa_1) = hf$$

(4.73)

It is important to note that the numerator f determines stability and an equilibrium point since $\dot{\psi}_{12} = 0$ if $f = 0$, $\dot{\psi}_{12} > 0$ if $f > 0$, and $\dot{\psi}_{12} < 0$ if $f < 0$. Further, applying L_{f1} in Equation 4.70 to f, we have

$$f = \kappa_1 L\left(1 - \frac{\psi_{12}^2}{6}\right) - 2\sin\psi_{12}$$

(4.74)

At equilibrium, we have $f = 0$ such that

$$\kappa_1 = \frac{2\sin\bar{\psi}_{12}}{L(1 - \bar{\psi}_{12}^2/6)}$$

(4.75)

where $\bar{\psi}_{12}$ is an equilibrium point. Thus, $\bar{\psi}_{12}$ can be solved numerically given κ_1. In order to find algebraic solutions for the equilibrium point, we approximate $\sin\psi_{12} = \psi_{12} - \psi_{12}^3/6 + \text{H.O.T.}$, such that

$$f \approx (L\kappa_1 - 2\psi_{12})(1 - \psi_{12}^2/6)$$

(4.76)

which is actually quite accurate since $|\psi| \le 0.637$ rad is always true due to the physical constraints of the robot. Thus, Equation 4.76 can be solved to find the unique equilibrium point

$$\psi_{12} = L\kappa_1 / 2 \equiv \bar{\psi}_{12} \qquad (4.77)$$

This result shows that ψ_{12} converges to an equilibrium point proportional to the path curvature κ_1 of the master axle.

Lyapunov's theorem [106] is used to show asymptotic stability of the equilibrium point. We first consider a sufficiently large domain, $D=\{\psi \in R| \; |\psi| < \pi/2\}$, which includes $|\psi| \le 0.637$. Again recall that h is a positive definite function since the denominator and v_1 are always positive here. Thus, stability of ψ_{12} depends upon only the numerator, f. Applying Equation 4.75 to Equation 4.74, we have

$$f(\psi_{12}) = \frac{\dot{\psi}_{12}}{h} = 2\sin\bar{\psi}_{12} \frac{6-(\psi_{12})^2}{6-\bar{\psi}_{12}^2} - 2\sin(\psi_{12}) \qquad (4.78)$$

In Figure 4.25, we evaluate $f = \dot{\psi}_{12} / h$ as a function of ψ_{12} given curvature. This result shows that $\bar{\psi}_{12}$ is a unique equilibrium point in D and that it satisfies physical steering limits, $|\psi| \le 0.637$. Most importantly, we have $\dot{\psi}_{12} = 0$ and $f = 0$ when $\psi_{12} = \bar{\psi}_{12}$, $\dot{\psi}_{12} > 0$ and $f > 0$ when $\psi_{12} < \bar{\psi}_{12}$, and $\dot{\psi}_{12} < 0$ and $f < 0$ when $\psi_{12} > \bar{\psi}_{12}$ in D. Thus, this result proves asymptotic stability in D. Further, the stability can be proven analytically using an energy-like Lyapunov function

$$V_\psi \equiv -\int_{\bar{\psi}_{12}}^{\psi_{12}} f(y)\,dy = \frac{2\sin\bar{\psi}_{12}}{6-\bar{\psi}_{12}^2}\left[\frac{(\psi_{12})^3 - \bar{\psi}_{12}^3}{3} - 6(\psi_{12}-\bar{\psi}_{12})\right] - 2\cos(\psi_{12}) + 2\cos(\bar{\psi}_{12})$$

$$(4.79)$$

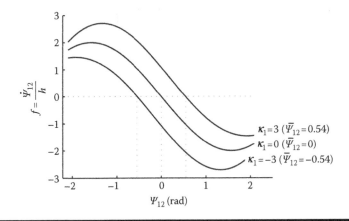

Figure 4.25 State equation for $\dot{\psi}_{12}$ as a function of ψ_{12} given curvature, $|\kappa_1| \le 3$ m⁻¹.

Note that $V\psi = 0$ for $\psi_{12} = \bar{\psi}_{12}$ and that $V\psi > 0$ in $D-\{\psi_{12} = \bar{\psi}_{12}\}$. Since $\dot{\psi}_{12} = 0$ for $\psi_{12} = \bar{\psi}_{12}$ and $\dot{\psi}_{12} \neq 0$ in $D-\{\psi_{12} = \bar{\psi}_{12}\}$, the derivative of $V\psi$ is negative definite

$$\dot{V}_\psi = \frac{\partial V_\psi}{\partial \psi} f = -f^2 < 0, \ \forall \ \psi_{12} \in D - \{\psi_{12} = \bar{\psi}_{12}\} \tag{4.80}$$

which proves asymptotic stability in D. We also evaluate the Jacobian, $\lambda_1 = [\partial \dot{\psi}_{12}/\partial \psi_{12}](\bar{\psi}_{12})$, based upon Equation 4.72 to prove exponential stability in the neighborhood of the equilibrium point. Figure 4.26 shows the eigenvalue λ_1 as a function of curvature κ_1. Since $\lambda_1 < 0$, ψ_{12} is exponentially stable near the equilibrium point.

This stability analysis confirms that ψ_{12} converges to $\bar{\psi}_{12}$ asymptotically and that the convergence is exponential near the equilibrium point. For the tracking problem where the reference path curvature varies, ψ_{12} tracks $\bar{\psi}_{12}$ with tracking errors proportional to curvature variations. It is important that the robot can easily track reference paths that consist of straight-line and circular-arc segments. This is because these segments can be readily combined by existing motion planners to generate optimal paths for a car-like vehicle [107].

Aforementioned results are readily extended to Axle i ($i \geq 2$). Supposing an equilibrium ($\dot{\psi}_{12} = 0$) in Equation 4.70 for Axle 2, we have $v_2 = v_1$ and $\kappa_2 = \kappa_1$ ($\dot{\phi}_2 = \dot{\phi}_1$). Likewise, subsequently expanding these results to Axle i, we have $\dot{\psi}_{i-1,i} \to 0$ such that $v_i \to v_{i-1} \to \cdots \to v_1$ and $\kappa_i \to \kappa_{i-1} \to \cdots \to \kappa_1$ as $t \to \infty$. Since each axle is essentially following their master in creeping-like steering, which all ultimately follow Axle 1, the entire robot tends to take the shape of the path executed by Axle 1, as shown by Figure 4.27. Thus, the robot configuration converges to a constant curvature path or tracks a path described by equilibrium steering angles. This is guaranteed by the path manifold controller specified in Section 4.3.2.1 since the path curvature always asymptotically converges to a steady state $|\kappa_1| \leq \kappa_{\max}$ in posture regulation, and $|\kappa_1| = |\kappa_{r1}| \leq \kappa_{\max}$ in path following and trajectory tracking.

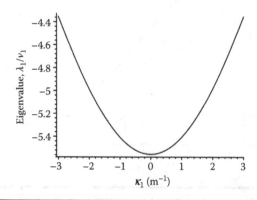

Figure 4.26 Eigenvalues for steering angle equation (4.72).

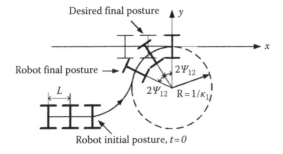

Figure 4.27   Basic creeping-like steering in posture regulation.

4.3.3.2 *Steering Algorithm for Posture Regulation*

Creeping motion provides good master tracking capability. However, it is limited in regulating the robot to a fixed posture aligned along a straight line. In order to solve this problem, we develop a steering algorithm that can converge the relative beam orientation, γ, to a constant. In this example, γ should converge to zero given a final posture along the x-axis, Figure 4.28. Toward this goal, we present two steering algorithms for posture regulation; extended creeping-like steering and sidewinding-like steering.

(a)

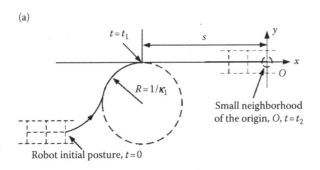

(b)

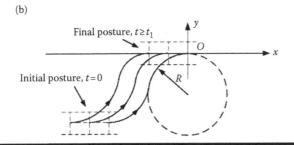

Figure 4.28   Steering algorithms for posture regulation. (a) Extended creeping-like steering via a linear path and (b) sidewinding-like steering.

4.3.3.2.1 Extended Creeping-like Steering

In this approach, similar to the basic creeping-like steering, we try to minimize wheel-traction forces while regulating γ to zero in finite time. Thus, we first apply $a=-1$ for steering commands. We then define the Lyapunov candidate function to investigate how γ_1 can be regulated as desired

$$V_{\gamma_1} = \frac{1}{2}\gamma_1^2 \text{ and } \dot{V}_{\gamma_1} = \gamma_1\dot{\gamma}_1 \tag{4.81}$$

Applying $\psi_{i,i-1}=-\psi_{i-1,i}$ and $\psi_{i-1,i}=\phi_{i-1}-\gamma_{i-1}$ from Equation 4.58 for the first beam module ($i=2$), expression (4.56) is reduced to

$$\dot{\gamma}_1 = \frac{(v_1 + v_2)\sin(\phi_1 - \gamma_1)}{L_{f1}} \tag{4.82}$$

Using LaSalle's theorem [106], an invariant set is $M=\{\gamma_1 \in R^1 | \gamma_1 = \phi_1, v_1 \neq 0, v_2 \neq 0\}$. This result indicates that a straight-line path is required to regulate γ_1 when we use $a=-1$. Recall that the basic steering motion is realized applying $a=-1$ to the controller in Section 4.3.2 as illustrated in Figure 4.27. Thus, in order to regulate γ_1 to zero in this algorithm, a trajectory path generated by creeping motion must be extended using a linear path as shown in Figure 4.28a. As a result, the extended creeping-like steering is presented here such that the final position of the robot is aligned along the x-axis.

Now, we show analytically that γ_1 asymptotically converge to zero in the extended creeping-like steering. Note that ϕ_1 converges to zero along the circular path manifold in creeping-like steering. Thereafter, following the linear segment, Axle 1 states are in the invariant set such that $\gamma_1=\phi_1=0$ for $t \geq t_1$. In creeping-like steering, controller equations (4.60 and 4.63) provide $v_2 \to v_1 \to v_{r1}$, $\dot{\phi}_1 \to 0$, and $\phi_1 \to 0$ in finite time, t_1. Further, $L_{f1} \approx L(=0.366\,\text{m})$ may be approximated for $|\psi| \leq 0.637$. Thus, we can rewrite Equation 4.82 by,

$$\dot{\gamma}_1 = -\frac{2v_{r1}}{L}\sin\gamma_1; \quad \forall\, t \geq t_1 \tag{4.83}$$

Given $v_{r1}>0$ for $t \geq t_1$, the derivative of the Lyapunov candidate function is negative definite on this linear path such that γ_1 is asymptotically stable by Theorem 4.10 [106]:

$$\dot{V}_{\gamma_1} = -\frac{2v_{r1}}{L}\gamma_1\sin\gamma_1 \leq 0, \quad \forall t \geq t_1 \tag{4.84}$$

Moreover, this result is applied to subsequent slave modules since a slave axle follows a master axle, ultimately the Axle 1. The relative orientation of Axle i is thus compensated (i.e., $\gamma_i=\phi_i=0$) and all axles of the robot are aligned along the x-axis.

We finally determine the linear segment length s required for the stabilization of γ based upon Axle 1 using Equation 4.83. A lower bound on s for the n-axle robot is

$$s = (n-1)\int_{t_1}^{t_2} v_{r1}\,dt = -\frac{(n-1)L}{2}\int_{\gamma_1(t_1)}^{\gamma_1(t_2)}\csc(\gamma_1)d\gamma_1 = \frac{(n-1)L}{2}\ln\left|\frac{\csc(\gamma_1(t_1))-\cot(\gamma_1(t_1))}{\csc(\gamma_1(t_2))-\cot(\gamma_1(t_2))}\right|$$

(4.85)

where $|\gamma_1(t_2)| < |\gamma_1(t_1)| < 0.637$, and $\gamma_1(t_2)$ determines the size of small neighborhood of the origin when $t = t_2$. In this case, the reference velocity for the linear segment is determined simply by

$$v_{r1} = 0.1\tanh(e_{r1}), \quad \kappa_{r1} = 0; \quad t \geq t_1$$

(4.86)

where e_{r1} is measured from the origin O, Figure 4.28a. It is important to note that this algorithm also demonstrates path tracking capability by simply providing a reference.

4.3.3.2.2 Sidewinding-Like Steering

Whereas the extended creeping-like steering satisfies minimum traction forces, it may require large steering space or provide slow convergence due to the extended path. Thus, we alternatively present the sidewinding-like steering algorithm, as illustrated in Figure 4.28b. In this algorithm, steering commands are formulated to converge all relative frame angles to zero simultaneously rather than using $a=-1$. For $i=2,\ldots,n$, the new steering command, $\psi_{i,i-1}$, is then presented by

$$\psi_{i,i-1} = \sin^{-1}\left(\cos\theta_{i-1}\frac{v_{i-1}\sin\psi_{i-1,i} + L\tanh(\gamma_{i-1})}{v_i}\right)$$

(4.87)

Unlike creeping motion, the trajectory path of a slave does not converge to that of a master since the slave follows the master in a different configuration shape commanded by Equation 4.87. Using the Lyapunov candidate function, Equation 4.81, we can prove asymptotic stability for γ. Applying Equation 4.87 to Equation 4.81, we have

$$\dot{V}_{\gamma_{i-1}} = \frac{-L\gamma_{i-1}\tanh(\gamma_{i-1})\cos\theta_{i-1} + v_{i-1}(1-\cos\theta_{i-1})\sin\psi_{i-1,i}}{L_{f,i-1}}$$

(4.88)

First, we consider Equation 4.88 for $i=2$. Note that θ_1, ψ_{12}, and v_1 converge to zero asymptotically but almost exponentially near the origin such that we have $\theta_1 \approx 0$, $\psi_{12} \approx 0$, and $v_1 \approx 0$ in finite time, t_1. Thereafter, the derivative of the Lyapunov function is negative definite

$$\dot{V}_{\gamma_1} = -\frac{L}{L_{f,1}} \gamma_1 \tanh(\gamma_1) \cos\theta_1 \leq 0 \qquad (4.89)$$

Thus, γ_1 converges to zero asymptotically, which leads to $\psi_{21} \to 0$, $\dot{\phi}_2 \to \dot{\phi}_1 \to 0$, and $v_2 \to v_1 \to 0$ in finite time per Equations 4.58, 4.60, 4.63, and 4.87. Aforementioned results then apply to a subsequent ith module such that we have $\gamma_{i-1} \to 0$, $\dot{\phi}_i \to \dot{\phi}_1 \to 0$, $\theta_i \to 0$ and $v_i \to v_1 \to 0$ in finite time. As a result, convergence rates then become faster and trajectory paths become shorter. However, this active control may require higher traction forces, whereas creeping-like steering requires minimum tractions, which will be demonstrated by experimental results in Section 4.3.4.2.

4.3.4 Controller Evaluation

4.3.4.1 Methods and Procedures

Simulation and experimental tests have been conducted for several different initial conditions and surfaces, Table 4.8, in order to evaluate the presented controller in ideal and nonideal scenarios. Note that the extended creeping and sidewinding algorithms provide posture regulation, whereas the basic creeping algorithm is suitable for path following and trajectory tracking. Since extended creeping uses a linear segment to regulate final posture, the algorithm also demonstrates tracking capability. Given the space limitations of our laboratory and the aforementioned factors, the presented steering algorithms are experimentally evaluated while performing posture regulation, which also demonstrates basic path following in the case of extended creeping. Further, more complicated tracking capability is evaluated in simulation.

References in path following are not explicit functions of time, whereas they are in trajectory tracking. Since the reference design is not the focus of this section, the reference path or trajectory is realized here by simply using linear and circular segments. In path following, the reference path is $v_r = v_{des}$ $\tanh(0.1/e)$, $\kappa_r = \kappa_{des}$ where v_{des} and κ_{des} represent desired path-segment velocity and curvature, respectively. In trajectory tracking, the reference trajectory is $\dot{x}_r = v_{des}\cos(\phi_r(t))$, $\dot{y}_r = v_{des}\sin(\phi_r(t))$, and $\dot{\phi}_r(t) = \kappa_{des}v_{des}$ where $x_r(0) = y_r(0) = 0$ m.

Initial conditions are selected to demonstrate maximum steering and maneuverability for each steering algorithm within the workspace shown in Figure 4.29, which highlights physical constraints of the robot. Further, an initial condition, IC (B), is applied to compare presented steering algorithms. Experimental results demonstrate application of the controller to an actual robot considering physical constraints. Carpet surface is used to illustrate performance under ideal circumstances with a high traction surface. Sand and sand/rock surfaces are then used to demonstrate performance in low traction conditions where physical constraints more closely match the specified velocity and curvature constraints, and wheel slippage can be significant.

Table 4.8 Final Posture Errors and Velocity Commands with IC (A) [$x_i(0)$, $y_i(0)$, $\phi_i(0)$] = [−1.2 m, −1.2 m, 0°], (B) [−1.4 m, −0.4 m, 0°], (C) [−1.4 m, −0.1 m, 0°], (D) [−1.0 m, −0.1 m, 0°], and (E) [−0.7 m, −0.1 m, 0°]; s=−0.8 m for Extended Creeping-Like Steering

No.	Steering	IC	Surface	Final Posture Errors				Velocity Commands		Norm
				$[e_1, e_2, e_3]$ (cm)	$[\theta_1, \theta_2, \theta_3]$ (°)	$[\alpha_1, \alpha_2, \alpha_3]$ (°)	$[\gamma_1, \gamma_2]$ (°)	$max(v_i)$ (m/s)	$Max(\dot{\phi}_i)$ (rad/s)	$\|e(t_f)\|$ (cm)
1	Basic creeping	(A)	Ideal (simulation)	[0.0, 10.6, 39.7]	[0, 101, 111]	[0, 68, 50]	[17, 47]	0.17	0.3	41.1
2			Sand/rock (odometry)	[2.9, 63.5, 80.5]	[−20, 114, 118]	[−32, 56, 69]	[79, 22]	—	—	102.6
3			Carpet (measured)	[4.5, 26.1, 62.0]	[108, 107, 115]	[88, 63, 43]	[34, 61]	0.22	0.34	67.4
4			Sand (measured)	[29.7, 42.9, 69.7]	[119, 114, 111]	[115, 71, 73]	[21, 39]	0.22	0.34	87.1
5			Sand/rock (measured)	[30.6, 47.8, 79.5]	[110, 107, 109]	[102, 58, 64]	[27, 47]	0.23	0.43	97.7
6	Basic creeping	(B)	Ideal (simulation)	[0.0, 4.7, 17.2]	[0, 94, 98]	[0, 80,74]	[7, 19]	0.16	0.13	17.8
7			Sand/rock (odometry)	[2.3, 12.8, 26.0]	[−15, 89, 93]	[−26, 77, 74]	[21, 20]	—	—	29.1
8			Carpet (measured)	[1.6, 13.8, 28.5]	[132, 103, 103]	[119, 85, 77]	[19, 22]	0.18	0.14	31.7

(Continued)

Table 4.8 (Continued) Final Posture Errors and Velocity Commands with IC (A) [$x_i(0)$, $y_i(0)$, $\phi_i(0)$] = [−1.2 m, −1.2 m, 0°], (B) [−1.4 m, −0.4 m, 0°], (C) [−1.4 m, −0.1 m, 0°], (D) [−1.0 m, −0.1 m, 0°], and (E) [−0.7 m, −0.1 m, 0°]; s = −0.8 m for Extended Creeping-Like Steering

| | | | | Final Posture Errors | | | | Velocity Commands | | Norm |
No.	Steering	IC	Surface	[e_1, e_2, e_3] (cm)	[θ_1, θ_2, θ_3] (°)	[α_1, α_2, α_3] (°)	[γ_1, γ_2] (°)	max(v_i) (m/s)	Max($\dot{\phi}_i$) (rad/s)	$\|e(t_f)\|$ (cm)
9			Sand (measured)	[1.2, 11.0, 22.5]	[−42, 107, 103]	[−55, 93, 81]	[17, 17]	0.18	0.13	25.1
10			Sand/rock (measured)	[4.1, 12.3, 21.1]	[110, 98, 98]	[99, 89, 76]	[13, 13]	0.18	0.14	24.8
11	Extended creeping	(B)	Ideal (simulation)	[0.0, 0.2, 2.1]	[0, 75, 90]	[0, 74, 85]	[0, 3]	0.06	0.21	2.1
12			Sand/Rock (odometry)	[3.6, 13.7, 3.9]	[0, −1, 0]	[0, −2, 1]	[−3, 9]	–	–	14.7
13			Carpet (measured)	[7.6, 5.1, 3.7]	[92, 105, 109]	[99, 112, 101]	[−4, −2]	0.17	0.34	9.9
14			Sand (measured)	[11.2, 10.4, 11.0]	[21, 49, 54]	[15, 52, 44]	[5, 2]	0.18	0.3	18.8
15			Sand/rock (measured)	[11.9, 10.6, 9.2]	[36, 55, 52]	[39, 60, 41]	[2, −3]	0.13	0.26	18.4
16	Side-winding	All	Ideal (simulation)	[0.0, 0.0, 0.0]	[0, 0, 0]	[0, 0, 0]	[0, 0]	0.16	0.13	0.0

(Continued)

Table 4.8 (*Continued*) Final Posture Errors and Velocity Commands with IC (A) $[x_i(0), y_i(0), \phi_i(0)] = [-1.2\,m, -1.2\,m, 0°]$, (B) $[-1.4\,m, -0.4\,m, 0°]$, (C) $[-1.4\,m, -0.1\,m, 0°]$, (D) $[-1.0m, -0.1\,m, 0°]$, and (E) $[-0.7\,m, -0.1\,m, 0°]$; s = −0.8 m for Extended Creeping-Like Steering

No.	Steering	IC	Surface	Final Posture Errors				Velocity Commands		Norm
				$[e_1, e_2, e_3]$ (cm)	$[\theta_1, \theta_2, \theta_3]$ (°)	$[\alpha_1, \alpha_2, \alpha_3]$ (°)	$[\gamma_1, \gamma_2]$ (°)	$max(v_i)$ (m/s)	$Max(\phi_i)$ (rad/s)	$\|e(t_f)\|$ (cm)
17		(B)	Carpet (odometry)	[2.9, 13.2, 13.2]	[−12, −164, 156]	[−24, −188, 166]	[−7,13]	—	—	18.9
18		(E)	Carpet (odometry)	[2.3, 5.5, 4.3]	[1, 130, 33]	[−7, 140, 22]	[7, −6]	—	—	7.4
19		(B)	Carpet (measured)	[7.1, 30, 31.8]	[−145, 127, 127]	[−191, 98, 143]	[49, 2]	0.2	0.29	44.3
20		(C)	Carpet (measured)	[2.7, 8.6, 6.7]	[27, 115, 144]	[16, 116, 140]	[12, −6]	0.18	0.21	11.2
21		(D)	Carpet (measured)	[3.4, 8.5, 6.4]	[−156, 120,151]	[−168, 120, 148]	[14, −6]	0.13	0.37	11.2
22		(E)	Carpet (measured)	[1.5, 9.8, 6.5]	[16, 104, 129]	[−1, 106, 124]	[15, −7]	0.12	0.7	11.9

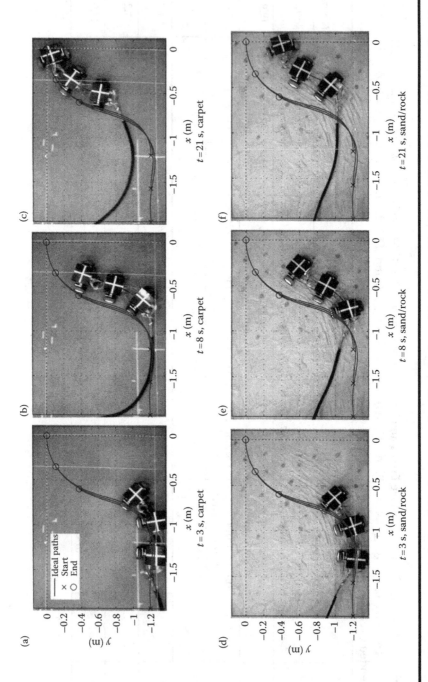

Figure 4.29 Posture regulation using basic creeping-like steering with IC (A) $[x_i(0), y_i(0), \phi_i(0)] = [-1.2\,\text{m}, -1.2\,\text{m}, 0°]$: Test No. 3 (a–c), Test No. 5 (d–f).

The controller is applied to the three-axle CFMMR using MATLAB and a dSPACE tethered to the robot for rapid control prototyping and controller evaluation similar to the two-axle CFMMR in the previous section. Since this section focuses on kinematic motion control algorithms that can produce references for the dynamic controller [68], traditional servo-type wheel controllers are used to drive the robot. Odometry data are simultaneously fed back to both kinematic and wheel controllers in cascade connection as presented in [68,69]. Further, in order to present experimental results precisely, actual final postures are manually measured using Cartesian coordinates established on the workspace. Furthermore, the master-slave controller combined with creeping-like steering is applied to a compliantly coupled two-axle robot with two Arduino Dues using a C/C++-based Arduino programming language to demonstrate microcontroller implementation.

4.3.4.2 Results and Discussion

From our tests, final robot postures and maximum velocity commands based upon Equations 4.60 and 4.63 are summarized in Table 4.8 to indicate performance of each algorithm and bounds of control inputs. Sequential snap shots from these tests, Figures 4.29 through 4.31, also demonstrate performance of the presented steering algorithms.

Path following and trajectory tracking are achieved using the basic creeping-like steering. The basic creeping-like steering is thus tested to demonstrate steering and tracking ability of Axle i to Axle 1 via the path manifold. An initial condition, IC (A), with large initial orientation errors, $\theta_i(0) = 45°$, is used in Tests 1–5 to illustrate steering and maneuverability of the robot and wheel slip in different surface conditions.

Test 3 (carpet), Figure 4.29a–c, shows modest errors compared to ideal paths, whereas Test 5 (sand/rock), Figure 4.29d–f, shows large steering and posture errors. These results confirm that the creeping steering can provide ideal performance as designed on a high-traction surface where wheel slips and sensing errors are minimized. From actual measurement of final robot posture in Table 4.8, Δe_1 (Axle 1 distance error increase relative to a test on carpet) is considerable on a low traction surface (~500%) while Δe_2 and Δe_3 are modest (≤83%); $\Delta e_1 \gg \Delta e_2 > \Delta e_3$. For IC(B) with smaller $\theta_i(0) = 16°$ where required traction forces are smaller, Δe_1 becomes much smaller (~150%). In the basic creeping-like steering, distance errors significantly increase for back axles. This is because the robot is steered to the fixed reference along the circular path manifold as described in Figure 4.27.

Figures 4.32 and 4.33 illustrate path following and trajectory tracking simulation using the same initial condition, IC (B). A reference path and trajectory are implemented as described in Section 4.3.4.1 by specifying $v_{des} = 0.1$ m/s and $\kappa_{des} = 1$ m^{-1}. As a result, the reference path shape is a circle with a 1 m radius. In trajectory tracking, the velocity command is typically higher and the curvature converges to a desired value faster to catch up to the reference trajectory commands.

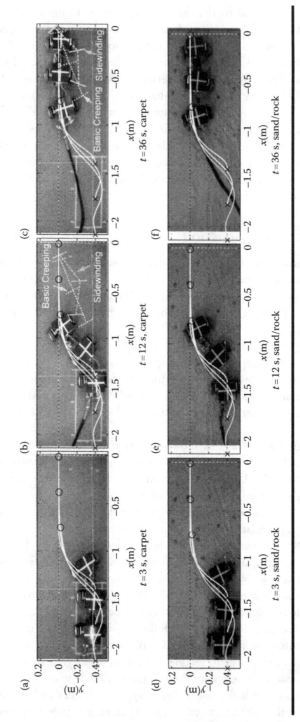

Figure 4.30 **Posture regulation using extended creeping-like steering with IC (B) [−1.4 m, −0.4 m, 0°]: Test No. 13 (a–c), Test No. 15 (d–f).**

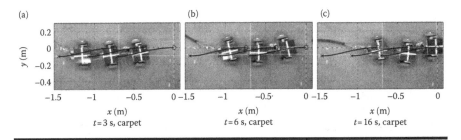

Figure 4.31   Posture regulation using sidewinding-like steering with IC (E) [−0.7 m, −0.1 m, 0°]: Test No. 22.

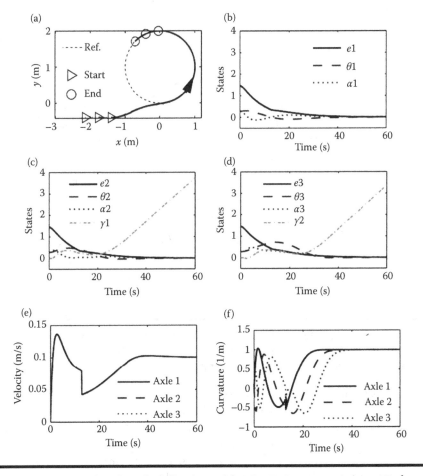

Figure 4.32   Simulated path following with IC (B) [−1.4 m, −0.4 m, 0°] for a circular reference path; $x_r^2+(y_r-1)^2=1$, $x_r(0)=y_r(0)=0$, $v_r=0.1$ tanh(0.1/e) m/s, $\kappa_r=1$ m⁻¹. (a) Trajectory path, (b) axle 1, C1, (c) axle 2, C2, (d) axle 3, C3, (e) control input, v, and (f) control input, κ.

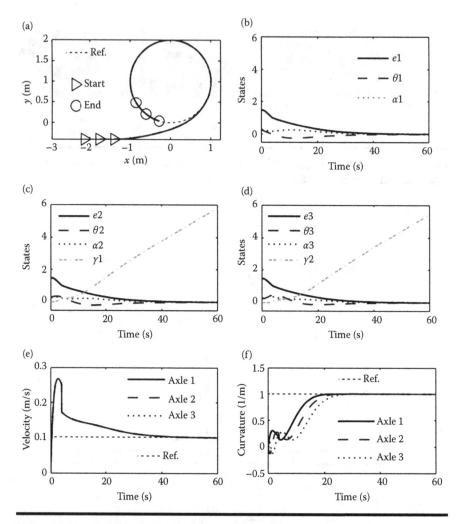

Figure 4.33 **Simulated trajectory tracking with IC (B) [−1.4 m, −0.4 m, 0°];** $v_r=0.1$ **m/s,** $\kappa_r=1$ **m⁻¹. (a) Trajectory path, (b) axle 1, C1, (c) axle 2, C2, (d) axle 3, C3, (e) control input,** v**, and (f) control input,** κ**.**

In both path following and trajectory tracking, trajectory paths converge to the reference and all state errors asymptotically converge to zero while γ changes proportionally to heading angles. Velocity commands of each axle are almost identical while curvature commands are slightly different to comply with compliance and nonholonomic constraints. Also note that these control commands asymptotically converge to those of Axle 1 and are well-bounded as designed.

Extended creeping-like steering is tested to converge the robot posture to the fixed reference by using a linear segment and to demonstrate path following capability. Considering the available workspace and the length of the three-axle CFMMR

(0.74 m), the linear segment length is selected to be $s = 0.8$ m for the extended creeping-like steering such that $|\gamma_1(t_2)| < 4.2°$ per Equation 4.85. Simulation results (Test 11) show sufficiently small final posture errors on second and third axles in spite of nonideal IC (B). Furthermore, modest errors are measured in experiment (Test 13–15). IC (B) is also applied to the other steering algorithms in order to compare performance (Test 6–17, 19). Figure 4.30b and c illustrate robot postures for all three steering algorithms simultaneously using IC (B). Norms of final posture, $\|e(t_f)\|$, on carpet are 9.9, 31.7, and 44.5 cm, respectively, for extended creeping-like, basic creeping-like, and sidewinding- like steering algorithms. These results demonstrate that the extended creeping steering provides the best regulation performance among presented algorithms. For the extended creeping-like steering, Δe_3 is relatively large on a low traction surface (~140%); $\Delta e_1 < \Delta e_2 < \Delta e_3$. This result indicates that slip effects are accumulated in rear axles.

Sidewinding-like steering is tested to show an alternative to extended creeping-like steering that can provide faster convergence and compact regulation paths. However, sidewinding-like steering shows poor performance for $\theta(0) > 10°$ in experiment (see Test 19) due to large traction force requirements ($F_T^{max} \sim 14$ N, Figure 4.35), although it provides ideal results in simulation (Test 16). In the CFMMR, Axles 1 and 3 are partially constrained by the frame while Axle 2 is tightly constrained by Beams 1 and 2. Thus, Axles 1 and 3 can rotate easily relative to Axle 2. As Axles 1 and 3 compensate for orientation errors simultaneously, the reaction torque on Axle 2 caused by Axles 1 and 3 may become extremely large such that it may prevent Axle 2 from compensating for orientation errors. Starting with large initial orientation errors, required traction forces on Axle 2 can easily exceed available traction limits. As a result, Axle 2 tracks the reference with offset, which accumulates errors on Axle 3.

Sidewinding-like steering is thus evaluated on carpet with IC (C)–(E) where $4.1° \leq \theta(0) \leq 8.1°$ in order to avoid a large traction force requirement during the motion (Test 18, 20–22). Norm of final posture, $\|e(t_f)\|$, is ~11 cm for IC (C)–(E), whereas $\|e(t_f)\| = 44.3$ cm for $\theta(0) = 16°$. This result verifies that small initial orientation errors should be used for sidewinding-like steering to reduce required traction forces. Although offset tracking on Axle 2 is still observed with small initial orientation errors, its effect is significantly reduced, Figure 4.31.

It is worth noting that ideal and actual velocity commands in the tests are well-bounded, as designed by values shown in Table 4.8. In experiment, actual velocity commands are commonly larger than ideal simulated commands because of sensing errors and disturbances from surface. Also note that $\theta_i(t_f)$ and $\alpha_i(t_f)$ in experiment approach approximately 90°, whereas e_i and γ_i converge to small values. This is because $\theta_i(t_f)$ and $\alpha_i(t_f)$ are numerically determined by position where $|y(t_f)| > |x(t_f)|$ in Cartesian coordinates as the robot approaches the small neighborhood of the reference or the origin. Deviations of posture errors estimated by odometry on the three different surfaces are consistently small given initial conditions. However, actual measurement shows considerable deviations from high traction to low traction surfaces as shown in Table 4.8. These results indicate that sensing errors caused by slip are significant. Large initial orientation errors that require high traction forces increase the propensity of wheel slip. In contrast, for small initial orientation errors, final posture error becomes smaller due to reduced traction force requirements. Almost similar test results are also obtained implementing posture regulation with creeping-like steering in microcontrollers for the two-axle robot, Figure 4.34. The robot is stabilized with modest errors to several different final postures starting from a given initial posture, which is also critically affected by initial posture and surface conditions. These results again verify the control algorithm presented here can easily be applied to microcontrollers without loss of control performance.

Figure 4.35 shows maximum required traction forces calculated from simulation data using Equation 4.66 for different steering algorithms and initial conditions. These results confirm that creeping-like steering requires lower traction forces, whereas sidewinding-like steering requires higher traction forces given identical initial conditions. These results also indicate that traction forces increase given larger initial orientation errors. These results also verify that traction forces have steady state values proportional to κ_r since $\kappa \to \kappa_r$ by applying the master controller Equation 4.60 to creeping-like steering. Note that when the reference is a fixed point where κ_r is arbitrarily defined, the path curvature converges to a finite

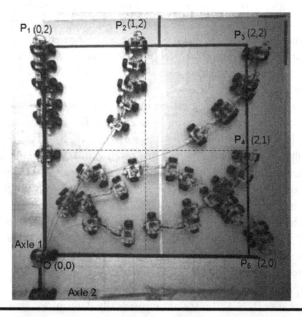

Figure 4.34 Trajectory paths of a two-axle robot implementing creeping-like steering in microcontrollers. The robot is stabilized using the initial posture, $P_0(x_0, y_0, \phi_0) = (0\,\text{m}, 0\,\text{m}, 90°)$ and several different final postures; $P_1(0, 2, 90°)$, $P_2(1, 2, 90°)$, $P_3(2, 2, 90°)$, $P_4(2, 1, 90°)$, and $P_5(2, 0, -90°)$.

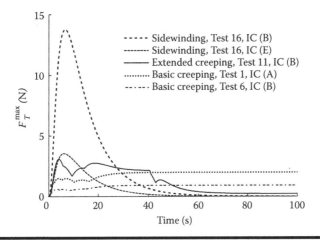

Figure 4.35 **Calculated maximum wheel traction forces based upon simulation.**

value according to the trajectory path generated by the master controller given a particular initial condition as shown in Section 4.2.4.2. In extended creeping-like and sidewinding steering where the robot is driven to a straight configuration, it is also validated that traction forces approach zero as the robot approaches the final posture.

In simulation and experiment, we demonstrate the presented steering algorithms combined with the distributed master and slave controllers (Equations 4.60 and 4.63) in several different scenarios. The results show that odometry and actual errors are modest on a higher traction surface, whereas they are significant on a lower traction surface when compared to ideal simulation. Note that larger traction forces are required for initial conditions with larger orientation errors. Also note that odometry data are used as a feedback to the controller. Thus, odometry errors, initial conditions, and surface condition critically impact actual performance. The basic creeping-like steering illustrates tracking capability as expected. The extended creeping-like steering then provides the best experimental results in regulating posture although it requires large steering space. Most importantly, the control algorithm described in this section provides reference inputs to a dynamic controller that considers disturbance and dynamic effects. Also note the simulation and experimental results here show ideal and actual performance, which highlights implementation issues related to kinematics and dynamics such as wheel-slippage due to surface conditions, coupling interactions, and traction forces.

Chapter 5

Sensory System

5.1 Introduction

In the architecture presented in Chapter 3, a sensory system is included for each axle module to provide accurate posture and velocity estimates. On rugged terrain, roll and yaw become coupled as the robot steers and accommodates terrain. In order to achieve a desired mobility task, such as path following or posture regulation, steering and maneuvering of the system are thus accomplished via coordinated control of the axles in Chapter 4. Accurate relative axle posture estimates, the primary focus of this chapter, are important to all these control algorithms since drift between the axle posture estimates produces antagonistic interaction forces between the axles and ultimately reduces maneuverability and mobility of the robot.

We first examine the snake-robot Genbu, which evolved from early snake robots to provide active wheeled and passive joint morphology for improved terrain adaptation and high speed locomotion. Genbu uses complex and expensive mechanisms to couple its axle modules. The coupling mechanisms of Genbu are instrumented in order to provide relative localization of its axle modules. This allows the axles to maintain spacing while traversing terrain and prevents antagonistic forces. Similarly treatment of the issue is made by the Omnimate robot [108] which uses multiple axles to support a moving platform for transport in a factory. In both cases, traditionally instrumented compliant linkages are used to accommodate and control drift between the axles.

Strain gauges are widely applied for measuring strain in order to determine the deflection of beams. They are the primary instrumentation used by most commercially available load cells. Unlike the applications in mobile robotics, load-cell stiffness is large, and the resulting deflections are quite small (<0.1 mm). Given the additional space required by load cells, strain gauges are commonly integrated directly into robotic mechanisms. This allows more compact end-effectors/fingers [109–112] links [113–117], and joints [112,118], to name a few applications and researchers.

The sensing issue discussed in this chapter has also appeared in compliant manipulators, links, which are usually motivated by space manipulators where workspaces are quite large and weight is limited. The result is long slender links with limited stiffness, inherent vibration, appreciable deflection, and potentially long settling times. Research in this area has been motivated by controlling these vibrations to provide fast and precise positioning. This research focused on damping out vibrations using strain data [114,116,117,119], accelerometer data [120–123], and combinations therein [122–125], to name a few.

Different from space manipulators, the nonholonomic constraints in the compliant mobile robot such as CFMMR combined with the effective inertia and damping of its actuators essentially prevent vibrations typical of space manipulators. A common theme between space manipulator and CFMMR, however, is that similar mathematical functions are used to predict beam deflection. That is to say, a polynomial of the same order as number of strain gauges can be used to directly fit strain gauge data. Assuming a linear stress-strain relationship, a curvature equation integrated piecewise to estimate deflection and force can then be derived [126]. Research by Piedbeouf [115] similarly applies a polynomial to directly determine tip displacement and orientation. Carusone [114] uses an equal number of Eigenmode functions and strain gauges to approximate deflection. Since the deflections of our target system are highly nonlinear (as much as ±75° in extremes) and the system may be in post-buckling, such modal-based approximations are not useful. While we build upon the work by Piedbeouf [115] to also obtain force estimates in [126], we only use position and orientation data here since our focus is on localization. While interaction forces between the axles are considered in other research for axle control [66], we apply a post-buckled stiffness model for simplicity.

Other methods of predicting tip position solve the beam partial differential equations (PDEs; typically Hamilton, Euler Bernoulli, or Timoshenko PDEs) and provide dynamic models of the system. Solution of the PDEs usually assumes deflection is approximated by spline functions [127,128], Eigen-mode functions [114,129], or experimentally derived modal analysis functions [130,131], to name a few. A variety of methods are then used to combine sensor data into these models. Cho examines observer-based deflection estimates derived from strain measurements and spline displacement functions [128]. Somolinos uses strain gauge data to predict tip deflection in conjunction with motor commands to provide simplified dynamic estimates [132]. Parsa uses accelerometer data to predict force and moment boundary conditions, which are then used as inputs to an extended Kalman Filter to predict dynamic motion [125]. Such algorithms provide flexural state information that is useful for dynamic control of manipulators. While the aforementioned spline functions can offer improved approximation at boundary conditions, we have selected a sufficient number of properly spaced strain gauges such that the polynomial functions provide a fast and accurate analysis of strain data without solving the PDEs governing dynamic motion [115].

Besides the strain and mechanism-based measurements described above, non-contact distance measurement techniques can also be used to deduce relative pose [133]. GPS, laser radar, and computer vision are probably the most popular alternatives in the robotics community. Laser radar systems are too costly for this application and are not suited for close proximity measurements. Likewise, GPS does not provide sufficient accuracy for our relative localization. Computer vision using monocular, stereo, and omni-directional vision is widely researched, but the common goal is global localization. Our goal is to localize one axle relative to another, which is more similar to group coordination research where relative posture is important. This has been studied using monocular vision where fiducials provide fixed-spacing dot patterns [134]. Other monocular vision algorithms focus on determining the relative position of two known points on an object, which are then interpolated to give the relative posture of the object [135]. Via appropriate rotation and translation transformations of these patterns, relative localization is provided. Either of these techniques may be applicable here, although the latter is more computationally efficient. Accuracy of the techniques and their ability to operate in adverse environments where mud, dirt, or leaves may obscure fiducials and cameras would limit vision-based relative localization, however.

Other common techniques proving distance measurements between discrete points are based upon Infra-Red (IR), Sonar, and Radio Frequency (RF) sensors. IR measurements offer the cheapest alternative, but the limited field of view of IR diodes and their related nonlinearity requires that complex arrays of emitters and transmitters be used. They are also highly susceptible to saturation in natural lighting environments, which typically precludes their use. Sonar sensors also behave nonlinearly as the object position in their field of view changes, and are thus undesirable. RF signal strength can be calibrated to distance [136], but field strength variations due to environmental factors produce poor results [137]. RF time of arrival (TOA) or time difference of arrival (TDOA) methods are thus used to determine the location of antennae, but these methods are most effective when distances are appreciable due to the propagation speed (3×10^8 m/s) of the signals [137]. The Angle of Arrival (AOA) technique circumvents timing problems, but it too creates complexity by requiring motorized directional antennae or complex antennae arrays.

Thus, in this chapter we implement a Relative Posture Sensor (RPS), introduced by Merrell and Minor [126], to produce more accurate relative posture estimates and reduce drift between the axles. The RPS consists of a series of strain gauges attached to the compliant frame of the robot, signal processing circuitry, and mathematical algorithms required for interpreting the signals from the circuits. The RPS is small and light enough to sit on the robot without limiting its full range of motion or impeding its travel in any way. The RPS can be used to predict interaction forces between the axles and has potential for extension to large deformation structural analysis such as that used in vehicle crash safety analysis. The RPS is also cost effective since it consists of inexpensive components and it is resistant to environmental wear, such as dirt, since it does not possess any mechanisms.

Once RPS provides multiple sensor data, the sensor fusion algorithms are necessary to obtain the most accurate relative posture estimates. It is worth noting that the IPEC algorithm was proposed in mobile robotics [108]. This algorithm works by detecting which axle has the least trustworthy posture estimate based on odometry and replacing that axle's posture estimate with the sum of the other axle's posture estimate plus the relative posture between the two axles calculated from the linkage potentiometers. This seems to be quite good at limiting the effect of odometry errors, but no attempt is made to maintain variance information about each axle's posture. Variance information is important to stochastic data fusion and can be vital to a path-planning algorithm in deciding whether the robot posture is known with sufficient accuracy to permit close quarters maneuvering around objects.

Another sensor fusion algorithm is the CI filter first proposed by Uhlman and Julier [138]. This filtering technique maintains consistent estimates without regard to the correlation between data sources. This is important because the correlation between data sources is often difficult or impossible to calculate. Because of this property, the CI filter has been used in attempts to solve the simultaneous localization and mapping (SLAM) problem. In this application, a mobile robot uses its sensory input to create a map of its environment and then uses the map to localize itself. The sensor data are therefore correlated with the robot's internally generated map, but it is very difficult to determine the degree of correlation. Moreover, Arambel et al. [139] proposed a CI filter being used in coordinating the motion of a constellation of deep space imaging satellites for the purpose of increasing the sensitivity of a space-based sensor over what a single satellite can accomplish.

Inspired by all the above literatures, a hierarchical data-fusion architecture is presented in Figure 5.1 to fuse all sensing data in the CFMMR. The data-fusion system is designed for modularity such that each axle is running a fusion system with an identical architecture. At the base of this structure is the well-known Extended Kalman Filter (EKF), which fuses data from sources on the axle module, such as wheel encoders, axle gyroscopes, accelerometers, or GPS. [140]. This particular EKF implementation is unique in that it uses constant acceleration terms in the discretized model to reduce the effect of sudden wheel slip. When multiple axle modules are joined by the RPS, though, a second tier of data fusion is necessary to facilitate data transfer from the RPS to the adjoining axle modules and between the joined axle modules themselves.

We introduced the relative measurement stochastic posture error correction (RMSPEC) for second-tier data fusion. The unknown correlations between data sources that results from relative posture information passed back and forth between axle modules and the RPS makes this level of the data fusion algorithm particularly challenging. In order for the EKF to be consistent in its state estimation, it is necessary that the correlation between data sources be known. At the

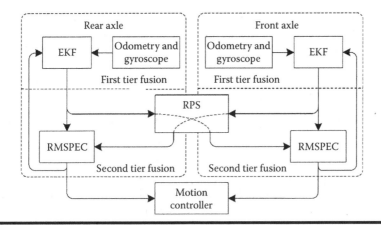

Figure 5.1   The tiered data-fusion structure.

heart of the RMSPEC is the Covariance Intersection (CI) filter, which assumes complete correlation and is therefore consistent in its estimation in the face of uncertain correlations [138]. The RMSPEC algorithm uses the CI filter to revise posture estimates by combining trustworthy axle data with RPS posture estimates. Similar to Borenstein's Internal Posture Error Correction (IPEC) algorithm [141], deviation angles determined by RPS and EKF data are used to characterize axle-level EKF data trustworthiness.

The hybrid RMSPEC-fusion approach provides the error-correction ability of the IPEC algorithm while maintaining the covariance propagation of the CI filter. This combination of data-fusion techniques is an approach that is required by the modular nature of the robot and the unique sensing capability of the RPS. Particularly, one aspect of this CI filter implementation is the approach used to optimize the CI update weighting factor in order to minimize odometry error between the axles. All of this is accomplished in real time without impeding the robot's motion controller.

The tiered data-fusion system described here should also be extended to other cooperative and distributed robotics applications. Any system that requires close cooperation of multiple independent systems to accomplish a task can benefit from this data-fusion architecture, such as cooperative robotic manipulators, cooperative mobile robots, or distributed sensor networks.

5.2 The Relative Position Sensor

It is desired to install proper sensors on the frame module such that the relative position, and orientation of one axle with respect to the other can be detected by sensor data from the flexible frame that is not dependent on the axle sensors in any way. To this end, the flexible frame is instrumented with strain gauges at regular intervals along its length. In this section, a theoretical foundation is derived for the RPS, and implementation is discussed.

5.2.1 Beam Model

In order to define the theoretical basis for the RPS, there are four assumptions to be made beforehand.

Assumption 1:
Small angle approximations are not applicable. The beam will be subjected to extreme bending conditions and the end point of the beam may be bent by greater than $40°$ relative to its root in the maneuvering mode.

Assumption 2:
The RPS will only detect posture estimates of the axles in a plane although the robot operating in rugged terrains will also be evaluated.

Assumption 3:
The sensor will consist of a series of strain bridges placed at known locations along the length of the beam to provide discrete strain measurements, $\varepsilon_1, \varepsilon_2, ..., \varepsilon_n$.

Assumption 4:
The frame must be able to measure a wider range of relative axle positions than the one commanded by the kinematic controller.

The next step in the RPS algorithm is to derive a smooth function based upon the data that interpolates the measurements along the length of the beam since the locations of the strains are all known according to Assumption 3. Due to its relative ease of calculation and its ability to exactly intersect the strain measurements, the polynomial interpolation

$$\varepsilon(x) = a_1 + a_2 x + \cdots + a_{n-1} x^{n-2} + a_n x^{n-1} \tag{5.1}$$

is selected where x represents the position along the length of the beam. Coefficients in Equation 5.1 are then determined by solving the following linear equations

$$\begin{bmatrix} 1 & l_1 & \cdots & l_1^{n-2} & l_1^{n-1} \\ 1 & l_2 & \cdots & l_2^{n-2} & l_2^{n-1} \\ 1 & l_3 & \cdots & l_3^{n-2} & l_3^{n-1} \\ \vdots & \vdots & & \vdots & \vdots \\ 1 & l_n & \cdots & l_n^{n-2} & l_n^{n-1} \end{bmatrix} \begin{bmatrix} a_1 \\ a_2 \\ a_3 \\ \vdots \\ a_n \end{bmatrix} = \begin{bmatrix} \varepsilon_1 \\ \varepsilon_2 \\ \varepsilon_3 \\ \vdots \\ \varepsilon_n \end{bmatrix} \tag{5.2}$$

where $l_1, ..., l_n$ are the discrete locations along the beam at which the strain is known.

The strain polynomial is then used to calculate the posture of one axle relative to the other without using small angle approximations. The starting point is the relationship between strain, ε, curvature, κ, and radius of curvature, ρ

$$\frac{1}{\rho} = \kappa = \frac{\varepsilon}{\tilde{y}} \tag{5.3}$$

where $\tilde{y}$ is the distance to the strained fiber from the neutral axis of the beam [142]. Since the beam has a simple rectangular cross section, axial loads are assumed to be negligible, and strain is measured at the surface of the beam, $\tilde{y}$ is assumed to be half of the beam thickness. The beam is then broken into small segments with length dL, Figure 5.2. Assuming that dL is sufficiently small, the change in curvature over the segment is negligible and assumed constant. Hence, the change in orientation $d\phi$ can be calculated from the arc length equation

$$d\phi = \frac{dL}{\rho} \tag{5.4}$$

which then provides the change in position for that segment

$$dx = \rho \sin(d\phi) \tag{5.5}$$

$$dy = \rho\left(1 - \cos(d\phi)\right) \tag{5.6}$$

Equations 5.4 through 5.6 are integrated piecewise over the length of the beam to determine the net change in position and orientation of the end point of the beam

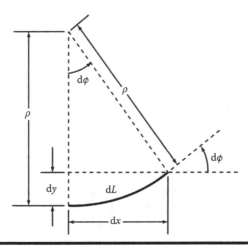

Figure 5.2   Curvature integration diagram.

with respect to its root. Since each segment is rotated with respect to its preceding segments, the vector [dx, dy] from each segment must be rotated

$$
\begin{bmatrix} dx_r \\ dy_r \end{bmatrix} = \begin{bmatrix} \cos(-\phi_p) & \sin(-\phi_p) \\ -\sin(-\phi_p) & \cos(-\phi_p) \end{bmatrix} \begin{bmatrix} dx \\ dy \end{bmatrix}
\tag{5.7}
$$

where [dx_r, dy_r] is the rotated position vector and ϕ_p is the sum of each $d\phi$ from all the previous segments. The dx_r and dy_r from each segment are then summed to calculate the total change in x and y over the length of the beam. Since the beam is clamped to the axles, it has small, rigid clamped sections at each end that are summed in as well. These rigid sections are handled similarly with the exception that because these segments are rigid, $d\phi$ is always zero. The result of the piecewise integration is a calculation of the relative pose of the center point of one axle with respect to the other. Thus, the relative posture of the front axle relative to the rear axle is reported by the beam sensor as

$$
\mathbf{x}_{RPS} = \begin{bmatrix} x_{RPS} \\ y_{RPS} \\ \phi_{RPS} \end{bmatrix} = \begin{bmatrix} \sum dx_r \\ \sum dy_r \\ \sum d\phi \end{bmatrix}
\tag{5.8}
$$

Associated with this data is the RPS covariance P_{RPS}, which reflects the amount of variation in the experimental data relative to the mean data. P_{RPS} is used during the second-tier data fusion described in Section 5.4 and is evaluated experimentally in Section 5.5.

Although the above RPS algorithm can also predict forces applied to the frame, this information is not used in the example of this book. This would be an alternative way to design the sensory system. The readers can refer to [126] for more detailed information, if interested.

5.2.2 Implementation

In this section, we give an example of an implementation of the RPS to illustrate how to consider both hardware and software issues. In order to capture a wide range of relative axle configurations, a minimum number of strain measurements must be provided. If the frame were ideally in pure bending, as commanded by the kinematic controller, this would necessitate only one strain gauge. However, more strain gauges would be demanded to accommodate uncertainties applied on relative axle postures for more accurate measurement. In this example, five equally spaced strain gauge locations were selected [115]. The beam itself is made of spring steel, is 0.71 mm thick, is 51 mm tall, and is 0.3464 m in length with strain gauges actually mounted at [0.0063, 0.0986, 0.1721, 0.2578, 0.3438] m along the beam.

Specific electrical requirements for implementing the RPS include signal amplification, signal conditioning, noise reduction, and consideration of signal loss. For example, if the CFMMR is controlled via a long (7.6 m) tether by a dSpace 1103 DSP from the MATLAB Simulink environment, the small 20 mV output from the strain bridges should be amplified on the robot to take advantage of the DSP's analog input range and to reduce the impact of electrical noise along the tether. An amplifier circuit was designed, and separate implementations of this circuit for each strain gauge bridge provide variable gain and offset for each bridge. Each amplifier was thus tuned to take advantage of the input range of the DSP and to minimize the effects of noise given the range of strain reported by each bridge for a large range of boundary conditions.

Once the gain and offset of the instrumentation amplifiers were adjusted, measured voltages were correlated to strain. In this process, the frame was deformed in pure bending and the output voltages were measured. Similar measurements were obtained for several boundary conditions. These voltages were then correlated statistically to the ideal strain levels to determine voltage-strain regression equations for each sensor. In the RPS algorithm, the strain measurements are then used to solve for the polynomial coefficients a_i in Equation 5.2, which ultimately allow for the piecewise integration of Equations 5.4 through 5.6, as described above.

Software implementation of the RPS algorithm presents challenges since evaluation of a_i and integration along the length of the beam must be performed in real-time at the sampling rate of the system. The number of beam segments used in the integration must be large enough to provide an accurate estimation of relative posture. On the other hand, a given robot controller must operate at some minimum speed for optimal performance, and a large number of segments could adversely affect the time step of the system. Evaluations of these factors on the accuracy of the RPS are described in Section 5.5.

5.3 First-Tier Data Fusion

In the first-tier algorithm, each axle module fuses the data from its wheel encoders and other onboard sensors using a kinematic-model–based Extended Kalman Filter (EKF) [140]. Specifically, seven axle states are used by each EKF to represent the motion of the axle in the global X–Y reference frame, Figure 5.3, and are represented by the vector

$$\mathbf{x}_i = \begin{bmatrix} x_i & y_i & \phi_i & V_i & \dot{\phi}_i & \dot{V}_i & \ddot{\phi}_i \end{bmatrix}^T \quad (5.9)$$

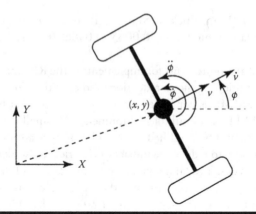

Figure 5.3   The seven single axle EKF states.

where $i=1$ and $i=2$ represent the front- and rear-axle states, respectively. The non-linear modeling systems for each axle are expressed as

$$\mathbf{x}_i^k = a_i\left(\mathbf{x}_i^{k-1},0,0,T\right)= \mathbf{x}_i^{k-1}+\delta\mathbf{x}_i^k \tag{5.10}$$

which are explicitly determined by

$$\mathbf{x}_i^k = \begin{bmatrix} x_i^k \\ y_i^k \\ \phi_i^k \\ v_i^k \\ \dot{\phi}_i^k \\ \dot{v}_i^k \\ \ddot{\phi}_i^k \end{bmatrix} = \begin{bmatrix} x_i^{k-1} \\ y_i^{k-1} \\ \phi_i^{k-1} \\ V_i^{k-1} \\ \dot{\phi}_i^{k-1} \\ \dot{V}_i^{k-1} \\ \ddot{\phi}_i^{k-1} \end{bmatrix} + \begin{bmatrix} \delta x_i^k \\ \delta y_i^k \\ \delta\phi_i^k \\ \dot{V}_i^{k-1}T \\ \ddot{\phi}_i^{k-1}T \\ 0 \\ 0 \end{bmatrix} \tag{5.11}$$

where δx_i^k, δy_i^k, and $\delta\phi_i^k$ are now derived assuming no wheel slip. Note that Equation 5.11 employs constant acceleration states (noted by the zeros in the last two elements of the $\delta\mathbf{x}_i^k$ vector) instead of constant velocities, which is discussed later in this section. The two velocity terms in Equation 5.11 are simply acceleration multiplied by sampling time, T, applied to both translational and rotational velocity.

Consider derivation of the posture states x, y, and ϕ in Equation 5.11. Figure 5.4 shows the path traveled by a single axle over one time step where the length of the path and change in orientation is exaggerated for clarity. Since the time step is usually very small, the difference in length between the straight line

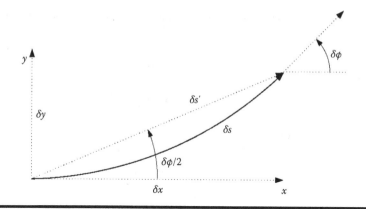

Figure 5.4   The kinematics of axle motion over a single step.

vector $\delta s'$ and the path the axle actually traveled, δs, can be negligible. Thus, $\delta s'$ can be calculated as

$$\delta s_i' = v_i^{k-1}T + \frac{\dot{v}_i^{k-1}T^2}{2} \qquad (5.12)$$

The change in orientation of the axle is then calculated by the angular velocity and acceleration in the previous time step

$$\delta \phi_i^k = \dot{\phi}_i^{k-1}T + \frac{\ddot{\phi}_i^{k-1}T}{2} \qquad (5.13)$$

The angle between the global x axis and the line $\delta s_i'$ can then be calculated by

$$\phi_i^{k-1} + \frac{1}{2}\left(\dot{\phi}_i^{k-1}T + \frac{\ddot{\phi}_i^{k-1}T^2}{2} \right) \qquad (5.14)$$

and δx_i^k and δy_i^k are predicted as the x and y components of the change in position vector $\delta s_i'$

$$\delta x_k = \left(v_{k-1}T + \frac{\dot{v}_{k-1}T^2}{2} \right)\cos\left(\phi_{k-1} + \frac{1}{2}\left(\dot{\phi}_{k-1}T + \frac{\ddot{\phi}_{k-1}T^2}{2} \right) \right) \qquad (5.15)$$

$$\delta y_k = \left(v_{k-1}T + \frac{\dot{v}_{k-1}T^2}{2} \right)\sin\left(\phi_{k-1} + \frac{1}{2}\left(\dot{\phi}_{k-1}T + \frac{\ddot{\phi}_{k-1}T^2}{2} \right) \right) \qquad (5.16)$$

which complete the state model Equation 5.11.

Each EKF propagates two types of information: the system states $\mathbf{x}_i$ and the covariance matrix P_i, which represents the uncertainty associated with the EKF estimates and the correlations between the states. Such information is updated over the time update as

$$\tilde{x}_i^k = a_i\left(\hat{x}_i^{k-1}, 0, 0, T\right) \tag{5.17}$$

$$\tilde{P}_i^k = A_i P_i^{k-1} A_i^T + Q_i \tag{5.18}$$

and the measurement update as

$$K_i^k = \tilde{P}_i^k H_i^T \left(H_i \tilde{P}_i^k H_i^T + R_i\right)^{-1} \tag{5.19}$$

$$\hat{\mathbf{x}}_i^k = \tilde{\mathbf{x}}_i^k + K_i^k \left(z_i^k - H_i \tilde{\mathbf{x}}_i^k\right), \text{and} \tag{5.20}$$

$$P_i^k = \left(I - K_i^k H_i\right) \tilde{P}_i^k \tag{5.21}$$

In these equations, $\hat{\mathbf{x}}$ denotes an estimate of the states and the tilde superscript indicates a prediction at the current time step, k. The matrix A_i represents a linearization of Equation 5.11 at the current time step; Q_i is the covariance associated with the uncertainties in the ith axle state model, f_i; and the matrix H_i maps the sensor inputs to the states.

Although wheel slip is not directly considered in this implementation, the constant acceleration terms in Equation 5.11 can be used to our advantage by a proper tuning of the matrix Q_i. The idea is that when the robot encounters a slick spot, and one of the wheels suddenly slips, the affected wheel will often experience a dramatic acceleration. If this acceleration can be shown to be significantly greater than the normal system accelerations, then it can be attenuated to some degree by the constant acceleration model in Equation 5.11. This is done by adjusting the two acceleration components of the Q_i matrix so that the speed with which a change in acceleration is incorporated into the system states is fast enough not to affect the normal system accelerations but slow enough to dampen the quick accelerations characteristic of a slipping wheel. The resulting Q_i matrix would become

$$Q_i = diag\left[\begin{array}{ccccccc} 0.001 & 0.001 & 0.001 & 0.1 & 0.1 & 10 & 10 \end{array}\right] \tag{5.22}$$

Finally, note that the P_i matrix is initially set to a diagonal matrix whose diagonal terms are all 0.001, which quickly converges to the actual variances of the system.

It is worth noting that in the phase of measurement update, the purpose of Equation 5.19 is to calculate the Kalman gain matrix, K, which is a measure of the relative difference in trust between the time update state prediction and the measurements. It also allows a mapping of the measurements to each of the system states. It is by the K matrix in Equation 5.20 that the EKF can estimate the acceleration states, even though the model assumes constant acceleration and the acceleration states are not directly measured. The H matrix is a mapping of the states to the measurements, and R_k is the covariance matrix associated with the measurements z_k. H can be found by taking the Jacobian of the measurement model h. The measurements include the left and right encoder counts, and the gyroscope voltage. The H matrices used for the front and rear axles respectively are shown in Equations 5.23 and 5.24

$$H_1 = \begin{bmatrix} 0 & 0 & 0 & \dfrac{C_E T}{2\pi r} & \dfrac{C_E B T}{2\pi r} & 0 & 0 \\ 0 & 0 & 0 & \dfrac{C_E T}{2\pi r} & -\dfrac{C_E B T}{2\pi r} & 0 & 0 \end{bmatrix} \tag{5.23}$$

$$H_2 = \begin{bmatrix} 0 & 0 & 0 & \dfrac{C_E T}{2\pi r} & \dfrac{C_E B T}{2\pi r} & 0 & 0 \\ 0 & 0 & 0 & \dfrac{C_E T}{2\pi r} & -\dfrac{C_E B T}{2\pi r} & 0 & 0 \\ 0 & 0 & 0 & 0 & C_G & 0 & 0 \end{bmatrix} \tag{5.24}$$

where C_E is the number of quadrature encoder counts in a single revolution of a wheel, r is the tire radius, B is the robot wheel base, and C_G is the gyroscope calibration coefficient. Table 5.1 contains the actual values used in the H matrix for our platform. In this case, the measurements are assumed to be independent such that R is a diagonal matrix with the variance of each sensor along the diagonal

$$R_1 = R_2 = diag(0.005, 0.005, 0.005) \tag{5.25}$$

Equation 5.20 then provides the state estimate for the current time step. The term in parentheses, $\left(z_i^k - H_i \tilde{x}_i^k\right)$, is known as the residual to indicate the difference between the predicted and actual measurements. The change in states for the time step is calculated by multiplying the residual by the Kalman gain, K_i. Equation 5.21 then calculates the final value of the state covariance matrix P_i.

Table 5.1 Parameter Values Used in the H Matrix

Variable	C_E	T	r	B	C_G
Value	1024 counts	0.01 s	0.073 m	0.343 m	1.39 rad/s/V

5.4 Second-Tier Data Fusion

5.4.1 Motivation for Covariance Intersection

In order to bring together all of the data sources on the robot including RPS, a second tier of data fusion is needed, Figure 5.1. Notice that the RPS is merely an observation of the relative pose $\mathbf{x}_{RPS}$ of the two axles without new information in terms of the global coordinate frame. Therefore, if the beam data is fused with the axle data using a traditional Kalman filter to decrease the variance of the axle pose, then such an estimate is not conservative.

This problem can be solved using the Covariance Intersection filter strategy that does not produce nonconservative estimates from data with unknown correlations [138]. Two simulations were conducted to verify the superiority of the CI filter compared to a Kalman filter for the second tier of data fusion. Similar to the CFMMR, the simulation used two axles connected by an RPS. Each axle used an EKF to estimate the axle states with the covariance matrix initialized to a diagonal matrix with the value 0.01 at each diagonal element. The simulated sensors, such as wheel encoders, and RPS strain bridges, were all set to report zero with the addition of a small amount of zero-mean, normally distributed noise. States for both axles were initialized to zero, which is contradictory to the fact that both axles could not be at the origin at the same time. This should be corrected by the second-tier data fusion algorithm based on the RPS.

The first simulation, Figure 5.5, used a CI filter for the second-tier filter, and the second simulation, Figure 5.6, used a Kalman filter. Even though both axles are

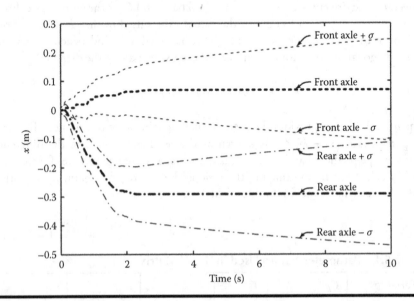

Figure 5.5 Using CI as the top-tier data-fusion method.

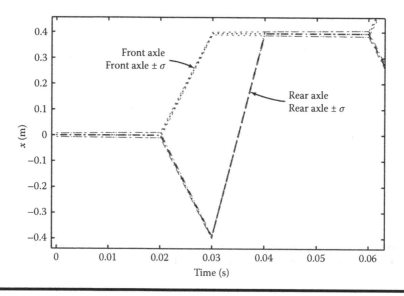

Figure 5.6 **Detail of using a Kalman filter as the top-tier data-fusion method.**

initialized to zero, the CI filter quickly converges and adjusts the x position of both axles such that they are separated by the distance reported by the RPS. Moreover, the standard deviations σ never drop below their initial values but steadily increase, as is expected in the absence of a direct and independent measurement of the x position state.

In contrast, Figure 5.6 shows the first six hundredths of a second of a simulation using the same initial conditions with a traditional Kalman filter as the second-tier data fusion method. As can be seen, the initial covariances are very small. In addition, Figure 5.7 shows the covariances remain so small that they are indistinguishable from the mean axle position for the duration of the simulation. Because the Kalman filter believes the RPS and encoder measurements to be independent measurements with respect to the global coordinate frame, the covariances are slashed with each measurement update, causing the filter to ignore new measurement inputs at the axle level. This behavior results in rapid divergence of the Kalman filter, Figure 5.7. This is clearly undesirable and conclusively shows the superiority of the CI filter for this application.

5.4.2 *Relative Measurement Stochastic Posture Error Correction (RMSPEC)*

In the second-tier data-fusion algorithm, the CI filter is used to update EKF posture estimates, $\mathbf{x}_j$, of the least trustworthy axle data using the RMSPEC algorithm. Similar to Borenstein [108, 141], RMSPEC employs the *growth rate* concept in

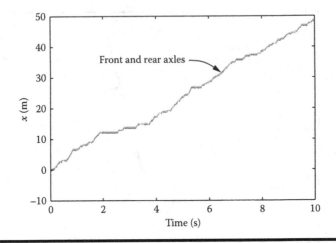

Figure 5.7   Using a Kalman filter as the top-tier data-fusion method.

order to determine which axle data is most likely to minimize relative posture estimate error between the axles. Since relative heading angle errors between coupled robots will typically cause the fastest divergence of the relative posture estimates, *growth rate* is characterized by the difference between the EKF predictions of relative axle postures and the estimates provided by the RPS. This difference is termed the *deviation angle* and can be evaluated directly from the EKF and RPS data in order to determine which axle is most trustworthy.

In order to calculate the *deviation angle* for each axle (represented by θ_1 and θ_2 in Figure 5.8 and Figure 5.9, respectively), first consider the relative position of the first axle relative to the second axle as provided by the EKF state estimates in the global coordinate frame

$$\Delta = \begin{bmatrix} x_1 - x_2 \\ y_1 - y_2 \end{bmatrix} = \begin{bmatrix} \Delta x \\ \Delta y \end{bmatrix} \tag{5.26}$$

The angle of Δ is thus estimated by the EKF to be

$$\gamma = a \ \tan2(\Delta y, \Delta x) \tag{5.27}$$

Similar relative position estimates are provided by the RPS, but we must first consider the fact that the RPS data is expressed relative to Axle 2. Thus, the angle of the relative position predicted by the RPS β is determined by

$$\beta = a \ \tan2(y_{RPS}, x_{RPS}) \tag{5.28}$$

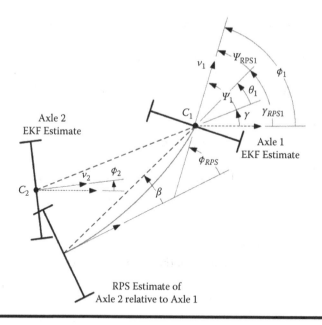

Figure 5.8   Illustration of deviation angle θ_1 calculation for Axle 1.

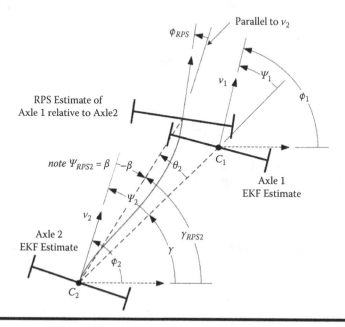

Figure 5.9   Illustration of deviation angle θ_2 calculation for Axle 2.

In the case of Axle 2, this directly estimates the relative heading of Axle 2

$$\psi_{RPS2} = \beta \tag{5.29}$$

as illustrated in Figure 5.9. The relative-position estimate provided by the RPS relative to Axle 2 is then determined by

$$\gamma_{RPS2} = \phi_2 - \psi_{RPS2} \tag{5.30}$$

The deviation between the EKF and RPS estimates relative to Axle 2 EKF data is then defined as

$$\theta_2 = \gamma_{RPS2} - \gamma \tag{5.31}$$

Substituting Equations 5.30 and 5.29, the deviation is calculated as

$$\theta_2 = \phi_2 - \psi_{RPS2} - \beta \tag{5.32}$$

Calculating the deviation angle relative to Axle 1 EKF data is slightly more complicated since the RPS data is expressed relative to Axle 2. In this case, however, it is noted that the RPS also provides an estimate, ϕ_{RPS}, of the relative headings of the two axles, Figure 5.8. Thus, the RPS estimate of the relative heading of Axle 1 is

$$\psi_{RPS1} = \phi_{RPS} - \beta \tag{5.33}$$

Likewise, the relative orientation using RPS data relative to Axle 1 is

$$\gamma_{RPS1} = \phi_1 - \psi_{RPS1} \tag{5.34}$$

Similar to Equation 5.31, the deviation between the EKF and RPS estimates of the relative position taken with respect to Axle 1 EKF data is defined as

$$\theta_1 = \gamma_{RPS1} - \gamma \tag{5.35}$$

Upon substituting Equations 5.33 and 5.34, the deviation angle reduces to

$$\theta_1 = \phi_1 - \phi_{RPS} + \beta - \gamma \tag{5.36}$$

which differs from Equation 5.32 due to the fact that RPS data is taken relative to Axle 2 and not Axle 1. Thus, deviation angles are determined from experimental data by Equations 5.32 and 5.36.

Taking note that $\gamma = \phi_i - \psi_i$, it is insightful to show that Equations 5.31 and 5.35 combined respectively with Equations 5.30 and 5.34 can be represented generically as

$$\theta_i = \psi_i - \psi_{RPSi} \qquad (5.37)$$

where i represents the ith axle. Thus, deviation angles indicate the differences between EKF and RPS estimates of relative axle headings, ψ_i and ψ_{RPSi}, respectively. Maintaining fidelity of these relative headings by minimizing deviation angles is critical for minimizing growth rate and maintaining robot configuration.

The axle with the smallest magnitude deviation angle will then provide the smallest growth rate when combined with RPS data. Thus, if $|\theta_1| < |\theta_2|$ then the EKF data $\mathbf{x}_1$ is combined with $\mathbf{x}_{RPS}$ to update posture estimates in $\mathbf{x}_2$. The opposite is true when $|\theta_2| < |\theta_1|$.

In order to combine EKF data and RPS data, the CI filter is used. The state vector used in the CI filter structure is composed of the position and orientation states of a single axle (x_i, y_i, and ϕs) because these are the only states that the RPS has the capacity to distinguish. The CI algorithm is stated as

$$C = \left(wA^{-1} + (1-w)B^{-1} \right)^{-1}$$
$$c = C \left(wA^{-1}a + (1-w)B^{-1}b \right) \qquad (5.38)$$

where $\{a, A\}$ and $\{b, B\}$ represent the {mean, variance} associated with datasets, and $\{c, C\}$ likewise represents the fusion of $\{a, A\}$ and $\{b, B\}$. The weighting factor w is chosen to minimize the trace of the resulting covariance matrix. Thus, the CI filter provides us with the ability to use the frame module to reduce odometric error and to maintain consistent covariance estimates.

The CI-based fusion algorithm operating on Axle 1 is stated as follows

If $|\theta_1| > |\theta_2|$, then Axle 2 is most Trustworthy. Update Axle 1 based upon RPS data:

Define CI input states

$$a = \begin{bmatrix} x_1 & y_1 & \phi_1 \end{bmatrix}^T \qquad (5.39)$$

$$b = \begin{bmatrix} x_2 \\ y_2 \\ \phi_2 \end{bmatrix} + \begin{bmatrix} x_{RPS} \\ y_{RPS} \\ \phi_{RPS} \end{bmatrix} \qquad (5.40)$$

and respective covariances

$$A = P_1[1,1:3,3] + \begin{bmatrix} 0 & 0 & 0 \\ 0 & 0 & 0 \\ 0 & 0 & 1 \end{bmatrix} \theta_1^2 \qquad (5.41)$$

$$B = P_2[1,1:3,3] + P_{RPS} \qquad (5.42)$$

Fuse data using Equation 5.38 to produce {c, C} based upon optimized and rate-limited w (discussed next).

Update Axle 1 EKF states and covariance

$$\mathbf{x}_1[1:3] = \begin{bmatrix} x_1 & y_1 & \phi_1 \end{bmatrix} = c \tag{5.43}$$

$$P_1[1,1:3,3] = C \tag{5.44}$$

Else do not update Axle 1 EKF states or covariance.

END

Note that Equation 5.33 is based on EKF data combined with RPS data derived in Equation 5.8. Covariances P_1 and P_2 are likewise derived from EKF data and are truncated here to the first 3×3 elements since these are the states updatable by the CI filter. The same method is applicable in the truncation of the $\mathbf{x}_1$ vector in Equation 5.37.

The CI-based fusion algorithm operating on Axle 2 is stated as follows

If $|\theta_1| \le |\theta_2|$, then Axle 1 is most Trustworthy. Update Axle 2 based upon RPS data:

Define CI input states

$$a = \begin{bmatrix} x_2 & y_2 & \phi_2 \end{bmatrix}^T \tag{5.45}$$

$$b = \begin{bmatrix} x_1 \\ y_1 \\ \phi_1 \end{bmatrix} - \begin{bmatrix} x_{RPS} \\ y_{RPS} \\ \phi_{RPS} \end{bmatrix} \tag{5.46}$$

and respective covariances

$$A = P_2[1,1:3,3] + \begin{bmatrix} 0 & 0 & 0 \\ 0 & 0 & 0 \\ 0 & 0 & 1 \end{bmatrix} \theta_2^2 \tag{5.47}$$

$$B = P_1[1,1:3,3] + P_{RPS} \tag{5.48}$$

Fuse data using Equation 5.38 to produce {c, C} based upon optimized and rate-limited w (discussed next).

Update Axle 2 EKF estimate

$$\mathbf{x}_2[1:3] = \begin{bmatrix} x_2 & y_2 & \phi_2 \end{bmatrix} = c \tag{5.49}$$

$$P_2[1,1:3,3] = C \tag{5.50}$$

Else do not update Axle 2 EKF states or covariance.

END

In calculating the w parameter for the CI filter, we take into account both accuracy and system limitations. It was desired to limit the number of calculations so as not to impact system performance. Experiments revealed that w often changes very rapidly for this system. To accommodate this fact, a three-part hybrid approach is used to estimate w. In this approach, C is calculated a maximum of 10 times for each time step, with the value of w that minimizes the trace of C being used as the final result. The first six calculations are a brute force approach in which C is calculated at w values of 0, 0.2, 0.4 0.6, 0.8, and 1. This is followed by a more dynamic approach in which C is calculated at the w used in the previous time step and at two additional points a small $\pm\delta w$ on either side of the w used in the previous time step. The final calculation is made by constructing a polynomial from three of the previously calculated values of w that meet the criteria of being adjacent, and producing the smallest values of the trace of C assuming that they bracket the minimum trace.

The challenge, however, is that the CI filter relies predominantly upon the EKF output until its variance approaches the same level as that of the RPS. Once above this level, the aforementioned algorithm abruptly changes w and causes a sudden change in posture estimates due to the RPS reigning in the relative postures of the axles. In order to smooth this transition to RPS data, a rate limiter is finally imposed on w to limit how much it may change in a single time step.

This fusion scheme is readily expandable to mobile robot configurations that have multiple axles and beam elements. In this situation, every axle would estimate its pose using a first-tier EKF and the sensors it has on board. Then, the RMSPEC second-tier algorithm is used to determine if any of the RPS outputs from neighboring axles is considered trustworthy. If so, then any number of trustworthy pose estimates extrapolated from adjoining axles can be fused together with the pose estimate from the axle's native sensor suite. This has the advantage that different axles can carry different sensors, yet all of the axles can benefit from the pose information provided. For example, if only one axle in a chain is equipped with a GPS, every axle will benefit from the absolute pose information returned by the GPS as the sensor data is propagated from one axle to the next via the integrated RPS sensors linking each axle.

After application of the RMSPEC fusion algorithm, the relative error in position between one axle and its neighbors is limited to the resolution of the beam as a sensor. This is true regardless of the amount of drift associated with the sensors on each individual axle. Without the RPS in the loop, the relative error between the axles would drift apart and large antagonistic forces would occur.

5.5 Static Testing of the RPS

5.5.1 Methods and Procedures

For the purpose of calibration and static evaluations, boundary conditions were imposed on the RPS using an instrumented fixture, Figure 5.10. The fixture

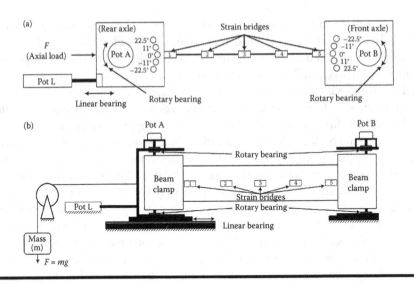

Figure 5.10   RPS test fixture schematic. (a) Top view and (b) side view.

supports the ends of the frame with low-friction ball bearings and measures angular deflection with highly linear potentiometers. One end of the frame, labeled Pot A, is also supported by a linear bearing to allow foreshortening as the frame deflects [43], which is measured by a linear displacement potentiometer. Both angular and prismatic displacement constraints can be imposed and accurately measured for calibration purposes. The fixture also allows for axial forces to be applied in order to evaluate the effects of foreshortening on traction forces. In all of these evaluations, the resulting RPS calculations for x_{RPS}, y_{RPS}, and ϕ_{RPS} describe the point B in the coordinate frame of A, as shown in Figure 5.11.

To evaluate the accuracy and efficiency of the RPS algorithms, experiments were conducted to determine the required number of discrete beam segments and the processor time required to implement the RPS algorithm. The test fixture was used to impose boundary conditions and measure actual displacements of the frame. Measured strain data was then used to evaluate accuracy of the RPS algorithm as the number of beam segments, n, was varied in the discrete integration. In order to evaluate a typical range of relative axle postures, several ratios of angular boundary conditions were evaluated. Mode 1 refers to the case where the beam was deflected in equal and opposite directions to provide pure bending where the A end was fixed at $\psi_{RPS2} = 22.5°$ and the B end at $\psi_{RPS1} = -22.5°$, as shown in Figure 5.11. For Mode 2, the boundary conditions were $\psi_{RPS2} = 0°$ and $\psi_{RPS1} = 22.5°$. For Mode 3, A and B were both pinned to 22.5°. The second experiment involved varying n and determining the amount of processor time required. These results were running on the 400 MHz CPU used on the dSpace 1103 DSP. As the new generations of hardware are much faster, the number of beam segments could be increased accordingly to achieve new balance of accuracy and computational efficiency.

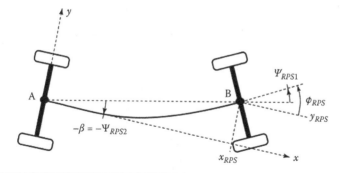

Figure 5.11   The pose of B in the coordinate frame of A.

A final group of experiments were conducted to evaluate the accuracy of the RPS algorithm with axial loads applied. This emulates the situation of nonzero F_x resulting from tracking error. According to Figure 5.10b, a string supporting a known weight is attached to the fixture to apply axial forces to the beam. The endpoints of the beam were deflected in Mode 1 at $-22.5°$, $-11°$, $0°$, $11°$, and $22.5°$. At each of these deflections, longitudinal loads of 0 N, 1.0 N, 2.0 N, and 3.9 N were applied. Due to a small amount of coulomb friction in the joints of the beam fixture, the beam comes to rest at a slightly different location if released slowly from tension than when released from compression. Hence, for each data point of this experiment, the RPS output was recorded after releasing the beam from behavior of tension and compression and then averaged. These small perturbing forces were applied manually several times in both tension and compression in addition to the aforementioned tensile forces to gain a sense of the nominal behavior. A more detailed study of the effects of compressive forces on post-buckled foreshortening can be found in [62]. To assure RPS convergence, $n = 100$ was used in these experiments. Percentages shown represent the mean RPS error at a given angular deflection relative to the actual values measured by the potentiometers.

5.5.2 Results and Discussion

Figure 5.12a–c shows the accuracy of the RPS predictions compared with the number of discrete beam segments, n, used in the spatial integration set to the integer values on the interval of 1 through 20, 100, 1000, and 10,000. All of the error plots indicate a rapid drop off in error for $n = 1–5$ followed by a very slow decrease in error thereafter. Based on this information $n \geq 5$ should be used. Also note that the RPS is generally most accurate in Mode 1, which is the steering configuration typically specified. Error shown for Mode 2 and Mode 3 is representative of error expected when non-ideal boundary conditions are present.

RPS processor time requirements are shown in Figure 5.13, where the solid line intersecting the data points is a linear curve fit where

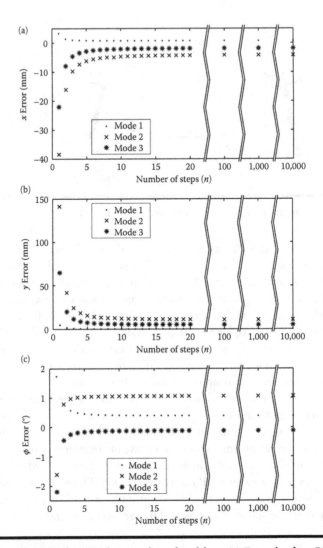

Figure 5.12 Error in the RPS integration algorithm. (a) Error in the xRPS component, (b) error in the yRPS direction, and (c) error in the ϕΡΠΣ.

$$\text{time (ms)} = 0.0025n + 0.018 \tag{5.51}$$

If the processing time required by the robot controller, the axle EKF, and the CI filter is known, then the upper bound on n can be estimated with the graphic in Figure 5.13. While as little as $n = 5$ could be used, $n = 100$ was implemented in the following experiments to assure convergence. Another possible improvement in accuracy could be to avoid discretization of $\kappa(x)$ in Equations 5.4 through 5.6, but the resulting computational burden for each step will increase.

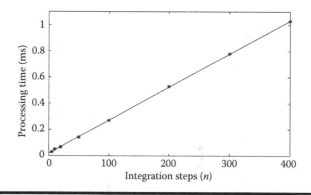

Figure 5.13   The RPS processing time required as *n* is varied.

Figure 5.14a–c shows the error associated with the *x*, *y*, and ϕ components of the relative position vector returned by the RPS algorithm. Several observations can be made that apply to all three plots. In spite of the difficulty in predicting the endpoint of a beam that is capable of deflections in excess of 45°, the RPS sensor performs quite well. Applying a force along a line between the attachment points of the beam does not seem to be detrimental to the accuracy of the RPS algorithm. It is good to know that the RPS is robust to this type of disturbance, as it will likely be common in practical application.

RPS error increases with larger deflections and is somewhat symmetric with respect to the zero deflection angle point. For moderate deflections (±22°), the net RPS posture error is symmetric and less than 4.1 mm and 1°. That symmetry is broken when the beam is deflected to ±45°, however. In this case, the percent error at −45° is half what it is at +45°. Thus, at large deflections, posture error is bounded by as much as 6.7 mm and 2°, or as little as 3.3 mm and 1.2°, depending on direction of deflection. Although RPS performance is not perfect, it does help tremendously to bound relative axle posture estimates.

It is believed that this asymmetry is due in part to a permanent strain in the beam. One indication of this is the fact that when the beam is placed on a flat surface it does not sit perfectly flat. Instead, the beam has a slight twist to it and one of the corners sits several millimeters off of the surface, which is a result of the manufacturing of the spring steel. It is also possible that this effect could be due to errors in the calibration process or errors in measuring the locations of the strain bridges.

Evaluation of the RPS covariance P_{RPS} is based upon the aforementioned experimental results. The covariance was evaluated for Modes 1, 2, and 3, and ultimately was based upon Mode 2 results since these represented worst case performance of the RPS:

$$P_{RPS} = diag \begin{bmatrix} 4.13 \times 10^{-04} & 1.30 \times 10^{-04} & 0.0115 \end{bmatrix} \qquad (5.52)$$

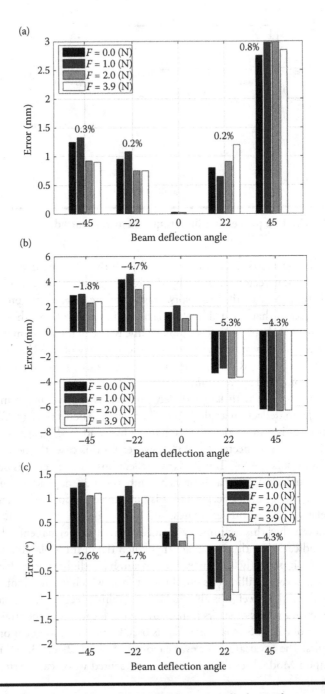

Figure 5.14 RPS error with various axial forces applied. (a) The *x* component of the RPS error, (b) the *y* component of the RPS error, and (c) the *φ* component of the RPS error.

5.6 Testing of the RPS and Data Fusion

5.6.1 Methods and Procedures

The robot was tested on three surfaces with increasing difficulty. The first surface was a tightly knit closed-loop carpet that provided excellent traction and very little slipping. This surface was used as the benchmark. The second surface consisted of sand at a uniform thickness of 10 mm spread on top of a plastic sheet. This surface resulted in a large amount of wheel slip. The final surface consisted of the sand from the previous testing with the addition of 10 to 20 mm thick rocks scattered in the path of the robot at approximately 70 mm intervals. These rocks are sand stone in origin with a rough surface to provide the robot with traction as it climbs over them. The size of the rocks was chosen to provide a significant obstacle when compared to the diameter of the wheels but not be so large as to be a barrier.

In the tests, the robot motion controller provided point stabilization using classical wheel velocity servos and a 100 Hz sampling rate. The robot was started at a distance of -1.000 m in y and -1.550 m in x from the origin. The controller caused the robot to travel an s-shaped path making first a left then a right turn as it tried to converge to the origin. Tests were done on each surface using four different sensor configurations. These sensor configurations were odometry only, odometry in conjunction with a gyroscope (BEI HZI-90–100A) on the rear axle only, and the previous two configurations with the addition of the RPS and the second-tier RMSPEC fusion algorithm. At the end of each run, the position and orientation of each axle was measured using a tape measure and a grid system of strings stretched just above the height of the robot. The actual final pose of the robot could then be compared to the pose as reported by the robot.

The objective is to show the improvement in relative off tracking afforded by the RPS. Therefore, the difference between the measured and sensed ending relative pose of each axle is reported. Measurements are taken manually using a tape measure at the end of each trial. Sensed relative posed data is derived from the CI/EKF/RPS algorithms presented in this chapter. The variables x_{REL}, y_{REL}, and ϕ_{PEA}, which describe the pose of the front axle in the reference frame of the rear axle, Figure 5.11, are used to communicate this information and are compiled in Table 5.2. At least five trials per test were conducted. While this is insufficient to draw statistically founded conclusions, we report mean and 95% confidence intervals ($\pm$ two standard deviations) for each metric to illustrate general trends. The confidence interval is included because in some cases the mean value of a metric was close to zero while the variation was large. It is also desired to show an improvement in the final global pose estimate of the robot. To show the improvement in final global pose estimation, e is reported as the distance from the origin to the mid-point between both axles, Figure 5.15. The variable γ is the orientation of a line drawn between the center points of both axles, Figure 5.15. Both e and γ are obtained from manual measurements using a tape measure.

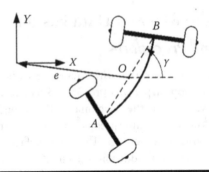

Figure 5.15   The global pose variables e and γ.

It should be noted that the rear axle also supported the RPS amplification circuit and two 7.2 Volt NiCad batteries that are its power source. This extra weight increased rear axle ground and traction forces.

5.6.2 *Results and Discussion*

Table 5.2 summarizes the results for all tests. In each data field, the top number is the mean of all trials and the bottom number is the 95% confidence interval. Again, since the numbers of trials were limited in each test, these values only indicate general trends regarding performance. The first row of the table shows the error in the relative x distance, x_{REL}, between the axles for all trials. Note the large decrease in both the mean and confidence interval of the error in the tests that used the RPS when compared with those that did not. The addition of the gyroscope without the RPS increased the error in this metric on the high-traction surface while decreasing the error on the low-traction surfaces. The effect is very likely due to the fact that for this experiment the gyro bias was assumed to be constant when in reality it is generally modeled as a first order Markov process. This phenomenon is also commonly referred to as gyroscope drift. The gyroscope data sheet states that the gyro bias stability over operating environments is <4.5°/s. The implication is that for a high-traction surface the odometry estimate of axle rotation rate is better than the gyroscope estimation due to the statistical variation in gyro bias with the result that the gyroscope degrades performance on the carpet surface. On the other hand, when maneuvering on a low-traction surface, such as sand, the gyroscope rotation rate estimate is superior to the rotation rate estimate from odometry, even with the gyro bias effects, and therefore improves the robot performance on the sand surfaces.

The second row of Table 5.2 shows the error in the relative y distance, y_{REL}, between the axles for all trials. Again, note the reduction in error with the addition of the RPS for all of the surfaces. The addition of the rear axle gyroscope seems detrimental to this metric, especially in the tests on sand and sand with rocks without

Table 5.2 The Error between Robot Ground Truth and Sensor-Driven Pose Estimate

| | Carpet | | | | Sand | | | | Rocks on Sand | | | |
| | No RPS | | With RPS | | No RPS | | With RPS | | No RPS | | With RPS | |
	No Gyro	With Gyro	No Gyro	With Gyro	No Gyro	With Gyro	No Gyro	With Gyro	No Gyro	With Gyro	No Gyro	With Gyro
x_{REL} (mm)	185±40.6	326±31.1	30.1±7.94	−15.7±3.77	399±201	−103±125	11.4±2.08	−0.41±2.52	−768±594	−270±160	14.9±10.6	37.0±20.8
y_{REL} (mm)	−359±32.7	165±11.8	−15.2±2.86	53.5±3.79	−24.6±290	−549±182	28.7±14.7	33.9±2.57	90.9±307	−1111±214	6.86±5.76	45.6±46.3
ϕ_{REL} (°)	−11.4±4.98	2.53±9.47	0.82±0.52	4.38±0.40	−2.38±10.2	−26.5±8.37	12.9±5.88	13.5±2.95	−270±248	−49.6±27.9	1.27±4.14	1.77±16.3
e (mm)	51.9±15.2	−4.60±4.42	−49.1±7.75	−78.8±5.93	−447±125	114±79.7	45.6±34.0	38.5±41.9	−131±182	500±182	43.4±64.6	96.7±67.2
γ (°)	−13.4±3.42	93.5±2.55	−8.94±0.41	−7.22±1.25	128±69.9	−77.2±24.9	−4.84±6.42	0.68±2.23	−6.57±27.0	−42.0±5.98	−0.49±0.84	−13.6±7.20

the RPS. In order to understand why this metric is degraded by the gyroscope it is important to consider how this metric is formed. The relative position metrics are all based on the posture of the front axle in the coordinate frame of the rear axle. Hence the y_{REL} metric is highly sensitive to perturbations in the orientation of the rear axle. Any effect that the gyroscope has on the orientation of the rear axle will be amplified by this metric's sensitivity to perturbations in the orientation of the rear axle.

The third row of Table 5.2 shows the error in the relative orientation, ϕ_{REL}, between the axles for all trials. For this metric, robot performance on carpet and sand was similar. This makes sense because the robot's motion controller is trying to control both axles in a Mode 1 configuration. At the same time, wheel slippage will have a tendency to move the robot closer to Mode 1, because this configuration requires the smallest traction forces to maintain its shape. For this reason, the relative orientation metric is less sensitive to low-traction surfaces than the previous metrics. There is a striking difference in ϕ_{REL} with and without the RPS on the sand with rocks surface. This can be attributed to the large disruption created by the rocks; in some cases the rear axle came to a complete stop on a rock. It can also be seen that even with the gyro bias problem, the gyroscope significantly improved the performance of the robot on the sand with rocks surface.

The fourth row of Table 5.2 shows the error in e for all trials. This metric is degraded slightly by the addition of the RPS on carpet. This is most likely due to the approximate 5% error in the RPS estimates. If the distance traveled on carpet were to be increased, it is likely that the error in this metric, for odometry only, would increase proportionally while the error with the RPS would remain bounded. The error in e is also improved significantly by the RPS on both sand and carpet. The addition of the gyroscope is inconclusive.

The fifth row of Table 5.2 shows the error in γ for all trials. This metric was improved by the addition of the RPS for all surfaces. The general trend for the addition of the gyroscope to increase the error in this metric is again due to the gyro bias.

Video footage was taken of the majority of the tests. Still frames from video at 3, 8, 21, and 45 seconds from representative tests of each surface and sensor configuration were assembled. These still frames are overlaid with the estimate of the robot's path as recorded by the sensors and data fusion architecture. A dashed line is used to represent the estimated path followed by the rear axle and a solid line is used to illustrate the estimated path followed by the front axle. Barely visible in the frames are two white lines. One runs horizontally across the top of the frames, and the other runs vertically down the right side. The intersection of these lines represents the location that the point stabilization controller is trying to drive the center point of the rear axle. Simultaneously the controller is trying to drive the front axle to a point on the horizontal line to the right of the line intersection in the frames.

Figure 5.16 shows progressive still frames from representative tests of all four sensor variations on the sand surface. The first two rows of still frames show the

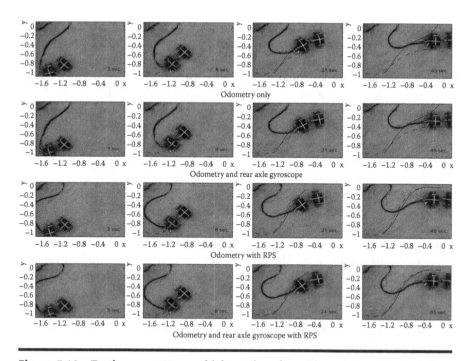

Figure 5.16 Testing on a 10 mm thick sand surface. The solid and dashed lines represent the front and rear axle paths, respectively, estimated by the CI filter.

robot's progression with odometry only and odometry with rear-axle gyroscope. In these two sensor configurations, the navigation pose of both axles drifts, but more particularly the front axle quickly drifts away. This divergence is caused by the large amount of wheel slip due to the low-traction sand surface. The rear axle does not drift as much because of the increased traction force due to the weight of the batteries and RPS support electronics carried by that axle. Because the front axle drifts at a greater rate than the rear, the relative pose between the two axles suffers greatly. This initiates antagonistic forces between the two axles, which compounds front axle wheel slip and drift. As can be seen in the final slides of the first two rows, the front axle pose estimate deviates significantly. With the loss of fidelity between the axles, the motion controller loses its ability to drive the navigation states to the origin.

The third and fourth rows of the still frames show the results with the addition of the RPS algorithm to the sensor suite. In these two series, the front and rear axles track each other very accurately. Because the RPS algorithm continually corrects the relative pose between the axles a high degree of fidelity is maintained between the front and rear axles. This allows the robot motion controller to maintain effective control authority regardless of the fact that the navigation states of the robot are still drifting away from the ground truth. This fidelity between the front and rear axle is required by the motion controller for stability, and is the primary benefit of the RPS and associated algorithms.

Figure 5.17 shows progressive still frames from representative tests of all four sensor variations on the sand and rocks surface. Note the more jagged appearance of all the navigation state lines is due to the rocks. In the first three rows of still frames, the rear axle got stuck on a rock and came to a halt. The front axle in these frames continues to spin its wheels in the sand but never manages to proceed any further. In the first two rows without the RPS, the trace of where the front axle thinks it is continues to progress even though the axle is stuck and spinning its wheels. This is a more extreme case of the potential difference in drift rates between front and rear axles than was seen in Figure 5.16.

In the third row of frames with the RPS in use, the front axle trace stops in place at the same time that the rear axle gets stuck. This occurs even though the front axle was spinning its wheels for the entire time it was stuck. This is an effective demonstration of the ability of the RPS to maintain fidelity between the front and rear axles. This type of performance can be extrapolated to extreme circumstances. For example, if one of the axles were to be kicked out of place in mid-maneuver, the RPS would detect the radical change in posture and correct the odometry, allowing the motion controller to maintain control authority. This

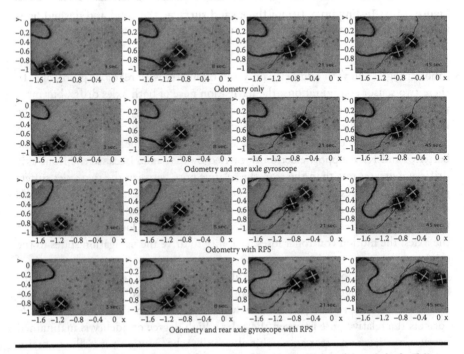

Figure 5.17 Testing on 10 mm thick sand with rocks. The solid and dashed lines represent the front and rear axle paths, respectively, estimated by the CI filter.

behavior makes the robot robust to surface conditions and the chaos in a dynamic environment.

In the fourth row of still frames, the robot performance on rocks is very similar to its performance on carpet, except that the axle traces are less smooth due to the rocky surface. The high degree of congruency between the front and rear axles seen in the final set of still frames in Figure 5.17 can be achieved only through the use of the RPS and associated data fusion algorithms. Figure 5.16 demonstrates that the RPS and RMSPEC algorithm vastly improved performance relative to the one without these sensors.

In summary, odometry works well for short runs on high-traction surfaces. However, it is highly possible that the performance of odometry degrades substantially for longer tests and certainly those on lower-traction surfaces. Hence, it is recommended that the odometry should be augmented with an additional posture-sensing mechanism.

The addition of the gyroscope to odometry is conflicting in its contribution. It improved some metrics on some surfaces while degrading others. Gyro bias was a significant factor in the performance of this sensor. Improvements must be made in the implementation of the gyroscope before it can make a positive contribution to estimating the posture of the robot. The most obvious improvement would be to use a better gyroscope. Another possibility would be to compensate for the gyro bias by including it as a state in the Kalman filter. Other possibilities include weighting the gyroscope information more when wheel slip is more likely such as when maneuvering quickly or when the wheel traction forces are high. The ability of the RPS seems to be only slightly affected by the addition of the gyroscope. Mostly, the RPS corrections overwhelm most of the detrimental effects of the gyro bias.

The RPS and RMSPEC algorithm improved performance in nearly all cases. This combination appears to be robust to seemingly catastrophic environmental conditions, such as a stalled axle on rocky terrain. It also appears to have the ability to place an upper bound on the relative position error between the two axles. While the bound on this error is not as small as predicted by the Mode 1 RPS test results, it is consistent with the bounds of the Mode 2 and Mode 3 results. This is to be expected since the wheel servo controller implemented is not robust to disturbances and these other modes can be witnessed in the still frame sequences just described. Combination of the RPS and RMSPEC algorithm within a formalized architecture discussed in Chapter 3 would highlight improved axle tracking and overall regulation accuracy, which will be presented in the following chapters.

The RPS ability to bound measurement error is an essential ingredient in providing the robot the ability to maintain fidelity between the axles during long-term maneuvers. Operational characteristics of the RMSPEC algorithm can be further appreciated in light of data derived from the tests. Figure 5.18 shows the control variables for the algorithm while operating on the sand surface and using the RPS, odometry, and RMSPEC algorithm. For convenience, the difference in deviation

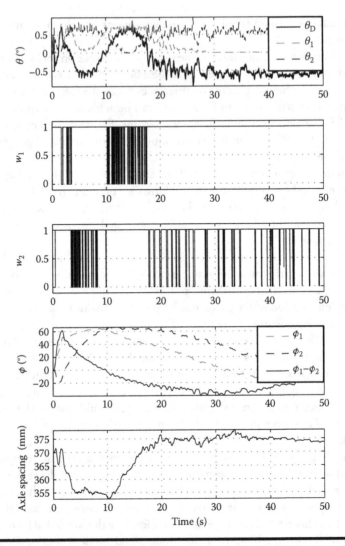

Figure 5.18 **RMSPEC control variables and output data while operating on sand with odometry and RPS sensors.**

angle magnitude, $\theta_D = |\theta_1| - |\theta_2|$, is shown to indicate which axle is most trustworthy. If $\theta_D > 0$ then $|\theta_1| > |\theta_2|$ and Axle 2 is most trustworthy and vice versa when $\theta_D < 0$. Thus, in the ~2–4 and ~10–17 s time periods of Figure 5.18, note that Axle 2 is most trustworthy. Interestingly, note that in these time periods the weighting factor w_2 is essentially unity, which indicates that Axle 1 posture data (covariance and mean) is being updated based entirely upon RPS estimates (Equations 5.40 and 5.42). Likewise, the weighting factor w_1 is varying appreciably during these periods where Axle 1 data is untrustworthy. This indicates that the covariance based method of calculating weighting factors described in Section 5.3 is also effective for identifying untrustworthy data.

In other time periods, such as ~4–10 s and ~17–50 s, $\theta_D < 0$ and Axle 1 is most trustworthy. Similarly, w_1 is unity during these periods and Axle 2 posture data is updated entirely by RPS posture estimates. Note that w_2 varies appreciably during these periods. Again, variation in weighting factor is an indicator of when axle data is untrustworthy.

These results also indicate, however, that weighting factors alone are insufficient for controlling the second-tier data fusion process. In particular, note that both w_1

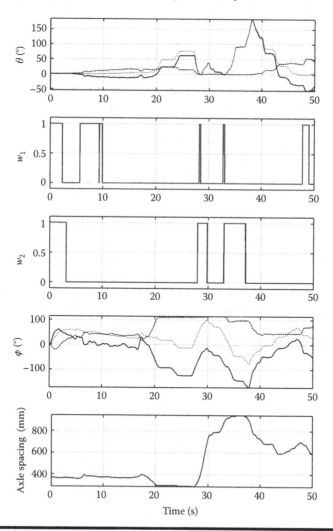

Figure 5.19 **RMSPEC control variables and data-fusion output while operating on sand with rock using only odometry, and first-tier EKF data fusion.**

and w_2 are intermittently unity during these tests, which indicates that a higher level deciding factor, such as deviation angle, is required to arbitrate the fusion process. Thus, the trustworthiness selection process based upon deviation angle is an important part of the RMSPEC algorithm that prevents the CI filters from competing.

Data derived from the robot on the sand-with-rock surface further highlight the ability of the RPS sensor and RMSPEC fusion algorithm to reject large disturbances and wheel spin. Figure 5.19 provides results based upon only EKF data fusion and odometry sensing. Note that deviation angles, θ, increase substantially and that estimates of axle spacing and orientation, ϕ, far exceed reasonable limits given the frame coupling the axles.

In striking contrast, Figure 5.19 shows data derived while also using the RPS and RMSPEC algorithm on the sand-with-rock surface. Note that deviation angles are still quite small, and that orientation and relative axle spacing data are quite reasonable. This is despite significant obstacles and slippery surfaces that caused appreciable out-of-plane motion and substantial wheel spinning. Note, however, that compared to similar data shown for the sand surface in Figure 5.18, deviation angles are larger and that θ_D varies between positive and negative more frequently. These characteristics are attributed to large disturbances (obstacles) that required the RMSPEC algorithm to switch more frequently. Nonetheless, the fusion architecture and RPS sensor discussed in this chapter far exceeded expectations for rejecting disturbances and out of plane motion.

There might be other possible extensions to incorporate more sensors using the discussed methodology. For instance, it would be worthwhile to investigate a full six degree of freedom IMU on each axle for navigation of three dimensional rough terrains. Another obvious sensor addition would be a GPS receiver on one of the axles. It would also be interesting to determine to what degree the RPS could propagate a GPS update from one axle to the other. The RPS itself could also be extended to detect rotations in roll between the two axles. This information could also prove useful when navigating rough terrain.

Chapter 6

Robust Motion Control

6.1 Introduction

According to the control architecture introduced in Chapter 3, we could apply a curvature-based *kinematic motion controller* [48], illustrated in Chapter 4, to specify individual axle motion such that the robot executes the desired net motion. These individual axle motions then provide real-time reference inputs to a *dynamic motion controller.* In Chapters 4 and 5, a perfect model of the robot was assumed in the dynamic controller, which ultimately led to tracking errors and necessary controller tuning for specific types of paths. Control of compliance in robotic systems has been predominant amongst flexible manipulators where oscillations are a primary concern [143,144]. Compliance control in outdoor mobile robots such as the CFMMR differs in two very substantial ways. First, CFMMR represents the modeling structure where the compliant frames encounter large deflections and may operate within post-buckled configurations during steering maneuvers. Therefore, it is difficult to model the compliant frame forces with great accuracy, although an approximate model of the compliant frame can be developed based on Finite Element Method (FEM) and the post-buckled frame element. Secondly, flexible manipulators do not possess nonholonomic constraints, which are one of the typical characteristics of mobile robots. Hence, the dynamic controllers developed for such outdoor mobile robots must consider nonlinear compliance effects and nonholonomic constraints typical of mobile robots, which prevent application of traditional dynamic controllers for flexible manipulators. Compliance amongst mobile robots cooperatively manipulating an object has also received attention [54], but these efforts have focused on motion planning and coordination issues rather than robust dynamic motion control subject to nonholonomic constraints, which is the subject of this chapter. The controller derived here could certainly benefit cooperative mobile robots, though.

In the last two decades, much attention has been paid to the motion control of mobile robots. Some research focuses only on the kinematic model (e.g., steering system) of a mobile robot where the input is velocity [145], and these can be called *kinematic motion controllers*. However, practically they need to take into account the specific dynamics that can produce the input velocity using wheel torque provided by the mobile robot. Thus, some research has been oriented toward torque-based control of dynamical models combined with kinematic models subject to nonholomomic constraints in order to improve tracking performance [53,146], which can be regarded as *dynamic motion control*. These efforts have focused only on rigid mobile robots not interacting cooperatively with other robots.

Control of the compliant mobile robots, however, requires us to consider compliant coupling (e.g., cooperation) between multiple axle modules.

In reality, many kinds of disturbances always exist. Therefore, a few nonlinear, robust, and adaptive *dynamic motion control* techniques have been developed in the presence of the uncertainties of mobile robots [147–152] to confront the negative effects caused by approximation. Other researchers proposed discontinuous robust and/or adaptive controllers that complicate the adjustment of control gains to deal with instability caused by discontinuity, where the bounds of the uncertainties must be known [148–150]. Fierro proposed robust adaptive controllers using online neural-networks. But time-consuming computation is required, and it is difficult to guarantee the convergence of neural network controllers in real-time [151,152]. Lin developed a robust damping control technique that does not require any knowledge of the bounds of the disturbances and had a fairly simple structure. Because of the complexity of the CFMMR dynamic model and the potentially large frame forces, the disturbances are unpredictable [147]. Hence, the robust controller presented here is based on extension of [147]. Note that the reference velocities provided by our curvature-based *kinematic motion control* algorithms for posture regulation and path following [48] are time-varying; however, constant reference velocities are assumed for simplicity in [147].

Therefore, this chapter mainly discusses the development of model-based distributed robust control for the CFMMR, which is generally applicable to any cooperative mobile robotic system with uncertain compliant interaction forces. Two significant issues considered in the development of the controller are modeling and control of highly nonlinear interaction forces, and dynamic tracking control of time-varying reference trajectories (velocity and posture specified as a function of time by a *kinematic motion controller*). In this chapter, we also present the experiments designed to validate the distributed robust controller performance with and without interaction force models and illustrate its capability to track time varying trajectories.

6.2 Kinematic and Dynamic Models

6.2.1 Modular Dynamic Models

The generic dynamic model has already been fully illustrated in Chapter 2 (Section 2.3.5). In this section, the generic dynamic model is reformed into the modular dynamic models. First, the dynamic model of single-axle module is presented based on Figure 6.1 [146]. The generic matrices are then assembled assuming a serial configuration. Considering the ith axle module, we let $\mathbf{V}_i\left(q_i, \dot{q}_i\right) = \mathbf{0}$ since centripetal and coriolis forces of each axle are relatively small due to the velocity and curvature constraints of our robot. Also, $\mathbf{G}_i(q_i) = \mathbf{0}$ since motion of robot system is assumed to be in the horizontal plane. The mass matrix and the input transformation matrix of this axle module are

$$\mathbf{M}_i\left(q_i\right) = \begin{bmatrix} m_i & 0 & 0 \\ 0 & m_i & 0 \\ 0 & 0 & J_i \end{bmatrix}, \quad \mathbf{E}_i\left(q_i\right) = \frac{1}{r_w} \begin{bmatrix} \cos\phi_i & \cos\phi_i \\ \sin\phi_i & \sin\phi_i \\ -d & d \end{bmatrix} \quad (6.1)$$

where m_i and J_i are mass and mass moment of the ith axle individually. The wheel torques applied to the ith axle module are denoted as $\tau_i = \begin{bmatrix} \tau_{L,i} & \tau_{R,i} \end{bmatrix}^T$, where $\tau_{L,i}$ and $\tau_{R,i}$ are motor torques acting on the left and right wheel, respectively. The corresponding frame reaction forces are then expressed as

$$\mathbf{F}_{K,i}(q_i, q_j) = \begin{bmatrix} F_{X,i} & F_{Y,i} & M_i \end{bmatrix}^T \quad (6.2)$$

where j denotes the numbers of all the axles connected with the ith axle, and the Lagrange multipliers are determined by

$$\lambda_i = -m_i\dot{\phi}_i\left(\dot{X}_i\cos\phi_i + \dot{Y}_i\sin\phi_i\right) + F_{X,i}\sin\phi_i - F_{Y,i}\cos\phi_i \quad (6.3)$$

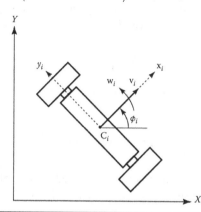

Figure 6.1   The *i*th axle module.

Therefore, the ith axle dynamic equation is expressed as

$$\mathbf{M}_i(q_i)\ddot{q}_i + \mathbf{F}(\dot{q}_i) + \tau_{d,i} + \mathbf{F}_{K,i}(q_i) = \mathbf{E}_i(q_i)\tau_i - \mathbf{A}_i^T(q_i)\lambda_i \qquad (6.4)$$

Hence, the whole dynamic system is assembled by the above axle module matrices as

$$\mathbf{M}(Q) = \begin{bmatrix} \mathbf{M}_1(q_1) & 0 & \cdots & 0 \\ 0 & \mathbf{M}_2(q_2) & 0 & \cdots \\ \cdots & 0 & \cdots & 0 \\ 0 & \cdots & 0 & \mathbf{M}_n(q_n) \end{bmatrix} \qquad (6.5)$$

$$\mathbf{E}(Q) = \begin{bmatrix} \mathbf{E}_1(q_1) & 0 & \cdots & 0 \\ 0 & \mathbf{E}_2(q_2) & 0 & \cdots \\ \cdots & 0 & \cdots & 0 \\ 0 & \cdots & 0 & \mathbf{E}_n(q_n) \end{bmatrix} \qquad (6.6)$$

$$\mathbf{F}_K(Q) = \begin{bmatrix} \mathbf{F}_{K,1} & \mathbf{F}_{K,2} & \cdots & \mathbf{F}_{K,n} \end{bmatrix}^T \qquad (6.7)$$

$$\tau = \begin{bmatrix} \tau_1 & \tau_2 & \cdots & \tau_n \end{bmatrix}^T \qquad (6.8)$$

6.2.2 Modular Kinematic Models

The kinematic model of the ith axle module is presented subject to nonholonomic constraints [146]. The generic kinematic matrices are then assembled similar to the dynamic matrices. Assuming pure rolling without slipping, the nonholonomic constraints of the ith axle module can be expressed in matrix form as

$$\mathbf{A}_i(q_i)\dot{q}_i = 0 \qquad (6.9)$$

where $\mathbf{A}_i(q_i) \in R^{1\times 3}$ is the matrix associated with the ith axle nonholonomic constraints

$$\mathbf{A}_i(q_i) = \begin{bmatrix} -\sin\phi_i & \cos\phi_i & 0 \end{bmatrix} \qquad (6.10)$$

Let $\mathbf{S}_i(q_i) \in R^{3\times 2}$ then be a full rank matrix formed by a set of smooth and linearly independent vector fields spanning the null space of $\mathbf{A}_i(q_i)$ such that

$$\mathbf{A}_i(q_i)\mathbf{S}_i(q_i) = 0 \qquad (6.11)$$

Equations 6.9 and 6.11 imply the existence of a two-dimensional velocity vector $\mathbf{v}_i(t) \in R^{2\times 1}$ such that, for all time, t

$$\dot{q}_i = \mathbf{S}_i(q_i)\mathbf{v}_i(t) \tag{6.12}$$

where

$$\mathbf{S}_i(q_i) = \begin{bmatrix} \cos\phi_i & 0 \\ \sin\phi_i & 0 \\ 0 & 1 \end{bmatrix} \tag{6.13}$$

$$\mathbf{v}_i(t) = \begin{bmatrix} v_i & \omega_i \end{bmatrix}^T \tag{6.14}$$

and v_i and ω_i represent the linear and angular velocities of the ith axle at point C_i.

Likewise, the n-axle matrix associated with the nonholonomic for the serial configuration can be assembled as

$$\mathbf{A}(Q) = \begin{bmatrix} \mathbf{A}_1(q_1) & \mathbf{0} & \cdots & \mathbf{0} \\ \mathbf{0} & \mathbf{A}_2(q_2) & \cdots & \vdots \\ \mathbf{0} & \mathbf{0} & \cdots & \mathbf{0} \\ \mathbf{0} & \cdots & \mathbf{0} & \mathbf{A}_n(q_n) \end{bmatrix} \tag{6.15}$$

There is also the existence of a $2n$-dimensional velocity vector, $\mathbf{v}(t) \in R^{2n\times 1}$, such that, for all time, t

$$\dot{Q} = \mathbf{S}(Q)\mathbf{v}(t) \tag{6.16}$$

where $\mathbf{S}(Q) \in R^{3n\times 2n}$ is a full-rank matrix formed by a set of smooth and linearly independent vector fields spanning the null space of $\mathbf{A}(Q)$ such that

$$\mathbf{A}(Q)\mathbf{S}(Q) = \mathbf{0} \tag{6.17}$$

and $\mathbf{S}(Q)$ and $\mathbf{v}(t)$ can be assembled as

$$\mathbf{S}(Q) = \begin{bmatrix} \mathbf{S}_1(q_1) & \mathbf{0} & \cdots & \mathbf{0} \\ \mathbf{0} & \mathbf{S}_2(q_2) & \cdots & \vdots \\ \mathbf{0} & \mathbf{0} & \cdots & \mathbf{0} \\ \mathbf{0} & \cdots & \mathbf{0} & \mathbf{S}_n(q_n) \end{bmatrix} \tag{6.18}$$

$$\mathbf{v}(t) = \begin{bmatrix} \mathbf{v}_1 & \mathbf{v}_2 & \cdots & \mathbf{v}_n \end{bmatrix}^T \tag{6.19}$$

6.2.3 Compliant Frame Model

As we mentioned in Chapter 2, it is difficult to model the compliant frame forces with great accuracy. However, we can approximate the forces to improve controller performance. The behavior of the compliant frame element is complicated because of the interaction of the axle modules and the nonlinear frame behavior. To simplify matters, an approximate model of the compliant frame module is developed based on the finite element method (FEM) and the post-buckled frame element. The model includes the transverse and bending forces of a compliant beam, which is used to develop the controller in the following subsections.

Given L, E, and I as the free length, Young's Modulus and area moment of inertia of the compliant frame, respectively, the frame model is expressed in the global coordinate frame with the local coordinate definition $w_i = w_j \equiv 0$, Figure 6.3, as

$$\mathbf{F}_K = \mathbf{R}^T \mathbf{K} \delta_L \tag{6.20}$$

Here, $\mathbf{R}$ is a rotation transformation matrix with θ defined as in Figure 6.2 such that

$$\mathbf{R} = \begin{bmatrix} \mathbf{R}_\theta & \mathbf{0} \\ \mathbf{0} & \mathbf{R}_\theta \end{bmatrix} \quad \text{and} \quad \mathbf{R}_\theta = \begin{bmatrix} \cos\theta & \sin\theta & 0 \\ -\sin\theta & \cos\theta & 0 \\ 0 & 0 & 1 \end{bmatrix} \tag{6.21}$$

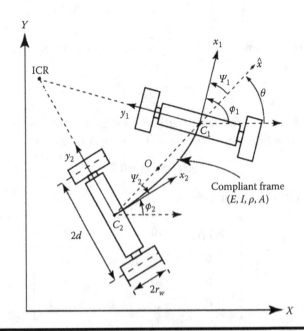

Figure 6.2   General configuration of a two-axle CFMMR.

For convenience, δ_L is measured relative to the ith node and described as a function of the axle configuration vectors to provide

$$\delta_L = \begin{bmatrix} 0 & 0 & \psi_i & -\Delta u & 0 & \psi_j \end{bmatrix} \qquad (6.22)$$

where the axial deflection caused by post-buckling Δu is defined as $L_f - (\hat{q}_j(1) - \hat{q}_i(1))$ and the displacements $\hat{q}_c(1)$, $c = i, j$ can be calculated from the node locations C_i and C_j by using the axle configuration vectors q_i and q_j, expressed in the local coordinate frame as

$$\begin{bmatrix} \hat{q}_c(1) & \hat{q}_c(2) & \psi_c \end{bmatrix} = \mathbf{R}_\theta q_c \quad c = i, j \qquad (6.23)$$

The foreshortened length L_f caused by bending moments is calculated as

$$L_f = L - \Delta L = L - \frac{2\psi_i^2 - \psi_i\psi_j + 2\psi_j^2}{30} L \qquad (6.24)$$

Note that for most cases, the compliant frame of the CFMMR is not straight due to steering maneuvers, and is essentially in a post-buckled shape. So the compliant frame is deflected by axial forces as well as bending moments. Therefore, the relationship between the final frame length $\hat{q}_j(1) - \hat{q}_i(1)$ and the undeformed length L is expressed as $\hat{q}_j(1) - \hat{q}_i(1) = L - \Delta L - \Delta u$, Figure 6.3.

For simplicity, we use a post-buckled axial stiffness that is linear and allows for a simple solution. The axial stiffness in post-buckling is modeled as $EI\pi^2 / 2L^3$, which is much more compliant than the traditional rigid bar model used in frame elements. Therefore, $\mathbf{K}$ is obtained as the modified post-buckling stiffness matrix where

$$\mathbf{K} = \begin{bmatrix} \mathbf{K}_{11} & \mathbf{K}_{12} \\ \mathbf{K}_{21} & \mathbf{K}_{22} \end{bmatrix}$$

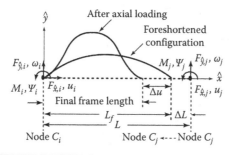

Figure 6.3 The general configuration of single finite element of the compliant frame module.

where,

$$\mathbf{K}_{11} = \frac{EI}{L^3}\begin{bmatrix} \pi^2/2 & 0 & 0 \\ 0 & 12 & 6L \\ 0 & 6L & 4L^2 \end{bmatrix}, \quad \mathbf{K}_{11} = \frac{EI}{L^3}\begin{bmatrix} -\pi^2/2 & 0 & 0 \\ 0 & -12 & 6L \\ 0 & -6L & 4L^2 \end{bmatrix} \quad (6.25)$$

$$\mathbf{K}_{21} = \mathbf{K}_{12}{}^T, \quad \mathbf{K}_{22} = \frac{EI}{L^3}\begin{bmatrix} \pi^2/2 & 0 & 0 \\ 0 & 12 & -6L \\ 0 & -6L & 4L^2 \end{bmatrix}$$

6.3 Single Axle Nonlinear Damping Control Design

Due to the increased complexity of the system equations, the system is separated into two parts: (1) curvature-based kinematic motion control and (2) robust dynamic motion control. Robust dynamic motion control is the main focus in this chapter since the curvature-based kinematic motion-control algorithms discussed in Chapter 4 are able to provide time-varying reference trajectories based on path state, s, and the robot configuration. These algorithms specify velocity trajectories for each axle to provide drift-free curvature-based steering algorithms for a two-axle CFMMR that minimize traction forces and account for frame foreshortening due to steering angles. The control system structure is presented in Figure 6.4, which is explained in the following subsections.

6.3.1 Structural Transformation of Single-Axle Module

Considering the ith axle module, we rewrite the ith corresponding dynamic equation for the control design. Differentiating Equation 6.12 with respect to time,

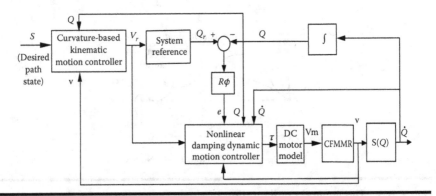

Figure 6.4   A motion and dynamic control structure of the CFMMR.

substituting this result into Equation 6.4, and then multiplying by $\mathbf{S}^{\mathbf{T}}{}_i(q_i)$, the constraint matrix $\mathbf{A}_i{}^T(q_i)\lambda_i$ can be eliminated. The ith-axle dynamic equation of the CFMMR is then given by

$$\mathbf{S}_i{}^T\mathbf{M}_i\mathbf{S}\dot{\mathbf{v}}_i + \mathbf{S}_i{}^T\mathbf{M}_i\dot{\mathbf{S}}\mathbf{v}_i + \mathbf{S}_i{}^T\mathbf{F}_i + \mathbf{S}_i{}^T\tau_{d,i} + \mathbf{S}_i{}^T\mathbf{F}_{K,i}(q_i,q_j) = \mathbf{S}_i{}^T\mathbf{E}_i\tau_i \quad (6.26)$$

where Lagrange multipliers are no longer required and applied wheel torque is now an input to the system as a function of system states. Here we assume $\mathbf{F}_i = B_i\dot{q}_i$, where B_i consists of constant friction coefficients. The nonlinear part of the friction forces is included in $\tau_{d,i}$. Then rewrite Equation 6.26 into the simplified form

$$\bar{\mathbf{M}}_i\dot{\mathbf{v}}_i + \bar{B}_i\mathbf{v}_i + \bar{\tau}_{d,i} = \bar{\tau}_i \quad (6.27)$$

where $\bar{\mathbf{M}}_i = \mathbf{S}_i{}^T\mathbf{M}_i\mathbf{S}_i, \bar{B}_i = \mathbf{S}_i{}^T(\mathbf{M}_i\dot{\mathbf{S}}_i + B_i\mathbf{S}_i), \bar{\tau}_{d,i} = \mathbf{S}_i{}^T(\tau_{d,i} + \mathbf{F}_{K,i}(q_i,q_j)), \bar{\tau}_i = \mathbf{S}_i^T\mathbf{E}_i\tau_i$

The next step is to specify the dynamic extension of the velocity input $\mathbf{v}_i \in R^{2\times1}$ such that the regular backstepping form can be obtained:

$$\dot{q}_i = \mathbf{S}(q_i)\mathbf{v}_i \quad (6.28)$$

$$\bar{\mathbf{M}}_i\dot{\mathbf{v}}_i + \bar{B}_i\mathbf{v}_i + \bar{\tau}_{d,i} = \bar{\tau}_i \quad (6.29)$$

These equations allow the two steering commands $\mathbf{v}_i(t)$ to be converted to desired wheel torques $\tau_i(t) \in R^{2\times1}$. The control objective is to derive a suitable $\tau_i(t)$ such that the CFMMR will track a specific smooth steering velocity $\mathbf{v}_{c,i}$ where

$$\mathbf{v}_{c,i}(t) = \begin{bmatrix} v_{c,i} & \omega_{c,i} \end{bmatrix}^T \quad (6.30)$$

This steering velocity as control input for the steering system (Equation 6.28) is chosen to achieve stable tracking of the reference trajectories, $q_{r,i}$. Then the CFMMR can make the trajectory tracking given the derived wheel torques $\tau_i(t)$.

Since the reference velocity $\mathbf{v}_{r,i}$ is given by the previously mentioned motion controller, the reference trajectories $q_{r,i}$ can be solved from

$$\dot{q}_{r,i} = S(q_{r,i})\mathbf{v}_{r,i} \quad (6.31)$$

Then the error-state model for tracking is defined as

$$e_i = \mathbf{R}_{\phi,i}(q_{r,i} - q_i) \quad (6.32)$$

where $q_{r,i}$ is the reference vector for the ith axle; $e_i \in R^{3\times1}$ is the error position vector for the ith axle; and

$$e_i = \begin{bmatrix} e_{X,i} & e_{Y,i} & e_{\phi,i} \end{bmatrix}^T \quad (6.33)$$

As [153] shows, an alternative $\mathbf{v}_{c,i}$ is chosen as

$$
\mathbf{v}_{c,i} = \begin{bmatrix} v_{r,i} \cos e_{\phi,i} + k_{X,i} e_{X,i} \\ \omega_{r,i} + k_{Y,i} v_{r,i} e_{Y,i} + k_{\phi,i} v_{r,i} \sin e_{\phi,i} \end{bmatrix}
\tag{6.34}
$$

where $k_{X,i}, k_{Y,i}, k_{\phi,i}$ are positive constants and $v_{r,i}$ are positive for the ith axle. The velocity control law $\mathbf{v}_{c,i}$ is thus proven [153] to make $e_i = 0$ a stable equilibrium point using the Lyapunov function

$$
V_{1,i}(e_i) = \frac{1}{2} e_{X,i}^2 + \frac{1}{2} e_{Y,i}^2 + (1 - \cos e_{\phi,i}) / k_{Y,i}
\tag{6.35}
$$

and $V_{1,i}(e_i)$ is used in subsequent controller development.

6.3.2 Properties and Assumptions of Single-Axle Controller

There are several properties and assumptions that are used in the following control design:

Assumption 1: $\tau_{d,i}$ and $\mathbf{F}_{K,i}(q_i, q_j)$ are bounded.
Property 1: $\left\| \bar{B}_i(q_i, \dot{q}_i) \right\| \leq b_i \left\| \dot{q}_i \right\| + c_i$, where b_i, c_i are nonnegative constants.
Property 2: $\mathbf{M}_i$ is a constant matrix.
Property 3: $\dot{\mathbf{v}}_{c,i} = A_{1,i} \mathbf{v}_{c,i} + A_{2,i} \mathbf{v}_{r,i} + A_{3,i} \dot{\mathbf{v}}_{r,i}$, where $\left\| A_{1,i} \right\|$, $\left\| A_{2,i} \right\|$, and $\left\| A_{3,i} \right\|$ are bounded.

Proof: Properties 1 and 2 can be proven by simple calculation assuming the same mass of each module. Thus, we focus on the proof of Property 3.

Differentiating Equation 6.34 yields

$$
\dot{\mathbf{v}}_{c,i} = \begin{bmatrix} k_{X,i} \dot{e}_{X,i} - v_{r,i}(\sin e_{\phi,i})\dot{e}_{\phi,i} + \dot{v}_{r,i} \cos e_{\phi,i} \\ \dot{\omega}_{r,i} + k_{Y,i} e_{Y,i} \dot{v}_{r,i} + k_{Y,i} v_{r,i} \dot{e}_{Y,i} + k_{\phi,i} v_{r,i}(\cos e_{\phi,i})\dot{e}_{\phi,i} + k_{\phi,i} \dot{v}_{r,i} \sin e_{\phi,i} \end{bmatrix}
$$

$$
= \begin{bmatrix} k_{X,i} & 0 & -v_{r,i}(\sin e_{\phi,i}) \\ 0 & k_{Y,i} v_{r,i} & k_{\phi,i} v_{r,i}(\cos e_{\phi,i}) \end{bmatrix} \begin{bmatrix} \dot{e}_{X,i} \\ \dot{e}_{Y,i} \\ \dot{e}_{\phi,i} \end{bmatrix}
$$

$$
+ \begin{bmatrix} \cos e_{\phi,i} & 0 \\ k_{Y,i} e_{Y,i} + k_{\phi,i} \sin e_{\phi,i} & 1 \end{bmatrix} \begin{bmatrix} \dot{v}_{r,i} \\ \dot{\omega}_{r,i} \end{bmatrix}
\tag{6.36}
$$

Substituting Equations 6.32 and 6.33 into Equation 6.36 and applying Equation 6.34, we can obtain

$$
\dot{\mathbf{v}}_{c,i} = \begin{bmatrix} k_{X,i} & 0 & -v_{r,i}(\sin e_{\phi,i}) \\ 0 & k_{Y,i}v_{r,i} & k_{\phi,i}v_{r,i}(\cos e_{\phi,i}) \end{bmatrix} \begin{bmatrix} \omega_i e_{Y,i} - v_i + v_{r,i}\cos e_{\phi,i} \\ -\omega_i e_{X,i} + v_{r,i}\sin e_{\phi,i} \\ \omega_{r,i} - \omega_i \end{bmatrix}
$$

$$
+ \begin{bmatrix} \cos e_{\phi,i} & 0 \\ k_{Y,i}e_{Y,i} + k_{\phi,i}\sin e_{\phi,i} & 1 \end{bmatrix} \dot{\mathbf{v}}_{r,i}
$$

$$
= \begin{bmatrix} -k_{X,i} & k_{X,i}e_{Y,i} + v_{r,i}\sin e_{\phi,i} \\ 0 & -k_{Y,i}v_{r,i}e_{X,i} - k_{\phi,i}v_{r,i}\cos e_{\phi,i} \end{bmatrix} \mathbf{v}_{c,i}
$$

$$
+ \begin{bmatrix} k_{X,i}\cos e_{\phi,i} & -v_{r,i}\sin e_{\phi,i} \\ k_{Y,i}v_{r,i}\sin e_{\phi,i} & k_{\phi,i}v_{r,i}\cos e_{\phi,i} \end{bmatrix} \mathbf{v}_{r,i} + \begin{bmatrix} \cos e_{\phi,i} & 0 \\ k_{Y,i}e_{Y,i} + k_{\phi,i}\sin e_{\phi,i} & 1 \end{bmatrix} \dot{\mathbf{v}}_{r,i}
$$

$$
\tag{6.37}
$$

Finally $\dot{\mathbf{v}}_{c,i}$ is simplified as

$$
\dot{\mathbf{v}}_{c,i} = A_{1,i}\mathbf{v}_{c,i} + A_{2,i}\mathbf{v}_{r,i} + A_{3,i}\dot{\mathbf{v}}_{r,i} \tag{6.38}
$$

where $A_{1,i}$, $A_{2,i}$, and $A_{3,i}$ are individually the coefficient matrix of $\mathbf{v}_{c,i}$, $\mathbf{v}_{r,i}$, and $\dot{\mathbf{v}}_{r,i}$.

Since $\|A_{1,i}\|$, $\|A_{2,i}\|$, and $\|A_{3,i}\|$ are checked to be bounded by inspection, Property 4 is proven.

Δ

6.3.3 Nonlinear Damping Control Design of Single-Axle Module

We now extend the nonlinear damping control scheme specified in [147] to a single-axle CFMMR configuration with time-varying reference velocities.

Define the velocity-error vector for each axle as

$$
\mathbf{e}_{c,i} = \begin{bmatrix} e_{v,i} \\ e_{\omega,i} \end{bmatrix} = \mathbf{v}_i - \mathbf{v}_{c,i}
$$

$$
= \begin{bmatrix} v_i - v_{r,i}\cos e_{\phi,i} - k_{X,i}e_{X,i} \\ \omega_i - \omega_{r,i} - k_{Y,i}v_{r,i}e_{Y,i} - k_{\phi,i}v_{r,i}\sin e_{\phi,i} \end{bmatrix}
$$

$$
\tag{6.39}
$$

Differentiating Equation 6.39 and substituting Equation 6.29 yields

$$
\overline{\mathbf{M}}_i \dot{\mathbf{e}}_{c,i} = \overline{\tau}_i - \overline{B}_i \mathbf{v}_i - \overline{\tau}_{d,i} - \overline{\mathbf{M}}_i \dot{\mathbf{v}}_{c,i} \tag{6.40}
$$

Then, choose the Lyapunov candidate for the dynamic model Equation 6.29 as

$$V_{2,i}(\mathbf{e}_{c,i}) = \frac{1}{2}\mathbf{e}^T_{c,i}\bar{\mathbf{M}}_i\mathbf{e}_{c,i} \tag{6.41}$$

Differentiating Equation 6.41 yields

$$\dot{V}_{2,i}(\mathbf{e}_{c,i}) = \mathbf{e}^T_{c,i}\bar{\mathbf{M}}_i\dot{\mathbf{e}}_{c,i} + \frac{1}{2}\mathbf{e}^T_{c,i}\dot{\bar{\mathbf{M}}}_i\mathbf{e}_{c,i} \tag{6.42}$$

By substituting Equation 6.40 into Equation 6.42, we obtain

$$\dot{V}_{2,i}(\mathbf{e}_{c,i}) = \mathbf{e}^T_{c,i}[\bar{\tau}_i - (\bar{B}_i\mathbf{v}_i + \bar{\mathbf{M}}_i\dot{\mathbf{v}}_{c,i} + \bar{\tau}_{d,i})] + \frac{1}{2}\mathbf{e}^T_{c,i}\dot{\bar{\mathbf{M}}}_i\mathbf{e}_{c,i} \tag{6.43}$$

Applying Property 2 yields

$$\dot{V}_{2,i}(\mathbf{e}_{c,i}) = \mathbf{e}^T_{c,i}[\bar{\tau}_i - (\bar{B}_i\mathbf{v}_i + \bar{\mathbf{M}}_i\dot{\mathbf{v}}_{c,i} + \bar{\tau}_{d,i})] \tag{6.44}$$

Then, applying Property 3 yields

$$\dot{V}_{2,i}(\mathbf{e}_{c,i}) = \mathbf{e}^T_{c,i}[\bar{\tau}_i - (\bar{B}_i\mathbf{v}_i + \bar{\mathbf{M}}_i A_{1,i}\mathbf{v}_{c,i} + \bar{\mathbf{M}}_i A_{2,i}\mathbf{v}_{r,i} + \bar{\mathbf{M}}_i A_{3,i}\dot{\mathbf{v}}_{r,i} + \bar{\tau}_{d,i})] \tag{6.45}$$

According to Properties 1 and 3 and Assumption 1, we obtain

$$\dot{V}_{2,i}(\mathbf{e}_{c,i}) \leq \mathbf{e}^T_{c,i}\bar{\tau}_i + \|\mathbf{e}_{c,i}\|\Big\{\Big\|\bar{B}_i\Big\|\|\mathbf{v}_i\| + \Big\|\bar{\mathbf{M}}_i\Big\|\|A_{1,i}\|\|\mathbf{v}_{c,i}\| + \Big\|\bar{\mathbf{M}}_i\Big\|\|A_{2,i}\|\|\mathbf{v}_{r,i}\|$$

$$+ \Big\|\bar{\mathbf{M}}_i\Big\|\|A_{3,i}\|\|\dot{\mathbf{v}}_{r,i}\| + \|\bar{\tau}_{d,i}\|\Big\}$$

$$\leq \mathbf{e}^T_{c,i}\bar{\tau}_i + \|\mathbf{e}_{c,i}\|\Big\{b_i\|\mathbf{v}_i\|\|\mathbf{v}_i\| + c_i\|\mathbf{v}_i\| + \Big\|\bar{\mathbf{M}}_i\Big\|\|A_{1,i}\|\|\mathbf{v}_{c,i}\|$$

$$+ \Big\|\bar{\mathbf{M}}_i\Big\|\|A_{2,i}\|\|\mathbf{v}_{r,i}\| + \Big\|\bar{\mathbf{M}}_i\Big\|\|A_{3,i}\|\|\dot{\mathbf{v}}_{r,i}\| + \|\tau_{d,i}\| + \|\mathbf{F}_K(q_i,q_j)\|\Big\}$$

$$= \mathbf{e}^T_{c,i}\bar{\tau}_i + \|\mathbf{e}_{c,i}\|\delta_i^T\xi_i \tag{6.46}$$

where

$$\delta_i^T = \Big\{b_i, c_i, \Big\|\bar{\mathbf{M}}_i\Big\|\|A_{1,i}\|, \Big\|\bar{\mathbf{M}}_i\Big\|\|A_{2,i}\|, \Big\|\bar{\mathbf{M}}_i\Big\|\|A_{3,i}\|, \|\tau_{d,i}\|, 1\Big\}$$

$$\xi_i^T = \Big\{\|\mathbf{v}_i\|\|\mathbf{v}_i\|, \|\mathbf{v}_i\|, \|\mathbf{v}_{c,i}\|, \|\mathbf{v}_{r,i}\|, \|\dot{\mathbf{v}}_{r,i}\|, 1, \|\mathbf{F}_{K,i}(q_i,q_j)\|\Big\} \tag{6.47}$$

Here, δ_i is bounded by the above properties and assumptions, and ξ_i is a known, positive definite vector. Hence, in order to make Equation 6.46 negative definite, choose

$$\bar{\tau}_i = -K_i \mathbf{e}_{c,i} \|\xi_i\|^2 \tag{6.48}$$

where $K_i = \begin{bmatrix} K_{1,i} & 0 \\ 0 & K_{2,i} \end{bmatrix}$ is the matrix control gain and $K_{1,i}$, $K_{2,i}$ are positive constants. The control input is then

$$\begin{aligned} \tau_i &= (\mathbf{S}_i^T \mathbf{E}_i)^{-1} \bar{\tau}_i \\ &= -(\mathbf{S}_i^T \mathbf{E}_i)^{-1} K_i \mathbf{e}_{c,i} \|\xi_i\|^2 \end{aligned} \tag{6.49}$$

Substitute Equation 6.48 into Equation 6.46

$$\begin{aligned} \dot{V}_{2,i}(\mathbf{e}_{c,i}) &= -\mathbf{e}^T{}_{c,i} K_i \mathbf{e}_{c,i} \|\xi_i\|^2 + \|\mathbf{e}_{c,i}\| \delta_i^T \xi_i \\ &\leq -\|K_i\| \|\mathbf{e}_{c,i}\|^2 \|\xi_i\|^2 + \|\mathbf{e}_{c,i}\| \|\delta_i\| \|\xi_i\| \\ &= -\|K_i\| \left\{ \|\mathbf{e}_{c,i}\| \|\xi_i\| - \frac{\|\delta_i\|}{2\|K_i\|} \right\}^2 + \frac{\|\delta_i\|^2}{4\|K_i\|} \end{aligned} \tag{6.50}$$

By using the Lyapunov function $V_i = V_{1,i} + V_{2,i}$ [106,147] $\mathbb{C}_i = \begin{bmatrix} \mathbf{e}_i & \mathbf{e}_{c,i} \end{bmatrix}^T$ is globally uniformly bounded, and the velocity-tracking error becomes arbitrarily small by increasing the control gain K_i.

Note that the reference-velocity vector is included in the control input since the motion controller could provide time-varying reference velocities. The compliant frame force $\mathbf{F}_{K,i}(q_i, q_j)$ is also taken into consideration in the controller, which is the topic of the next subsection.

6.3.4 Compliant Frame Effect on Control Design

There are two cases to consider for the CFMMR in terms of the compliant frame effect on control design. On one hand, the approximate model of the compliant frame force, $\mathbf{F}_{K,i}(q_i, q_j)$, may be used, and the inaccurate part of this model will become part of the disturbance $\tau_{d,i}$, and δ_i and ξ_i are chosen per Equation 6.47. On the other hand, $\mathbf{F}_{K,i}(q_i, q_j)$ may be considered to be totally unknown, and δ_i and ξ_i will be redefined as

$$\begin{aligned} \delta_i^T &= \left\{ b_i, c_i, \|\bar{\mathbf{M}}_i\| \|A_{1,i}\|, \|\bar{\mathbf{M}}_i\| \|A_{2,i}\|, \|\bar{\mathbf{M}}_i\| \|A_{3,i}\|, \|\tau_{d,i} + \mathbf{F}_{K,i}(q_i, q_j)\| \right\} \\ \xi_i^T &= \left\{ \|\mathbf{v}_i\| \|\mathbf{v}_i\|, \|\mathbf{v}_i\|, \|\mathbf{v}_{c,i}\|, \|\mathbf{v}_{r,i}\|, \|\dot{\mathbf{v}}_{r,i}\|, 1 \right\} \end{aligned} \tag{6.51}$$

which helps to decrease computational requirements since $\mathbf{F}_{K,i}(q_i, q_j)$ is not calculated between time steps.

We apply both control inputs determined by Equations 6.47 and 6.51 to the experimental platform and compare them in Section 6.5 in order to determine the characteristics of performance, tracking errors, and computations.

6.4 Multi-Axle Distributed Control Design

The distributed controller is designed for a multi-axle CFMMR based on the above single-axle controller. That is to say, the distributed controller is composed of n independent controllers τ_j, $j = 1 \sim n$ as:

$$\tau_j = -(\mathbf{S}_j^T \mathbf{E}_j)^{-1} K_j \mathbf{e}_{c,j} \left\| \boldsymbol{\xi}_j \right\|^2 \tag{6.52}$$

Proposition: The multi-axle CFMMR can achieve stable trajectory tracking with the distributed controller (Equation 6.52) if the response of each module is globally uniformly bounded by its corresponding single-axle controller.

Proof: Choose the composite Lyapunov function candidate

$$\begin{aligned} V &= V_1 + \cdots + V_i + \cdots + V_n \\ &= V_{1,1} + V_{2,1} + \cdots + V_{1,i} + V_{2,i} + \cdots + V_{1,n} + V_{2,n} \end{aligned} \tag{6.53}$$

Substituting Equations 6.35 and 6.41 into Equation 6.53 produces

$$\begin{aligned} V &= \frac{1}{2} e_{X,1}^2 + \frac{1}{2} e_{Y,1}^2 + (1 - \cos e_{\phi,1}) / k_{Y,1} + \frac{1}{2} \mathbf{e}_{c,1}^T \bar{\mathbf{M}}_1 \mathbf{e}_{c,1} + \cdots \\ &\quad + \frac{1}{2} e_{X,i}^2 + \frac{1}{2} e_{Y,i}^2 + (1 - \cos e_{\phi,i}) / k_{Y,i} + \frac{1}{2} \mathbf{e}_{c,i}^T \bar{\mathbf{M}}_i \mathbf{e}_{c,i} + \cdots \\ &\quad + \frac{1}{2} e_{X,n}^2 + \frac{1}{2} e_{Y,n}^2 + (1 - \cos e_{\phi,n}) / k_{Y,n} + \frac{1}{2} \mathbf{e}_{c,n}^T \bar{\mathbf{M}}_n \mathbf{e}_{c,n} \end{aligned} \tag{6.54}$$

Differentiating Equation 6.54 and applying Equations 6.32 and 6.50 yields

$$\begin{aligned} \dot{V} &\leq -k_{X,1} e_{X,1}^2 - \frac{k_{\phi,1}}{k_{Y,1}} v_{r,1} \sin^2 e_{\phi,1} - \|K_1\| \left\{ \|\mathbf{e}_{c,1}\| \|\boldsymbol{\xi}_1\| - \frac{\|\delta_1\|}{2\|K_1\|} \right\}^2 + \frac{\|\delta_1\|^2}{4\|K_1\|} - \cdots \\ &\quad -k_{X,i} e_{X,i}^2 - \frac{k_{\phi,i}}{k_{Y,i}} v_{r,i} \sin^2 e_{\phi,i} - \|K_i\| \left\{ \|\mathbf{e}_{c,i}\| \|\boldsymbol{\xi}_i\| - \frac{\|\delta_i\|}{2\|K_i\|} \right\}^2 + \frac{\|\delta_i\|^2}{4\|K_i\|} - \cdots \\ &\quad -k_{X,n} e_{X,n}^2 - \frac{k_{\phi,n}}{k_{Y,n}} v_{r,n} \sin^2 e_{\phi,n} - \|K_n\| \left\{ \|\mathbf{e}_{c,n}\| \|\boldsymbol{\xi}_n\| - \frac{\|\delta_n\|}{2\|K_n\|} \right\}^2 + \frac{\|\delta_n\|^2}{4\|K_n\|} \end{aligned} \tag{6.55}$$

where $K_1,\ldots,K_n$ are positive definite matrices, $k_{X,1},\ldots,k_{X,n},k_{Y,1},\ldots,k_{Y,n},k_{\phi,1},\ldots,k_{\phi,n}$ are positive constants, and $\|\delta_1\|,\ldots,\|\delta_n\|$ are bounded. Therefore

$$\dot{V} \le -k_{X,1}e_{X,1}^2 - \frac{k_{\phi,1}}{k_{Y,1}}v_{r,1}\sin^2 e_{\phi,1} - \cdots - k_{X,i}e_{X,i}^2 - \frac{k_{\phi,i}}{k_{Y,i}}v_{r,i}\sin^2 e_{\phi,i}$$

$$-\cdots - k_{X,n}e_{X,n}^2 - \frac{k_{\phi,n}}{k_{Y,n}}v_{r,n}\sin^2 e_{\phi,n}$$

$$= -W(\mathbf{e}) \tag{6.56}$$

when

$$\|\mathbf{e}_{c,1}\| \ge \frac{1}{\|K_1\|}\frac{\|\delta_1\|}{\|\xi_1\|},\ldots,\|\mathbf{e}_{c,n}\| \ge \frac{1}{\|K_n\|}\frac{\|\delta_n\|}{\|\xi_n\|} \tag{6.57}$$

where $\mathbf{e} = [C_1 \quad \cdots \quad C_n]^T$, $C_j = [\mathbf{e}_j \quad \mathbf{e}_{c,j}]^T$, $j = 1 \sim n$, and $W(\mathbf{e})$ is a continuous positive definite function.

Hence, we conclude $\mathbf{e}$ is globally uniformly bounded [106]. According to Equation 6.57, the tracking-error bounds of each module become smaller as the norm of the corresponding control gain matrix, K_i, is increased. However, tracking-error bounds for the multi-axle CFMMR become more complicated. The modules are interconnected by compliant frames, so the behavior of each module can affect the others. Increasing the control gain for one axle may increase the tracking error of another. Second, the tracking-error bounds are increased as the term δ_i increases, which may be caused by increased disturbances or model uncertainty. Therefore, it is proper to minimize the tracking errors for the entire system by experimentally tuning the set of control gains, $K_1,\ldots,K_n$.

$$\Delta$$

6.5 Controller Evaluation

6.5.1 Methods and Procedures

The distributed nonlinear damping controller for the two-axle CFMMR was simulated in MATLAB and Simulink. The reference velocities $\mathbf{v}_r$ of both axles are generated by a drift-free curvature-based kinematic motion-control algorithm guiding midpoint, O, of the robot to follow the desired path [48]. The velocity trajectories are specified for each axle such that the distance between points C_1 and C_2 remains consistent with the ideal foreshortened length L_f of the frame given the current axle headings. As we mentioned in Section 6.4, the control gains need to be tuned to minimize the tracking-error bounds. The gains were first tuned in simulation until the tracking errors were within 10^{-3} with a similar time step size, 10^{-3}. These gains were then verified in experiment.

Several experiments were conducted on a two-module CFMMR experimental platform at the University of Utah. The robot is controlled via tether by a dSpace 1103 DSP board and an external power supply. Each wheel is actuated by a geared DC motor with voltage input V_m, Figure 6.4. The real-time position of each wheel is detected by an encoder, and odometry is used for predicting axle posture. Video is used to illustrate robot performance. Here we apply controllers with and without beam-force compensation to consider their effect on performance.

The prototype parameters, Table 6.1, and the parameters of the compliant frame, Table 6.3, are used for both simulations and experiments. Three different path shapes, a straight line, a circle, and a sine wave, were used with nonzero initial positions of midpoint O, Table 6.2. The straight line is the simplest path, where the reference is only a constant linear velocity. The circle is more complicated since the reference is ultimately constant linear and angular velocities. The sine wave is the most

Table 6.1 Prototype of a Two-Module CFMMR

Parameter	Value	Units	Description
r_w	0.073	m	Wheel radius
d	0.162	m	Axle width (half)
m_i	4.76	kg	Mass of each axle
J_i	0.0186	kg/m²	Mass moment of inertia of each axle

Table 6.2 Initial Positions of Three Different Shapes

Path	x	y	ϕ
Line	−0.1	0.1	0
Circle	1.05	−0.2	$\pi/2$
Sine wave	−0.09	−q0.04	$\pi/4$

Table 6.3 Parameters of Compliant Frame

Parameter	Value	Units	Descriptions
L	0.37	m	Length
w	0.05	m	Width
t	0.7	mm	Thickness
E	2.0×10^{11}	Pa	Young's modulus
A	3.5×10^{-5}	m²	Cross-sectional area
ρ	7.8×10^3	kg/m³	Density
I	1.4292×10^{-12}	m⁴	Area moment of inertia

complicated, since the path consists of time-varying linear and angular velocities. Therefore, the tracking performance of the robot can be evaluated comprehensively.

6.5.2 Results

Using the tuned gains $K_1 = K_2 = \begin{bmatrix} 30 & 0 \\ 0 & 5 \end{bmatrix}$, the simulation results predict that the robot follows the corresponding desired paths perfectly. Experimental odometry results corroborate the simulated results well except for some chattering and apparent wheel slippage.

Figure 6.5 shows the experimental posture data (according to odometry) of path following both with and without beam-force compensation. The desired position is

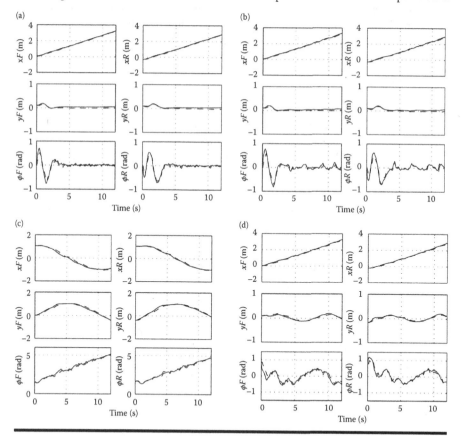

Figure 6.5 Experimental posture data for path following, where solid lines represent the desired position and dashed lines represent the experimentally determined position. (a) Line path with beam-force compensation, (b) line path without beam-force compensation, (c) circular path with beam-force compensation, and (d) sinusoidal path with beam-force compensation.

represented by the solid lines, and the experimentally determined position is represented by the dashed lines. Figure 6.6 shows the position errors of each axle and the reference velocity $\dot{s}$ of the midpoint O, where the position error of the rear axle is represented by the solid line and the position error of the front axle is represented by the dashed line. Figure 6.7 shows the experimental path following results without beam-force compensation, where the desired trajectory of the midpoint O of the robot is represented by the solid line, the experimental trajectory of the midpoint O is represented by the dashed line, and the trajectory of the wheels is represented by dotted lines. Figure 6.8 shows the snapshots of the video for line path following. The dotted lines are from simulation results, which represent the path of the midpoint O and each wheel, respectively. The white line illustrates the actual path that the robot converges to, which is parallel to the desired path (along the x-axis), but offset by -0.06 m. Note that according to odometry, however, the robot converges to the specified paths quite well, Figure 6.5. All of these results were conducted with the robot on a smooth, flat, high-traction carpet surface.

6.5.3 Discussion

As Figure 6.5 indicates, the system performed well while following the paths; even with nonzero initial error states and uncertain disturbance due to model inaccuracy. Note that compared with the pure model-based back-stepping controller presented in [44], the nonlinear damping controller derived here compensates

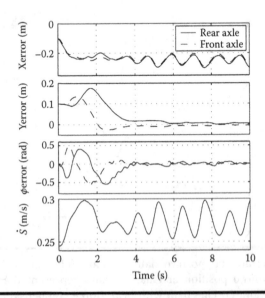

Figure 6.6 Experimental-position errors of each axle and reference velocity of middle point O while line path following according to odometric data.

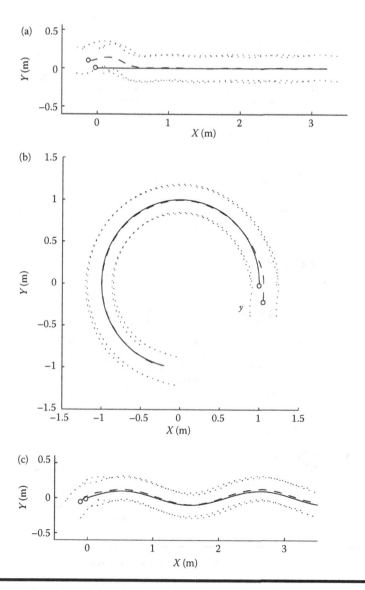

Figure 6.7 **Experimental path following results without beam-force compensation according to odometric data. (a) Line path following, (b) circular path following, and (c) sinuisoidal path following.**

model uncertainty and does not need to adjust the control gains during the experiments. Thus, once the control gains are tuned properly in simulation, they can be used in experiment directly without off-tracking, as witnessed in previous results. This critical characteristic demonstrates the robustness of the controller applied to groups of axle modules bound by uncertain interaction forces.

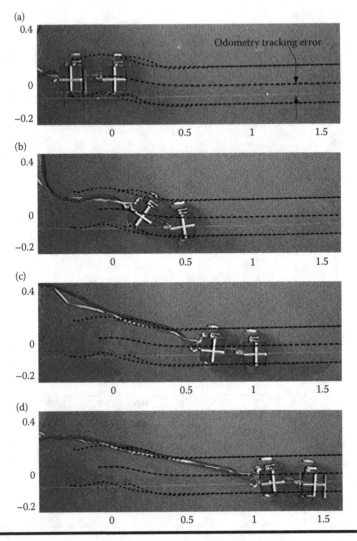

Figure 6.8 Snapshots of line path following without beam compensation; (a) $t=0$ s, (b) $t=1.2$ s, (c) $t=2$ s, and (d) $t=2.5$ s.

As Figure 6.5a and b indicate, while line path following the controller with beam-force compensation can achieve tighter performance and less tracking error, more computation is required to predict those forces. The controller without beam-force compensation is less aggressive at the cost of increasing the tracking error slightly. Both of them work well with the two-axle CFMMR. However, as the configuration and the environment become more and more complicated, the compliant frame forces will play more important roles in the robot performance. The controller with beam-force compensation will be preferable even though more computation will be required. Therefore, the controller with beam-force compensation should be used for the two-axle CFMMR on the rough terrain, such as on sand or with scattered rocks. Additional relative-position sensors should then be introduced to help measure the relative position between the adjacent modules and predict the compliant frame forces more accurately.

As Figure 6.6 indicates, the actual X position lags the reference position and oscillates. The Y position errors converge to a small value close to zero. The ϕ errors converge well except for a small chattering. Note that the reference velocity $\dot{s}$ of the middle point O has oscillations that cause the oscillation of X position errors. These oscillations also cause, in part, the saturation of the wheel torques, Figure 6.9, which are discussed later. In the design of a curvature-based kinematic motion controller, a positive constant ε was introduced to make this controller smooth. This introduction of ε causes the lagged X position, however. Readers could make some improvements to the kinematic motion control to solve the lag problem.

The 0.06 m-odometry-error is observed in Figure 6.8, which is mainly caused by wheel slippage. The apparent wheel slippage happened in the first second because of the fast maneuvering turn of the robot. The torque saturation was also observed in the experiments, see Figure 6.9d. First, the saturation is caused by phase lag in the odometry measurement system. In the odometry system, second-order filters are

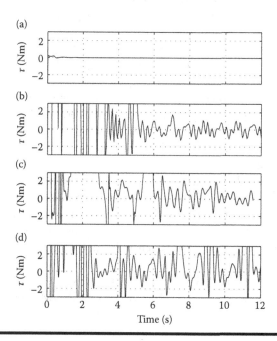

Figure 6.9 **Experimental and simulation results illustrating torque saturation of the front-left wheel while line path following; (a) In simulation, (b) no ground contact, (c) on sand, and (d) on carpet.**

Table 6.4 Analysis Data of Average Torque Saturation

Condition	In Simulation	No Ground Contact	On Sand	On Carpet
Saturation percentage	0	19	28	32

used to decrease measurement noise. The filter also increases phase lag and makes the system closer to marginal stability. In this case, the filter was chosen to reduce the noise, but introduced the corresponding oscillations and aggravated saturation. Additional sensor fusion algorithms should be used to reduce the odometry problems in this situation.

As Figure 6.9 indicates, unmodeled uncertainties of the robot also contribute to torque saturation. In order to evaluate this problem, a series of line path following experiments were performed on surfaces with increasing traction characteristics, such as with no ground contact, on sand, and on carpet. In the case of no ground contact, the robot was put on the box so that all the wheels are free to rotate without any surface interaction. It was used to narrow down the possible causes of torque saturation. Figure 6.9a shows the simulation results of the wheel torques. Figure 6.9b–d shows the experimental results in the three mentioned conditions. The average percent saturation for all the wheels in each case is investigated as well, Table 6.4. As Figure 6.9 and Table 6.4 show, b–d have saturation that does not appear in simulation, which predicts that the unmodeled plant characteristics (such as backlash, unmodeled frame forces, or friction) cause the saturation. Comparing (c) and (d) with (b), note that (b) has the fewest uncertainties caused by the flexible frame and friction, and therefore has the least saturation. Comparing (b) and (c) with (d), note that (d) has the highest traction on carpet, and therefore has the most saturation. Hence, the torque saturation increases as the number of uncertainties of the robot increases. Hence, it is concluded that torque saturation is caused, in part, by model uncertainty.

This chapter introduces a distributed nonlinear damping controller for dynamic motion control of wheeled compliant framed modular mobile robots to compensate for model uncertainty with unknown bounds. Simulation and experimental results for a two-axle CFMMR configuration demonstrate the robustness of the proposed controller. This control algorithm is generally applicable to other mobile robots, which have unknown or partially known uncertainties. The readers could focus on improving the kinematic motion control, additional sensor algorithms incorporating relative position sensors, and the behavior of the CFMMR on the rough terrain to improve the system performance.

Chapter 7

Overall Evaluation

7.1 Introduction

In the previous chapters (from Chapters 2 to 6), we discussed the methodologies of mechanism design, overall control architecture, kinematic and dynamic motion control and the sensory system in the example of CFMMR. The kinematic motion control, dynamic motion control, and sensory system were evaluated independently. For instance, in the evaluation part of the kinematic motion controller in Chapter 4, the experiments mainly focused on performance of the kinematic motion-control algorithm that could produce references for the dynamic controller while robot dynamics and disturbances were not considered as Chapter 6 presented. Traditional servo-type wheel controllers based on filtered wheel encoder odometry were used to drive the robot without using the sensory system designed in Chapter 5. Therefore, the overall architecture as well as the algorithms and controllers discussed in the previous chapters for each component are implemented and evaluated integrally in this chapter.

7.2 Experiment Evaluation

7.2.1 Methods and Procedures

The distributed, cooperative motion-control system, including the algorithms from Chapters 4 to 6 for the two-axle CFMMR, was simulated in MATLAB and Simulink to adjust control gains prior to the experiments. Experiments were conducted on the same two-module CFMMR experimental platform, Figure 1.12, at the University of Utah. The robot is controlled via tether by a dSpace DSP, and power is supplied externally. Geared DC motors actuate each wheel and encoders provide the original position and velocity. Odometry and the relative-position sensor are used in the sensing system. Two 7.2v RC car batteries are mounted on the rear axle to power the RPS amplifying circuit. The sampling frequency of the experiments was 100 Hz in order to arrive at a compromise between the computational limits of the DSP, velocity sensor noise attributed to higher sampling rates, and robust controller chatter at lower sampling rates.

The purpose of the control system is to perform posture regulation. The evaluations were conducted on surfaces with increasing difficulty and realism: flat carpet (C), sand (S), and sand with scattered rocks (SR). Carpet provides high traction and emphasizes the capability of the kinematic and dynamic motion controllers under ideal circumstances. Sand provides lower traction and emphasizes the importance of the sensory system. Sand-and-rock introduces difficulty and demonstrates robustness of the whole system to disturbances.

Nonideal algorithms were also evaluated to justify the control system presented in this book. These include a nonideal kinematic motion controller, a traditional backstepping dynamic motion controller, and a traditional odometry-based sensor system. Comparison experiments were operated on sand or carpet depending on whether controller or sensory-system performance was being evaluated. The nonideal kinematic motion controller (FB) in Ref. [64] had the actual velocity fed into the kinematic controller, which does not satisfy the requirement (3) in Chapter 3 (Section 3.3). The dynamic motion controller (NR) was not robust, which violates the requirement (3) in Chapter 3 (Section 3.4). The odometry sensor system (OD) did not have any cooperative sensors, which does not satisfy requirement (2) in Chapter 3 (Section 3.5).

Overall, seven experimental tests are reported here with each test consisting of five trials. The initial posture of the middle point R for each test is $[x \quad y \quad \phi] = [-1.342 \text{ m} \quad -1.342 \text{ m} \quad 0°]$. At the end of each trial, the final robot posture is manually measured relative to a string-grid system suspended just above the robot to determine the actual final position error, E, and off-tracking, $\Delta = \gamma - \phi$. Under ideal circumstances when pure bending is maintained, the orientation of the line $\overline{C_1 C_2}$, represented by γ, equals the actual heading angle ϕ of the velocity at point R, Figure 2.12. Off-tracking, Δ, indicates the ability of the dynamic controller and sensor system to maintain pure bending. Standard deviations σ_E and $\sigma\Delta$ are reported for manual measurements to indicate consistency. For each test, we also record the position error magnitude and orientation provided by the kinematic controller $[E_k, e_k^\phi]$, dynamic controller $[E_d, e_d^\phi]$, and sensory system $[E_s, e_s^\phi]$. A successful trial is defined only if the robot can complete the posture regulation task in this trial. The success rate is defined as the number of all successful trials over the total number of trials.

7.2.2 Experimental Results and Discussion

Table 7.1 shows the final posture errors for all the tests according to odometry and manual measurements, where kin denotes kinematic controller, dyn denotes

Table 7.1 Experimental Final Posture Error

No.	Surf.	System kin+dyn+sens	Kinematic. Contr. Err.		Dyn. Contr. Err.		Sensor Error		Actual Error			
			E_k (cm)	e_k^ϕ (°)	E_d (cm)	e_d^ϕ (°)	E_s (cm)	e_s^ϕ (°)	$E \pm \sigma_E$ (cm)	$\Delta \pm \sigma\Delta$ (°)	Inct.err. (%)	Succ. Rate (%)
1	C	1+1+1	0	0	1.4	9.2	9.8	0.6	9.9 ± 1.0	-2.0 ± 3.5		100
2	C	FB+1+1	17.3	-2.0	4.6	27.9	4.0	-36.6	21.9 ± 0.8	30.8 ± 8.8	121	100
3	C	1+NR+1	0	0	34.5	12.0	24.8	-5.2	17.5	0.6	76	40
4	C	1+1+OD	0	0	4.4	6.6	9.2	7.1	10.6 ± 3.4	-8.3 ± 4.4	7	100
5	S	1+1+1	0	0	0.6	13.2	18.2	-15.6	17.9 ± 1.6	0.9 ± 2.0	80	100
6	S	1+1+OD	0	0	0.5	11.0	21.3	-8.0	21.6 ± 8.5	-8.3 ± 18.4	21 (wrt No. 5)	100
7	SR	1+1+1	0	0	0.8	15.8	18.0	-16.2	17.6 ± 8.3	6.1 ± 2.2	78	100

dynamic controller and sens denotes sensor system. According to Table 7.1, the techniques discussed in this book (Tests 1, 5, 7) perform as expected. In all of these tests, the kinematic controller produces zero position error, E_k, and zero orientation error, e_k^ϕ. Errors produced by the dynamic motion controller (E_d, e_d^ϕ) and the sensor system (E_s, e_s^ϕ) both contribute to the actual error measured at the final posture. The system performance is relatively consistent with expectations. Relative to carpet (Test 1), E is increased by 80% on sand (Test 5) and 78% on sand–rock (Test 7). Increased disturbance is expected on these surfaces, although larger error is expected on sand–rock. Consistent with expectations, though, off-tracking is the least on sand. The sand allows the wheels to slip and reduces traction forces attributed to off-tracking. Overall, it can be observed from E_k, E_d, and E_s that the major source of error is produced by the sensing system, while a small amount of error results from the dynamic controller.

The nonideal kinematic motion controller with velocity feedback was used in Test 2. Compared to Test 1, E is increased by 121% and off-tracking Δ is increased by 1440% in Test 2. Velocity feedback also perturbed the kinematic motion controller and increased kinematic controller error (E_k, e_k^ϕ) significantly. Since the kinematic controller provides the reference trajectories to the dynamic controller, the dynamic control errors also became larger, (E_d, e_d^ϕ). The posture errors were therefore increased significantly.

The nonrobust dynamic motion controller used in Test 3 also increased error and most of the trials failed. Position error E is 76% larger than Test 1. More importantly though, 60% of the trials failed to complete because the wheels collided during the maneuver due to off-tracking caused by nonrobustness of the

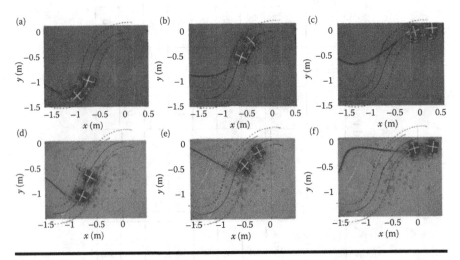

Figure 7.1 Robot paths during posture regulation on carpet and on sand-and-rock. (a) $t=4$s (on carpet), (b) $t=12$s (on carpet), (c) $t=60$s (on carpet), (d) $t=6$s (on sand–rock), (e) $t=12$s (on sand–rock), (f) $t=60$s (on sand–rock).

controller. In the trials that did complete, the off-tracking is actually quite small, but this is *not* representative of this controller's performance. It is thus concluded that the system performance with nonrobust control is unreliable.

The sensor system is evaluated with just odometry feedback in Tests 4 and 6 on carpet and sand, respectively. Given the high traction provided by the carpet (Test 1), error E is only increased by 7% while off-tracking Δ is increased by 315%. This large increase in Δ illustrates the importance of the cooperative sensor. The sand surface (Test 6) underscores the importance of the cooperative sensing. Compared to Test 5, E is increased by 21% and Δ is increased by 822%, both with significantly increased standard deviations.

Figure 7.1 shows the robot using the control system discussed in this book during posture regulation on carpet (Test 1) and sand with rock (Test 7). The white lines represent the string grids and the black lines represent sensor system data. The solid black line represents the predicted position of the middle point R and the dashed black lines represent estimated positions of the wheels. The system performs nearly as well with sand–rock as it did with the ideal high-traction carpet surface. This is a significant improvement over the other traditional methods without the architecture introduced in this book, where the error on sand with rock was as large as 66cm. Overall, all these results demonstrate the superiority of the discussed distributed cooperative motion control and sensing system to robustly maneuver nonideal terrain with significant disturbances.

LOCALIZATION AND MAPPING

Chapter 8

Terrain-Inclination–Based Localization and Mapping

8.1 Introduction

Autonomous localization and mapping is one of the vital and challenging problems for outdoor mobile robots because outdoor scenarios always include more complex and larger-scaled environments. From the beginning of this chapter, we start a new part: Part IV Localization and Mapping. In this chapter, we introduce a less computationally-demanding and more accurate 3D localization and mapping approach with terrain-inclination assistance for outdoor mobile robots navigating on inclined terrains.

In the last decade, significant investigation of mobile robot localization and mapping has been performed [154]. The simultaneous localization and mapping (SLAM) was proven to be effective in generating large, consistent maps, and in achieving localization, especially for indoor applications [155,156]. Different sensors have been used to obtain the surrounding information, such as laser range finders [155,157,158], vision systems [156,159,160], and sonar [161,162]. These sensors are used to generate a series of local maps as the robot is moving. Such overlapped local maps need to be matched so as to obtain the relative rotation and translation for localization and in order to build a global map of the whole navigation area [163].

Among these sensors, laser range sensors are very popular because they can provide more reliable perception and a wider view of the surrounding environment in facilitating localization and mapping. Some researchers have proposed the combination of a 3D laser range scanner with a 2D simultaneous localization and mapping algorithm for autonomous navigation in uneven environments [157,158]. Hence, this chapter also talks about a 3D laser range scan system. However, the computational cost of dealing with point clouds is very expensive, especially for poorly structured outdoor scenarios, which results in large time-consumption in relation to task execution.

Traditionally, the Iterative Closest Points (ICP) algorithm [164] is used to align the overlapped local maps, whereby the overhanging obstacles are generally treated as landmarks [157]. ICP has been proven to be very effective in building the global map of the surrounding area by dealing with serial overlapped local maps. The inherited disadvantages of ICP, however, are slow convergence and locally optimal solutions. In order to overcome these shortcomings, some researchers have developed different variations of the ICP algorithms [157,165]. Notice that it is much more challenging to achieve efficient localization and mapping in most outdoor environments. Sparse or unconstructed overhanging obstacles can greatly harm precision, and complex point clouds data can increase the time-consumption of ICP algorithms. Hence, Kummerle et al. proposed the outdoor localization and mapping assisted by terrain with a multilevel surface [166]. Lee et al. have made an effort to improve the performance of ICP-based localization and mapping using terrain classification [163]. In unstructured outdoor environments, even one ICP matching was very time-consuming (more than 30 s) [167]. Later, Nüchter et al. proposed an approximate kd-tree that reduced the time consumption of each ICP matching to roughly 75% [168]. Furthermore, Nüchter et al. proposed a new approach called the "cached kd-tree" for large environments and compared the proposed cached kd-tree with several different methods in terms of their computational costs, such as point reduction and kd-tree, while the average distance between two consecutive 3D scans was 2.5 m [169]. They found out in [169] that each ICP matching took one second with the cached kd-tree after point reduction. This is a very fast ICP matching for unstructured outdoor applications, although the time consumption of each ICP matching could be milliseconds for many indoor scenarios. However, if more accurate localization and mapping results are needed, ICP matching has to be applied for more instances, such that the computation cost becomes much more expensive [170]. Therefore, frequent ICP matching still results in expensive computational costs, although the matching time for each alignment can be reduced to a reasonable range. Moreover, the consumption of each scan is not negligible (usually more than 3 s) [168,169]. Hence, the substantial time consumption of scans can also increase the total task execution period, especially while exploring large-scale environments.

In order to balance the accuracy and computational load as well as to take advantage of ICP matching, we introduce a different method in this chapter, terrain-inclination–aided 3D localization and mapping technique (TILAM), to combine the ICP algorithm and the inclination of the terrains the robot is navigating so as to achieve autonomous 3D localization and mapping. Using this method, fewer local maps are required to be generated by the 3D laser-scan system. Hence, the time-consuming ICP matching is ultimately applied far fewer times in building a joint global map. Terrain inclinations are used to achieve local localization based on the ground points extracted from the previous laser scan data during the interval between two laser scans. The idea of this terrain-inclination–based localization presented by the co-authors of this book has proven to be accurate and fast [171]. The time consumption is therefore reduced by preventing frequent scan-and-alignments of large point clouds. Experiments then verify the discussed approach and demonstrate accurate and fast localization and mapping on outdoor inclined terrains.

8.2 Three-Dimensional Terrain-Inclination–Based Localization

8.2.1 Robot Terrain-Inclination–Model Extraction

Two frames are defined here: inertial frame and body frame. The inertial frame O is fixed to the earth-surface-ellipsoid at the estimated initial position of the robot with three orthogonal axes (x, y, z), Figure 8.1a. The axis y always points to the North Pole and the axis z points upward, away from the Earth's center. The body frame B is fixed to the midpoint of the rear axis of the robot with three orthogonal axes (x_b, y_b, z_b), Figure 8.1a. The axis x_b is always consistent with the direction of the robot velocity, whereas the axis z_b is vertical to the robot plane. The robot path is represented by the trajectory of the origin in the body frame B. Roll, pitch, and yaw are with respect to x_b, y_b, and z_b, respectively. It is assumed that the mobile robot could be treated as a plane if the robot height is negligible relative to the scale of its travel distance, and that the traversing terrain is rigid.

Notice that the plane of the topographical map (Figure 8.1b) is the same as the x–O–y plane of the inertial frame. Assume that a pre-planned path $(E_1'F_1'...E_j'F_j')$ is given on the topographical map, which is the projection of the actual robot terrain path $(E_1F_1...E_jF_j)$ onto the x–O–y plane, Figure 8.2a. The path on the x–O–y plane is first segmented into a series of line segments with a fixed interval L_l/k where L_l is the length of the robot and $E_j'F_j'$ represents the jth line segment, Figure 8.2a. A series of rectangles on the x–O–y plane such as

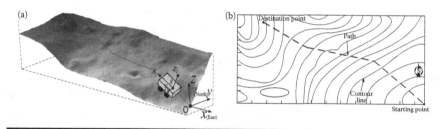

Figure 8.1 Outdoor scenario. (a) 3D inclined terrain and (b) terrain map.

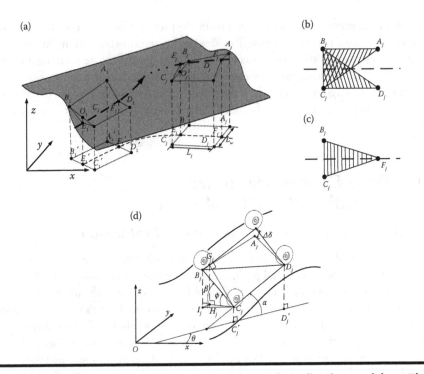

Figure 8.2 **Geometric extraction of the robot-terrain inclination model. (a) The path on the *x–O–y* plane is segmented into a series of quadrangles, (b) four-wheeled robot, (c) three-wheeled robot, and (d) geometric extraction ($\Delta\delta$ represents the distance between the off-land wheel and the terrain point A_j).**

$A_j'B_j'C_j'D_j'$ can be plotted according to the geometrical relationship where L_w is the width of the robot. The points A_j', B_j', C_j', D_j', E_j', and F_j' are the projections of the terrain points A_j, B_j, C_j, D_j, E_j, and F_j, respectively. The z value of these terrain points can be obtained by a weighted average interpolation method, an "Inverse Distance to a Power" from the topographical map [172]. When the four-wheeled robot moves on the inclined 3D terrain, not all four wheels will touch the terrain. The center of gravity (CG) of the robot would help analyze the ground contact points once the robot platforms are confirmed. If the CG is located at the center of the robot, three terrain points among A_j, B_j, C_j, D_j with larger z components will be treated as the ground contact points. In this chapter, the CG of our platform is close to the rear axis. So the rear wheels of the robot are assumed to always touch the ground. One of the front wheels might touch the ground, whereas the other one would be suspended. When the robot moves above the *j*th quadrangle $A_j'B_j'C_j'D_j'$ along the path on the topographical map, the terrain points B_j and C_j represent the ground contact points of two rear wheels. Once another ground contact point (A_j or D_j) is determined, the robot plane at this moment will be obtained. Compare the z values of the terrain points A_j and D_j. If $z_{A_j} > z_{D_j}$, the left front wheel of the robot will touch the terrain point A_j and the right front wheel will be suspended. In this case, A_j will be the ground contact point, and the triangle $A_jB_jC_j$ will be used to represent the robot plane, Figure 8.2b. If $z_{D_j} > z_{A_j}$, then the right front wheel of the robot will touch the terrain point D_j and the triangle $B_jC_jD_j$ will be used to represent the robot plane at this moment, Figure 8.2b. When the three-wheeled robot moves on the 3D terrain, all three wheels will touch the terrain at the ground points B_j, C_j, and F_j where B_j and C_j represent the ground contact points of two rear wheels, respectively, and F_j represents the ground contact points of the front wheel. Hence, the triangle $B_jC_jF_j$ will be used to represent the robot plane in the case of the three-wheeled robot, Figure 8.2c.

Once the robot plane is obtained, the next step is to extract the Robot-Terrain Inclination model (RTI model). In this section, a four-wheeled robot is used as the example for extraction of the RTI model. Suppose the triangle $B_jC_jD_j$ represents the robot plane, and the $\overline{C_jD_j}$ represents the direction of the robot motion, Figure 8.2d. Notice that the origin of the body frame of the robot is coincident with the midpoint O_j of the terrain points B_j and C_j if the robot height is negligible. So the coordinates of O_j will be treated as the position of the robot. The coordinates of the points B_j, C_j, D_j, and O_j relative to the inertial frame are represented as (x_B, y_B, z_B), (x_C, y_C, z_C), (x_D, y_D, z_D), and (x_j, y_j, z_j), respectively. Then a Robot-Terrain Inclination model $RTI\_Model : (x_j, y_j, z_j) \rightarrow \gamma_M$ for the jth quadrangle will be derived as a correlation function between the system states and the measurements for the particle filter presented later. In this model, $\gamma_M = \begin{bmatrix} \theta_j & \alpha_j & \phi_j \end{bmatrix}^T$ represent the orientation angles of the robot plane according to the terrain information on the topographical map. These angles ϕ_j, α_j, and θ_j will be directly related to the roll, pitch, and yaw angles of the robot, respectively.

8.2.2 Particle-Filter Terrain-Inclination Localization

Assume that the robot follows a given path where the terrain surface inclinations are not always zeros and that the robot can measure its attitude and velocities. The 3D robot position is defined as the system state X_t, which will be estimated using a Monte-Carlo approach [173]. The basic idea of the Monte-Carlo approach is to estimate the state X_t by a weighted set of M particles. The state transition of a single particle m through motion is described as

$$X_t^{[m]} = \begin{bmatrix} x_t^{[m]} \\ y_t^{[m]} \\ z_t^{[m]} \end{bmatrix} = \begin{bmatrix} x_{t-1}^{[m]} \\ y_{t-1}^{[m]} \\ z_{t-1}^{[m]} \end{bmatrix} + TA \begin{bmatrix} v_{x_b} \\ v_{y_b} \\ v_{z_b} \end{bmatrix} \tag{8.1}$$

where

$$
A = \begin{bmatrix} c\theta\, c\alpha & -c\theta\, s\alpha\, s\phi - s\theta\, c\phi & -c\theta\, s\alpha\, c\phi + s\theta\, c\phi \\ s\theta\, c\alpha & -s\theta\, c\alpha\, s\phi + c\theta\, c\phi & -s\theta\, s\alpha\, c\phi - c\theta\, s\phi \\ s\alpha & c\alpha\, s\phi & c\alpha\, c\phi \end{bmatrix}_{t-1}
$$

The c and s are the abbreviations for cos and sin, respectively, and T is the sampling period. The linear velocity vector $\begin{bmatrix} v_{xb} & v_{yb} & v_{zb} \end{bmatrix}^T$ is with respect to the body frame of the robot (x_b, y_b, z_b) defined in Section 8.2.1.

The RTI model extracted from the terrain map in Section 8.2.1 is treated as the measurement model. Therefore, the measurement prediction can be described for each particle m as

$$
\hat{z}_t^{[m]} = \begin{bmatrix} \hat{\theta}_t^{[m]} \\ \hat{\alpha}_t^{[m]} \\ \hat{\phi}_t^{[m]} \\ \hat{dist}_t^{[m]} \end{bmatrix} = \begin{bmatrix} RTI\_Model_\theta(x_t^{[m]}, y_t^{[m]}, z_t^{[m]}) \\ RTI\_Model_\alpha(x_t^{[m]}, y_t^{[m]}, z_t^{[m]}) \\ RTI\_Model_\phi(x_t^{[m]}, y_t^{[m]}, z_t^{[m]}) \\ dist(p(x,y,z) - p(x_t^{[m]}, y_t^{[m]}, z_t^{[m]})) \end{bmatrix} \tag{8.2}
$$

where RTI_Model_θ, RTI_Model_α, and RTI_Model_ϕ consists of the RTI model extracted in the previous section. $p(x_t^{[m]}, y_t^{[m]}, z_t^{[m]})$ represents the position of the particle m, and $p(x, y, z)$ represents the terrain point on the robot path closest to this particle that is gained from the map. $\hat{dist}_t^{[m]}$ is the distance between the particle m and the point $p(x, y, z)$.

To carry out the particle-filter-resample step, the weighting factor of each sample $w_t^{[m]}$ will be computed according to the sensor model

$$
z_t = [\theta_t, \alpha_t, \phi_t, dist_t] \tag{8.3}
$$

where $[\theta_t, \alpha_t, \phi_t]^T$ is the measurement vector obtained from the onboard inertial sensors at the time interval T. The distance $dist_t$ is not a real sensor measurement but a virtual measurement to keep all samples along the path at this moment. So $dist_t$ is always zero [174]. The $w_t^{[m]}$ is computed by

$$
w_t^{[m]} = \left| 2\pi Q_t \right|^{-\frac{1}{2}} \exp\left\{ -\frac{1}{2}\left(z_t - \hat{z}_t^{[m]}\right)^T \right\} Q_t^{-1}\left(z_t - \hat{z}_t^{[m]}\right) \tag{8.4}
$$

The variation Q_t represents the uncertainty of the RTI model and the map inaccuracy.

The heading angle θ_j is defined as the angle between the $\overline{C_j'D_j'}$ and the x axis. The heading angle is exclusively determined by the path. The angle α_j is defined as the one between the robot direction $\overrightarrow{C_jD_j}$ and the x–O–y plane. The plane $H_jI_jC_j$ is parallel to the x–O–y plane. The β_j is the angle between the line $\overrightarrow{C_jI_j}$ and $\overrightarrow{C_jB_j}$. The ϕ_j is the angle between the $\overrightarrow{C_jB_j}$ and the line $\overrightarrow{C_jH_j}$ (Figure 8.2d). Then the angles α_j and ϕ_j can be obtained from the following equations

$$\alpha_j = \sin^{-1}\left(\frac{(z_D - z_C)}{\left|\overrightarrow{C_jD_j}\right|}\right) \tag{8.5}$$

$$\phi_j = \sin^{-1}\left(\frac{\sin\beta_j}{\cos\alpha_j}\right) \tag{8.6}$$

$$\beta_j = \sin^{-1}\left(\frac{(z_B - z_C)}{\left|\overrightarrow{B_jC_j}\right|}\right) \tag{8.7}$$

$$\left|\overrightarrow{C_jD_j}\right| = \sqrt{(x_C - x_D)^2 + (y_C - y_D)^2 + (z_C - z_D)^2} \tag{8.8}$$

$$\left|\overrightarrow{B_jC_j}\right| = \sqrt{(x_B - x_C)^2 + (y_B - y_C)^2 + (z_B - z_C)^2} \tag{8.9}$$

Therefore, a number of angles $(\theta_j, \alpha_j, \phi_j)$ can be extracted from the serial quadrangles $A'_jB'_jC'_jD'_j$, Figure 8.2a. Then the robot position (x_j, y_j, z_j) at each quadrangle corresponds with each group $(\theta_j, \alpha_j, \phi_j)$. By linear interpolation of the above discrete relationship, $\begin{bmatrix} \theta_k & \alpha_k & \phi_k \end{bmatrix}^T = RTI\_Model(x_k, y_k, z_k)$ can be obtained, $k = 1, 2, \ldots, N$. The number N can be adjusted for the accuracy requirement. Hence, we finally get a series of discrete relationships between the robot attitude and the robot position.

8.3 Mapping

8.3.1 Data Acquisition and Point Clouds Separation

8.3.1.1 Data Acquisition

In the system presented here, a 3D laser scan system was built on the top of the mobile robot to obtain the point clouds of the environment during the robot navigation. The 3D laser scan system consists of a 2D laser scanner (SICK LMS200) and a turntable driven by a servo motor.

Three coordinate systems are defined in this chapter. They are the world coordinate system (x, y, z), the robot coordinate system (x_b, y_b, z_b), and the laser coordinate system (x_l, y_l, z_l). The world coordinate system is fixed to the tangential plane of the earth-surface-ellipsoid at the estimated initial position of the robot with three orthogonal axes (x, y, z). The axis y always points to the North Pole and the axis z points upwards, away from the Earth's center. The robot coordinate system is fixed to the midpoint of the rear axis of the robot with three orthogonal axes (x_b, y_b, z_b). The axis x_b is always consistent with the direction of the robot velocity, whereas the axis z_b is vertical to the robot plane. The laser coordinate system is fixed to the mirror wheel center of the laser scanner. The direction of the axis x_l is always the same as that of the axis x_b, whereas the axis z_l is coincident with the axis z_b.

In this chapter, scanning the environment with a mobile robot is done in a stop-scan-go fashion. The laser scan is applied every few meters. After the robot stops, the laser scanner is rotated by the turntable from $0°$ (positive direction of the x_l axis) to $180°$ (negative direction of the x_l axis). Hence, we can get the 3D coordinate values of each point cloud in the laser coordinate system as

$$z_l = R \times \sin \gamma \tag{8.10}$$

$$y_l = R \times \cos \gamma \times \cos \varphi \tag{8.11}$$

$$x_l = R \times \cos \gamma \times \sin \varphi \tag{8.12}$$

where (x_l, y_l, z_l) are the coordinate values, R is the distance from the laser to the object, γ is the angle between the scan line and the $x_l o_l y_l$ plane, and φ is the rotation angle of the turntable.

8.3.1.2 Point Clouds Separation

The point clouds representing the environmental information contain both the terrain points and nonterrain points (overhanging points). Rather than the traditional approaches, the terrain points and nonterrain points both contribute to the localization and mapping in the methodology discussed here. Hence, those points need to be extracted separately from the point clouds map.

In order to separate this point data, a modified filter is applied on each scan line based on so-called "pseudo scanning lines" by slopes and elevations [175]. Since a scan line is composed of many points ordered by the scanning sequence, we can arbitrarily choose two adjacent points P_{i-1} and P_i. Then, dz_i and S_i represent the elevation difference and the slope between the points P_i and P_{i-1}. If dz_i and S_i are both less than the threshold $Limit\_dz$ and $Limit\_S$, then the point P_i is treated as the terrain point. Otherwise, it is a nonterrain point. According to Figure 8.3, the calculation formula of the elevation difference dz_i and the slope S_i are shown as

$$dz_i = |z_i - z_{i-1}| \tag{8.13}$$

$$S_i = \frac{z_i - z_{i-1}}{\sqrt{(x_i - x_{i-1})^2 + (y_i - y_{i-1})^2}} \tag{8.14}$$

where (x_i, y_i, z_i) is the world coordinate of the point P_i and $(x_{i-1}, y_{i-1}, z_{i-1})$ is the world coordinate of the point P_{i-1}. Figure 8.4 shows the results of the data separation on a local point clouds scan where the light and dark colors represent the terrain points and the nonterrain points, respectively.

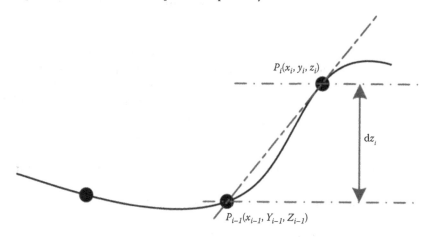

Figure 8.3 Relationship between two points.

Figure 8.4 Data separation result.

8.3.2 ICP-Based Mapping

In this chapter, we use the ICP algorithm to align each pair of the local point clouds maps to finally build the global map of the navigation area. The ICP is based on a point-to-point correspondence between two partially overlapped scans. It starts with two meshes and an initial guess in order to get the relative transform between them. This is different from most traditional approaches where the initial guess is given by odometry; the initial guess, in this technique, comes from the results of the terrain-inclination–aided localization applied in the previous time interval. Next, the initial transform is refined iteratively by repeatedly generating pairs of the corresponding points on the meshes and minimizing an error metric [176]. According to the literature [157], ground information is not effective in achieving good matching in an outdoor environment, while nonground features like trees or buildings can get good and fast results. Point reduction and the cached kd-tree are both applied here to reduce the time consumption of the ICP matching to around 1 s [169].

Figure 8.5 illustrates the matching of two local point cloud maps using nonterrain points and the initial guess from the terrain-inclination–aided localization. Figure 8.5a shows two local point cloud maps before matching where the grey points represent the cloud map from the nth scan and the black points represent that from the $(n+1)$th scan. The matching results are shown in Figure 8.5b after the alignment of two maps.

8.4 Experimental Results and Discussion

8.4.1 Methods and Procedures

The experiments were conducted on the platform, a pioneer 3DX robot equipped with a 3D laser scan system. The NAV440 from Crossbow Technology was used as the inertial measurement unit (IMU) that mounted on the robot in order to measure the roll, pitch, yaw angles, and the angular velocities ω_{x_b}, ω_{y_b}, ω_{z_b}. The forward speed v_{x_b} with respect to the robot coordinate system was provided by the encoders of the robot. v_{y_b}, v_{z_b} are both zero with respect to the robot coordinate system with no-slip assumption.

An outdoor environment is selected around the library of the Shenzhen University Town with the 3D terrains covered with the grass and surrounded with the trees. This environment is one kind of typical inclined terrains with natural landmarks (trees) where the TILAM presented in the chapter could be validated. This selected region is approximately 15 m × 10 m. The horizontal opening angle of the 3D laser scan system is 180°, whereas the vertical opening angle is 80°. One scan map is obtained roughly every 6 m for the TILAM. In order to do a comparison, a fast ICP-based SLAM with point reduction and a cached kd-tree [169]

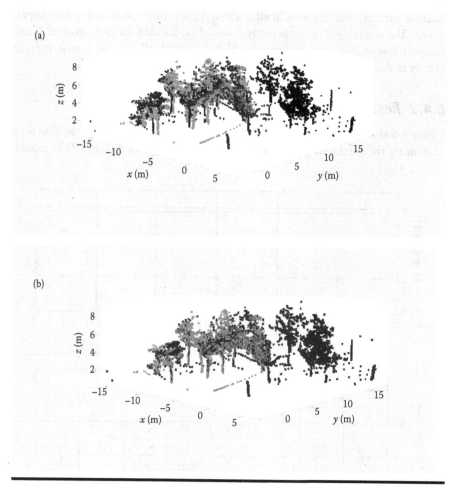

Figure 8.5 **Illustration of the alignment of two local point clouds maps. (a) Before matching and (b) after matching.**

is applied at the same region where the robot stops and scans every three meters to update the estimation of the robot position. Note that this method is known as a very fast ICP variation in the literature so far. The robot moved on this terrain at a speed of 0.1 m/s. The sampling period $\Delta t = 0.1$ s is chosen for all experiments so as to be consistent with the sampling period of IMU.

A PhaseSpace motion capture system was applied here to obtain the reference positions of the robot during the navigation. PhaseSpace is an optical motion capture system used to estimate the position, velocity, and acceleration of an object to which LED markers are attached. Its measurement accuracy is 1 mm. Notice that the continuous ground truth value is difficult to obtain online since the motion capture system cannot cover the whole navigation area at one time. Hence, a few discrete artificial markers were labelled along the real robot path during each experiment. The corresponding time interval was also recorded for each marker. Next, the positions of those markers were measured individually by the motion capture system as the reference values after each experiment were done.

8.4.2 Results and Discussion

Figure 8.6 shows the robot-terrain–inclination model extracted from the first scan map using the method in Section 8.2. Based on this robot-terrain (RTI) model,

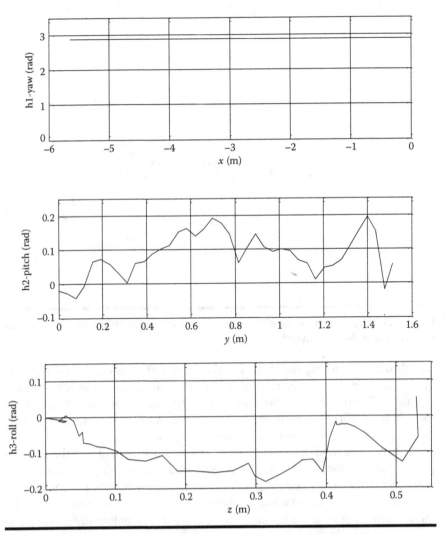

Figure 8.6 **Robot-terrain–inclination model based on the first scan map.**

the terrain-inclination–aided localization was achieved online during the interval between the first scan ($T = 0$) and the second scan ($T = 1$ min), where T is the clock-time ticking from the beginning of the movement. At $T = 1$ min, the robot stopped and did the second scan. Afterwards, the ICP-based alignment between the first scan and the second scan was finished to generate a joined local map using the localization results at $T = 1$ min as the initial condition of the ICP, Figure 8.5. Likewise, the terrain-inclination–aided localization was applied again during the next interval between the second scan ($T = 1$ min) and the third scan ($T = 2$ min). A global map of this region was finally built after three scans while the online localization was also achieved during the whole navigation. The estimation of the robot position by the proposed technique (solid line) is compared with the dead-reckoning results (dash-dot line) and the reference positions (circle signs) in Figure 8.7. According to Figure 8.7, the position estimation by our presented technique is much closer to the ground truth values in such outdoor scenarios. In order to consider the ability of dealing with the associated uncertainties, the localization performance using different filter algorithms such as the Extended Kalman Filter (EKF) and the particle filter have also been compared in Figure 8.7. Figure 8.7 indicates the position estimation based on the particle-filter–based TIL (solid line), the method introduced in this chapter, is much smoother than the one estimated by EKF (dotted line). Figure 8.9b and c show the mapping results of the region

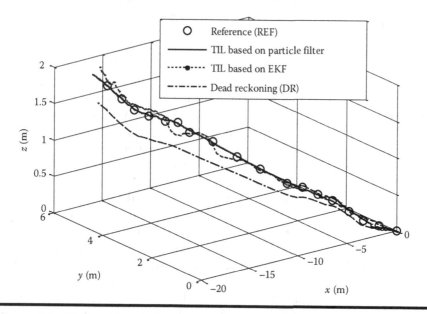

Figure 8.7 **The position estimation comparison of the robot-Scenario 1. TIL stands for Terrain Inclination Localization. Solid line represents the proposed method in this chapter while the dotted line represents the results when the particle filter is replaced by EKF.**

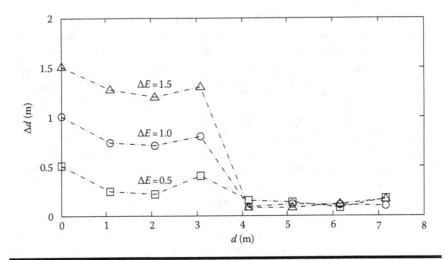

Figure 8.8 Position estimation errors at different initial errors, ΔE, along the trip.

in Figure 8.9a using our TILAM and the ICP-based SLAM, respectively. Twelve discrete ground truth values were measured in total during each experimental trial as the references (the mini-flags in Figure 8.9a).

In order to evaluate how the initial-position error, ΔE, would affect the robot performance, the 3D Euclidean distance between the estimated position and the reference position, Δd, is defined as the position-estimation error, whereas the distance of the estimated position in the world coordinate is d. When the robot encountered the inclination variation of the terrain (i.e., crossing a contour line), the position-estimation error was reduced quickly afterwards (e.g., after the distance of 3 m in Figure 8.8). According to Figure 8.8, the convergence of the position-estimation errors is robust to large initial-position errors up to 1.5 m.

According to Figure 8.9, there is no big difference between the discussed TILAM and the ICP-based SLAM in terms of the global map accuracy. Each of them can successfully build the global map. However, the position estimation by the technique discussed in this chapter is much closer to the ground truth values than the traditional ICP-based SLAM in such an outdoor scenario as Figure 8.10. In order to further examine how different the localization performance is between TILAM and the traditional ICP-based SLAM, five repeated experimental trials were carried out. The average mean and the variance of the position-estimation errors in three individual axes and in the Euclidean distance d are shown, respectively, in Table 8.1. According to Table 8.1, the position-estimation error in the Euclidean distance using the discussed TILAM is 82% smaller than that using the ICP-based SLAM. The distribution of the position errors from the TILAM is also 43% more narrow than the ICP-based SLAM.

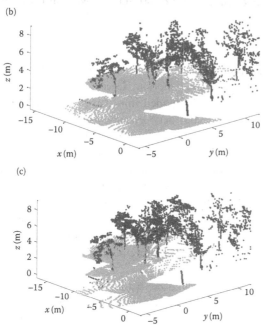

Figure 8.9 The mapping result comparison. (a) Experimental environment, (b) mapping used TILAM, and (c) mapping used the ICP-based SLAM.

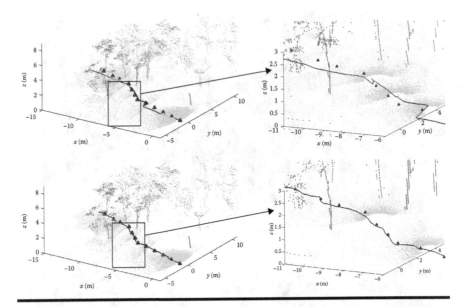

Figure 8.10 Localization and mapping results for the outdoor environment. (a) ICP-based SLAM, (b) Zoom-in-view of (a), (c) TILAM, and (d) Zoom-in-view of (c).

Moreover, there is a difference between the discussed TILAM and the ICP-based SLAM in terms of the time consumption, Table 8.2. According to Table 8.2, the time consumption of TIALM is divided into two parts: terrain-inclination–aided localization during the interval between any pair of two laser scans, and ICP-based matching. Two ICP alignments were needed for the entire 15-m path using the TILAM approach. The time consumption of an ICP-based SLAM is also divided into two parts: odometry-based localization and ICP-based matching, where five ICP alignments were needed in order to achieve satisfying localization results. Although the terrain-inclination–aided localization took longer (0.09 s in average) than the odometry-based localization (0.02 s in average), the overall computational cost of TILAM (2.67 s) was still 56% lower than the ICP-based SLAM (6.1 s) because of a lower ICP alignment requirement with even better localization performance.

In order to evaluate how the initial estimation error would affect the robot performance, the convergence periods are shown in Table 8.3 with different initial position estimations. Notice that the convergence period is less than 4 s if the initial estimation error at each axis is less than 0.2 m. Moreover, it takes longer for the system to settle down as the initial estimation error increases. Hence, the technique discussed in this chapter is sensitive to larger initial errors, although it only affects the localization accuracy at the beginning of the first scan interval and could not

Table 8.1 Localization Error Comparison

No	Method	Error Mean x-Axis (m)	Error Variance x-Axis (m)	Error Mean y-Axis (m)	Error Variance y-Axis (m)	Error Mean z-Axis (m)	Error Variance z-Axis (m)	Error Mean d (m)	Error Variance d (m)
1	TILAM	−0.0126	0.0898	0.0326	0.0105	−0.0165	0.0018	0.0386	0.0904
2	ICP-based SLAM	−0.0125	0.1324	−0.2016	0.0842	−0.0781	0.0288	0.2166	0.1595

Table 8.2 The Computation Time Comparison

No.	Test Distance (m)	Method	The Consuming Time for Localization	The Matching Time	Total Time (s)
1	15	TILAM	0.09 (s) × 3 times = 0.27 (s)	1.2 (s) × 2 times = 2.4 (s)	2.67
2	15	ICP-based SLAM	0.02 (s) × 5 times = 0.1 (s)	1.2 (s) × 5 times = 6 (s)	6.1

Table 8.3 Convergence Periods with Different Initial Estimation Errors

No.	Robot Speed (m/s)	Initial Estimation Error (m)	Convergence Period (s)
1	0.1	(0.1, 0.1, 0.1)	3.5
2	0.1	(0.2, 0.2, 0.2)	4
3	0.1	(0.3, 0.3, 0.3)	28
4	0.1	(0.4, 0.4, 0.4)	32

harm the performance afterwards. Particle filters could be used to improve the robustness of this technique; they are discussed in the next chapter. It is, therefore, concluded that the terrain-inclination–aided localization and mapping algorithms can improve localizations on 3D-inclined terrains and efficiently build the global map of the surrounding area.

Chapter 9

Cloud-Based Localization Architecture in Large-Scale Environments

9.1 Introduction

In Chapter 8, we introduced a terrain-inclination- and laser-based localization and mapping of a mobile robot in an outdoor environment where the complex terrain conditions are the focus, but the scenario was relatively small. But field robots such as rescue, surveillance, and military robots are often required to work in large-scale environments. Therefore, in this chapter, we deal with this situation: a robot operating in a large-scale outdoor environment using techniques other than those illustrated in Chapter 8. Robot localization, especially for large-scale explorations, has traditionally been limited by inherent physical constraints, since all the computations have to be conducted in the onboard computers/microchips of the robot with limited computing capabilities. Hence, this chapter presents a cloud-based architecture to achieve large-scale localization of mobile robots in outdoor environments, taking advantage of the powerful computation, storage, and other shared resources of the cloud.

In the last decade, many researchers have started to focus on robot localization in outdoor environments. Many outdoor-environment localization algorithms depend on GPS. However, in some urban circumstances, e.g., urban canyons, service ways, and tunnels, the GPS signal may be severely blocked. In these situations, the estimation error can reach more than 10 m [177–179]. Outsourcing map-based localization is a relatively novel method for estimating robot position. Christian et al. proposed a novel approach to take advantage of a road network structure and its height profile for position estimation when the GPS signal was lost [174]. Zhu et al. also proposed a new localization method with less occupied memory, where the topographical map was utilized as the prior available terrain map for localization [180,181]. But these methods may fail when a robot encounters ambiguous routes with parallel roads. Xu et al. presented an outsourcing map-based algorithm with vision and road curvature estimation for localizing a vehicle to solve the ambiguous routes problem [182]. Recently, Majdik et al. proposed an air-ground image-matching algorithm to localize and track the pose of a micro aerial vehicle (MAV) flying in urban streets without GPS [183]. This method also took outsourcing data such as ground-level Street View images for localization where these images have been previously back-projected onto a cadastral 3D city model. But their method is limited by high computational complexity and is unable to be readily used in real-time applications [183].

However, in the case of large-scale exploration, all the preceding efforts are not enough. A large-scale environment is defined as one whose spatial structure is at a significantly larger scale than the horizon sensors could observe [184]. Large-scale localization is challenging because of the demand for expensive computational power and huge memory storage due to the large amount of data to be processed [185]. For example, the Stanley and Boss who won the DARPA Grand and Urban Challenge, respectively, were equipped with an array of 6–10 computers and more than 1TB of hard drive storage was needed for data processing and logging [12,186]. In order to reduce the memory requirement, Lankenau et al. presented a new algorithm called RouteLoc for the absolute self-localization of mobile robots in a large-scale environment [187] represented by a hybrid topological-metric map. However, this method can be used only in structured environments. In order to deal with the complexity of an unstructured large-scale environment, Bonev et al. proposed a scalable machine-learning approach to distinguish the similarity of consecutive images over long trajectories for robot localization with vision sensors [179]. Bradley et al. presented a new method using "Weighted Gradient Orientation Histograms" in which features are extracted from the images and the robot estimates position by matching these features [188]. This method could effectively reduce computational consumption in large outdoor environments. However, it was hard to discriminate between visually similar locations and to match the features under extreme illumination changes [189]. Xie et al. introduced a coarse-to-fine matching method for global localization and kidnapped problem of a mobile robot with laser sensor in large-scale unstructured outdoor environments [190]. However, the proposed localization approach would fail if the environments changed significantly or the onboard laser sensors were "blocked" by the surrounding crowd.

Cloud robotics, a concept first introduced by Kuffner at Google, provides a very promising solution to the problems faced by large-scale or long-term autonomous robots [191,192]. Cloud robotics applies cloud computing concepts to a robot in order to augment the capabilities of the robot by offloading computation and sharing the huge data or new skills via the Internet. Only a few papers on cloud robotics have been reported so far, such as cloud-based simultaneous localization and mapping (SLAM), object grasping, and multi-robotics. In order to tackle the challenges of the intensive mapping data and computation load during SLAM, Arumugam et al. built a cloud computing infrastructure "DAvinCi" to improve the implementation speed of the SLAM algorithm [193]. Riazuelo et al. described a visual SLAM system based on the cloud where the expensive map optimization and storage was allocated in the cloud and a light camera-tracking client ran on the onboard computer of the robot [194]. Kehoe et al. developed the architecture of a cloud robotics system to recognize and grasp common household objects [195]. In order to reduce the demand of manually labeled training data, Lai and Fox used objects from Google's 3D warehouse to help classify 3D point clouds collected by a robot [196]. Multiple robot cooperation is another area that could benefit from cloud robotics [197,198]. Hu et al. proposed a cloud robotics architecture to handle the constraints faced by networked robots and described some specific challenges and potential applications in cloud robotics [197]. In order to improve efficiency and to share data among different robots, Wang et al. introduced a generic infra-structure for a cloud robotic system to enable several poorly equipped robots to retrieve location data from a dynamically updated map built by a well-equipped robot [198].

In this chapter, we introduce a different cloud-based localization architec-ture using outsourced road network maps and reference images in the cloud (CLAOR) to achieve real-time autonomous navigation of a mobile robot in large-scale outdoor environments. The road network maps and reference images are first extracted by Google Earth, OpenStreet Map, or other commercially avail-able resources such that new road information could be added into the database in the cloud. The terrain-inclination-based localization algorithms discussed in Chapter 8 [181] will then be extended to achieve large-scale online localization, only taking advantage of the road network maps stored in the cloud. A vision-based supplement is presented to further improve the performance using the reference images stored in the cloud. The main advantages of this cloud-based structure are threefold: (1) In the cloud-based architecture, a ground mobile robot can achieve accurate, real-time localization in different large-scale chal-lenging scenarios where the GPS signal is often shadowed or completely unavail-able. (2) The methodology presented here allows the mobile robot, which is just equipped with minimal hardware and onboard sensors, to access a large amount of data stored in the cloud. On the other hand, network delays caused by data interchanging between the cloud and robot are compensated successfully. (3) A technique of the vision-based supplement is used to effectively solve the problem of location ambiguity resulting from the cumulative error of onboard sensors when the robot travels along a very long, straight, and flat road segment. This technique guarantees a limited localization error within 0.5 m during the whole long-term operation.

9.2 Cloud-Based Outsourcing Localization Architecture

The cloud-based architecture presented in this chapter (CLAOR) has two phases: offline and online, as Figure 9.1 shows. Each phase is illustrated in detail in the following subsections.

9.2.1 Offline Phase

The offline phase consists of two parts: the extraction of road network information and the construction of reference images. The former extracts new road networks and updates the existing road network map stored in the cloud. In order to build the road networks, first a set of reference points are labeled along the new road. Then, the geodetic coordinates (latitude, longitude, altitude) of these points, along with the road's name, are extracted from Google Earth or other Geographic Information System (GIS) software, as Figure 9.2 depicts. A higher density of these reference points would result in a higher localization accuracy. Finally, the latest road information is integrated into the road network database, which is stored and maintained in the cloud.

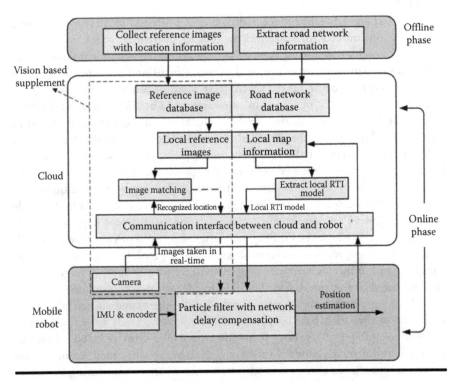

Figure 9.1   Cloud-based localization architecture.

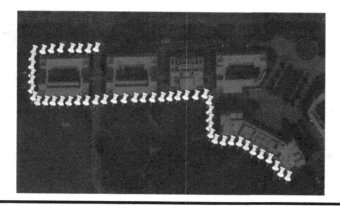

Figure 9.2 Extraction of point set on a pre-planned path.

To further improve localization accuracy for mobile robots, the second part of the offline phase is to construct a reference image database in our framework. An image of a specific location in the road network is taken as a reference for localization. Each image is tagged with location information as a prior. In order to increase the accuracy and robustness of image matching, the reference images are always taken with salient features that are easily identifiable from the open source GIS software (e.g., Google Earth or OpenStreet Map), such as an image of building with sharp edges, landscapes with obvious markers or color shifts, Figure 9.3. The reference images could also be taken manually if the area is not covered by the existing database. These images will be updated and integrated into the reference image database stored in the cloud as well.

9.2.2 Online Phase

The online phase is for mobile robot localization based on the cloud. According to Figure 9.1, the architecture consists of two ends: the cloud and the mobile robot. On the cloud end, the robot terrain inclination (RTI) model [181] can be extracted from the road network map and used to describe the relationship between the robot altitude and the robot position. On the other hand, image matching between an image taken by a mobile robot in real-time and the local reference images is also implemented on the cloud for a vision-based supplement to improve localization performance. An interface is designed for all the communication between the cloud and the robot. On the mobile robot end, onboard sensors (IMU, encoder, and camera) are equipped and a particle-filter-based localization algorithm with network delay compensation is used to estimate the robot position.

The whole procedure is as follows: When the robot moves on a road, the initial position estimated by GPS is sent to the cloud. All the local road information

Figure 9.3 Some examples of reference images along the road, (a) a building with sharp edge, (b) ground with distinct boundary and markers, (c) unique statue or object, and (d) crossroads with plenty of textures.

and reference images within an area of radius δ centered at the initial position are automatically searched from the road network database and the reference image database, respectively, on the cloud. The RTI model for the corresponding road segments is extracted. Then, the local RTI model for the road network is sent back to the robot. At the same time, images are received sequentially from the moving mobile robot and compared with the local reference images on the cloud. Once image matching is successful, the corresponding geodetic information of the reference image will be sent back to the robot. Finally, the robot will fuse the preceding local RTI model and the recognized location from the vision-based supplement with the motion model in a particle filter to estimate the robot's current position. Notice that network delay is fully considered in the particle filter algorithm. Hence, most of the computation load as well as storage load can be distributed on the cloud in the cloud-based architecture presented here such that the onboard microchip/ computer of the robot will not be overloaded even if the exploration area expands larger and larger.

9.3 Cloud-Based Localization Algorithms

9.3.1 Algorithms in the Cloud

9.3.1.1 RTI Model

The RTI (robot terrain inclination) model has been fully illustrated and discussed in Chapter 8. Readers can refer to Section 8.2.1 for more details.

9.3.1.2 Image Matching

In the reference image database, each image is linked to a specific geodetic coordinate in the map. An image taken by the mobile robot in real-time is matched with reference images stored in the cloud. Once there is a successful match, the corresponding coordinates will be sent to the robot to help update the position estimation. The matching process is based on the Speeded-Up Robust Features (SURF) detector/descriptor [199]. The U-SURF detector/descriptor is used to extract key points from images and to compute the 64-dimensional non-rotation-invariant descriptors for these regions. Note that non-rotation-invariant descriptors can reduce the matching time remarkably and enable real-time application. In this section, the matching process is done in two directions. That is to say, for each feature point in a matching image, the two closest neighbors should be found in the reference image. Similarly, the two closest neighbors should be found in the matching image as well for a feature point in the reference image. A mutual ratio is defined as the ratio of the distance between the feature point in a matching/reference image and the closest neighbor in the reference/matching image over the distance for the next closest one. If the mutual ratio is lower than a given threshold, then the closest neighbor point can be accepted as a good candidate. But if the mutual ratio is larger than the threshold, both neighbor points are rejected to avoid wrong matching, which has removed a large number of unreliable matches. Then, two good match sets are obtained: one is from the matching image to the reference image, whereas the other is from the reference image to the matching image. A match pair is accepted only if these two match sets have a one-to-one correspondence. Finally, the random sample consensus (RANSAC) method is used to compute the fundamental matrix that checks whether the matches satisfy the epipolar constraint. Once a successful match is found, the location is recognized, and the corresponding geodetic coordinate will be sent to the mobile robot.

9.3.2 Localization Algorithm on the Robot

9.3.2.1 Particle-Filter-Based Localization

In this section, we introduce the particle-filter-based localization algorithm designed on the robot to estimate its position. The detailed algorithm is summarized in

Table 9.1. Algorithm: particle-filter-based localization. The system state X_{t-1} represents the three-dimensional position of the robot in the inertial Cartesian frame (x, y, z) at the time $t-1$. Q_t is the covariance matrix of the system. Z_t is the system measurement vector. The IMU and encoder measurements from time $t-k$ to t are stored in Z_{backup} and v_{backup}, respectively, where k stands for the network time delay caused by the data exchange between the robot and the cloud. Z_{backup}, v_{backup}, and X_{t-k-1} are used for network delay compensation that will be presented in the following subsection. An index VI (Line 3, Table 9.1) is used to indicate whether the robot receives the recognized location result from the cloud. When VI is equal to 0 (i.e., when it is not receiving feedback from the cloud), the algorithm from Line 4 to 17 will be used to estimate the robot position X_t at the time t. Otherwise, a network delay compensation algorithm is proposed to be implemented additionally because the vision-based supplement would induce non-negligible network delay.

The motion model for one particle is shown in Line 5, Table 9.1, where the superscript $[m]$ denotes the particle m. M is the total number of the particles. T is the sampling period, and v_t is the linear velocity in the direction of the robot movement. The measurement prediction is depicted in Line 6, Table 9.1 where RTI_θ and RTI_α are the RTI models downloaded from the cloud, which are treated as part of the measurement model. $\hat{d}_t^{[m]}$ is the Euclidean distance between the particle m and the point $p(x, y, z)$, where $p(x_t^{[m]}, y_t^{[m]}, z_t^{[m]})$ represents the position of the particle m, whereas $p(x, y, z)$ represents the road point on the robot path closest to this particle that is gained from the map. $\hat{V}_t^{[m]}$ represents the measurement prediction of the robot position in the geodetic coordinates obtained from the cloud only in case of successful image matching ($VI=1$). Then the state update is depicted in Lines 7~17 where θ_t and α_t are the measurements of yaw and pitch obtained from the onboard inertial measurement unit (IMU) at time t. The distance d_t is not a real sensor measurement but a virtual measurement to keep all samples along the path at time t [174]. V_t is the recognized location result from the cloud. Line 8 in Table 9.1 indicates the weight calculation of each particle, where $w_t^{[m]}$ is the weighting factor of the particle m.

It is worth mentioning that if the initial position estimated by the GPS is far from the real position, the robot has to re-localize itself. Moreover, when the robot

Table 9.1 Algorithm: Particle-Filter-Based Localization

1	$(X_{t-1}, Z_t, V_t, X_{t-k-1}, Z_{\text{backup}}, V_{\text{backup}})$
2	$X_{t-1} = \left\langle \chi_{t-1}^{[1]}, \chi_{t-1}^{[2]}, \ldots, \chi_{t-1}^{[M]} \right\rangle, Z_t = \{\theta_t, \alpha_t, d_t, V_t\}, Q_t, \overline{X}_t = X_t = \varnothing,$ $X_{t-k-1} = \left\langle \chi_{t-k-1}^{[1]}, \chi_{t-k-1}^{[2]}, \ldots, \chi_{t-k-1}^{[M]} \right\rangle, Z_{\text{backup}} = \{Z_{t-k-1}, Z_{t-k}, \ldots, Z_t\},$ $V_{\text{backup}} = \{V_{t-k-1}, V_{t-k}, \ldots, V_t\}.$

(Continued)

Table 9.1 (*Continued*)   Algorithm: Particle-Filter-Based Localization

3	if $VI=0$ do
4	for $m=1$ to M do
5	$\chi_t^{[m]} = \begin{bmatrix} x_t^{[m]} \\ y_t^{[m]} \\ z_t^{[m]} \end{bmatrix} = \begin{bmatrix} x_{t-1}^{[m]} + \cos\theta_{t-1} \cdot \cos\alpha_{t-1} \cdot v_{t-1} \cdot T \\ y_{t-1}^{[m]} + \sin\theta_{t-1} \cdot \cos\alpha_{t-1} \cdot v_{t-1} \cdot T \\ z_{t-1}^{[m]} + \sin\alpha_{t-1} \cdot v_{t-1} \cdot T \end{bmatrix}$ //sample new pose
6	$\hat{Z}_t^{[m]} = \begin{bmatrix} \hat{\theta}_t^{[m]} \\ \hat{\alpha}_t^{[m]} \\ \hat{d}_t^{[m]} \\ \hat{V}_t^{[m]} \end{bmatrix} = \begin{bmatrix} RTI_\theta(x_t^{[m]}, y_t^{[m]}, z_t^{[m]}) \\ RTI_\alpha(x_t^{[m]}, y_t^{[m]}, z_t^{[m]}) \\ dist[p(x,y,z), p(x_t^{[m]}, y_t^{[m]}, z_t^{[m]})] \\ 0 \end{bmatrix}$ //measurement prediction
7	$Z_t - \hat{Z}_t^{[m]} = \begin{bmatrix} \theta_t - \hat{\theta}_t^{[m]} \\ \alpha_t - \hat{\alpha}_t^{[m]} \\ d_t - \hat{d}_t^{[m]} \\ V_t - \hat{V}_t^{[m]} \end{bmatrix}$
8	$w_t^{[m]} = \left| 2\pi Q_t \right|^{-\frac{1}{2}} \exp\left\{ -\frac{1}{2} \left(Z_t - \hat{Z}_t^{[m]} \right)^T \right\} Q_t^{-1} \left(\left(Z_t - \hat{Z}_t^{[m]} \right) \right)$, //weight calculation
9	add $\chi_t^{[m]}$ and $w_t^{[m]}$ to $\bar{X}_t$
10	Endfor
11	if $\sum w_i > K$, for $m=1$ to M do
12	draw i with probability $\propto w_t^{[i]}$
13	add $\chi_t^{[i]}$ to X_t
14	Endfor
15	Else
16	replace particles with more reliable ones //sensor resetting
17	Endif
18	return $X_t = \left\langle \chi_t^{[1]}, \chi_t^{[2]}, \ldots, \chi_t^{[M]} \right\rangle$
19	if $VI=1$ do
20	network delay compensation
21	Endif

moves along a very long straight and flat road without identifiable visual features for the vision-based supplement, the distribution of the particle sets might be deviated from the real position. Such situations are similar to the robot kidnapping problem and could make the implementation of the particle filter fail [200]. Hence, in order to adapt to the preceding situations, additional hypotheses generated from sensing are inserted for sensor-based resampling to the particle-filter localization when wrong estimations are detected [201]. This process is called *sensor resetting* (Line 16 in Table 9.1). If the sum of the particle weight, $\sum w_i$, is above a threshold K, all the samples are kept. Otherwise, a wrong estimation detection is assumed, and the sensor-based resampling will start. By matching the sensor measurement with the RTI model in a certain range, a best-matching position can be found. Then, a fixed number of samples will be added after resampling.

9.3.2.2 The Network Delay Compensation

The assumption in this chapter is that the cloud and the robot are able to connect with each other through a wireless network. The cloud server creates a listener socket that is waiting for connections from remote clients. The client issues the connect() socket function to start the TCP handshake. This socket contains many client parameters such as IP address, the port number, and so on. If these parameters are the same as those in the listener socket, then the cloud server issues an accept() socket function to accept the connection request. Thus, the communication between the cloud and the robot can be established. In this chapter, network delays caused by data exchange could affect the real-time performance of the robot localization procedure, even though data processing in the cloud is much less time-consuming and would not generate any apparent delay. Moreover, network delay would be larger as exchanging data between the cloud and the robot increase in size.

In the architecture presented in Section 9.2, two types of data are exchanged between the cloud and the robot, i.e., the local RTI model, and the images in the vision-based supplement part. The network delay caused by the local RTI model is always negligible for robot localization because most data and algorithms are designed to be relocated into the cloud, and data exchange between the cloud and the robot has been minimized to reduce time delay within a range of negligibility. On the other hand, network delay in the vision-based supplement part has a significant effect on the localization because real-time image transmission from the robot to the cloud would result in non-negligible network delay. Hence, a network delay compensation algorithm is used when *VI* is equal to 1 (Lines 19–20, Table 9.1). The detailed algorithm is summarized in Table 9.2.

Assume that the robot receives the recognized location result from the cloud at the current time t. Then it is inferred that this recognized location is associated with the image taken from the on-board camera of the robot at the time $t-k$. The main idea of the compensation is to take advantage of the backup sensor data

Table 9.2 Algorithm: Network Delay Compensation

1	$(X_{t-k-1}, Z_{backup}, V_{backup})$
2	for $i=t-k$ to t do //state re-update during network delay intervals
3	for $m=1$ to M do
4	$\chi_i^{[m]} = \begin{bmatrix} x_i^{[m]} \\ y_i^{[m]} \\ z_i^{[m]} \end{bmatrix} = \begin{bmatrix} x_{i-1}^{[m]} + \cos\theta_{i-1} \cdot \cos\alpha_{i-1} \cdot v_{i-1} \cdot T \\ y_{i-1}^{[m]} + \sin\theta_{i-1} \cdot \cos\alpha_{i-1} \cdot v_{i-1} \cdot T \\ z_{i-1}^{[m]} + \sin\alpha_{i-1} \cdot v_{i-1} \cdot T \end{bmatrix}$
5	$\hat{Z}_i^{[m]} = \begin{bmatrix} \hat{\theta}_i^{[m]} \\ \hat{\alpha}_i^{[m]} \\ \hat{d}_i^{[m]} \\ \hat{V}_i^{[m]} \end{bmatrix} = \begin{bmatrix} RTI_\theta(x_i^{[m]}, y_i^{[m]}, z_i^{[m]}) \\ RTI_\alpha(x_i^{[m]}, y_i^{[m]}, z_i^{[m]}) \\ dist[p(x,y,z), p(x_i^{[m]}, y_i^{[m]}, z_i^{[m]})] \\ IL[p(x_i^{[m]}, y_i^{[m]}, z_i^{[m]})] \end{bmatrix}$
6	$Z_i - \hat{Z}_i^{[m]} = \begin{bmatrix} \theta_i - \hat{\theta}_i^{[m]} \\ \alpha_i - \hat{\alpha}_i^{[m]} \\ d_i - \hat{d}_i^{[m]} \\ V_i - \hat{V}_i^{[m]} \end{bmatrix}$
7	$w_i^{[m]} = \left|2\pi Q_i\right|^{-\frac{1}{2}} \exp\left\{-\frac{1}{2}\left(Z_i - \hat{Z}_i^{[m]}\right)^T\right\} Q_i^{-1}\left(\left(Z_i - \hat{Z}_i^{[m]}\right)\right)$
8	add $\chi_i^{[m]}$ and $w_i^{[m]}$ to $\bar{X}_i$
9	Endfor
10	for $m=1$ to M do
11	draw j with probability $\propto w_i^{[j]}$
12	add $\chi_i^{[j]}$ to X_i
13	Endfor
14	Endfor
15	return $X_t = \left\langle \chi_t^{[1]}, \chi_t^{[2]}, ..., \chi_t^{[M]} \right\rangle$

during the delay time (the interval between the instant of taking the image and the moment of receiving the feedback from the cloud) to re-update the system state. When the robot receives the recognized location feedback from the cloud, another particle filter is used to fuse the feedback and the backup sensor data to re-update the estimated position of the robot, Table 9.2. The algorithm is similar to the one depicted in Table 9.1. The main difference is the introduction of a measurement function $IL[p(x_i^{[m]}, y_i^{[m]}, z_i^{[m]})]$ for the vision-based supplement (Line 5, Table 9.2), which is the transformation function from the ENU Cartesian coordinates to the geodetic coordinates. The conversion can be done by the following two steps: (1) convert the local ENU coordinate to the Earth-Centered Earth-Fixed (ECEF) coordinate as

$$
\begin{bmatrix} X_i^{[m]} \\ Y_i^{[m]} \\ Z_i^{[m]} \end{bmatrix} = \begin{bmatrix} -\sin \lambda_r & -\sin \varphi_r \cos \lambda_r & \cos \varphi_r \cos \lambda_r \\ \cos \lambda_r & -\sin \varphi_r \sin \lambda_r & \cos \varphi_r \sin \lambda_r \\ 0 & \cos \varphi_r \sin \lambda_r & \sin \varphi_r \end{bmatrix} \begin{bmatrix} x_i^{[m]} \\ y_i^{[m]} \\ z_i^{[m]} \end{bmatrix} + \begin{bmatrix} X_r \\ Y_r \\ Z_r \end{bmatrix}
$$

$$(9.1)$$

where (X_r, Y_r, Z_r) represents the initial coordinate of the robot in the ECEF coordinate; λ_r and φ_r represent the longitude and latitude respectively. $(X_i^{[m]}, Y_i^{[m]}, Z_i^{[m]})$ represents the position of the particle m in the ECEF coordinates at the time i, (2) Convert the ECEF coordinate to the geodetic coordinate as

$$\lambda_i^{[m]} = \arctan(Y_i^{[m]} / X_i^{[m]})$$

$$(9.2)$$

$$\varphi_i^{[m]} = \arctan \left\{ \frac{Z_i^{[m]} + be' \sin^3 U}{\sqrt{(X_i^{[m]})^2 + (Y_i^{[m]})^2} - ae^2 \cos^3 U} \right\}$$

$$(9.3)$$

$$h_i^{[m]} = Z_i^{[m]} / \sin \varphi_i^{[m]} - N(\varphi_i^{[m]})(1 - e^2)$$

$$(9.4)$$

where $N(\varphi_i^{[m]}) = a / \sqrt{1 - e^2 \sin^2 \varphi_i^{[m]}}$, $U = \arctan(Z_i^{[m]} a / \sqrt{(X_i^{[m]})^2 + (Y_i^{[m]})^2} b)$, $b = \sqrt{(1 - e^2)a^2}$. The parameter a represents the semi-major axis of the ellipsoid, whereas e and e' are the first and second numerical eccentricity of the ellipsoid, respectively [34]. Time consumption of this compensation algorithm is relatively negligible compared with network delay because all sensor data in the previous few sampling intervals has been added to the backup space automatically. Therefore, the side effect of network delay is efficiently eliminated while the network delay compensation will not introduce additional delay.

9.4 Experiments and Discussions

9.4.1 Methods and Procedures

The experiments were conducted on a Summit XL outdoor mobile robot with a smartphone-level onboard processor. The cloud service was run on a desktop PC

(Intel Xeon CPU X5650 at 2.67 GHz, 4GB RAM) offered by the National Super Computer Center in Shenzhen. The network chosen was China Telecom's TD-LTE and FDD-LTE network, where the theoretical uplink (from the subscriber to the Internet) peak rate was 50 Mbps and the downlink (from the Internet to the subscriber) peak rate was 100 Mbps. The NAV440 from Crossbow Technology was used as the IMU that was mounted on the top surface of the robot in order to measure roll, pitch, and yaw angles. The measurement accuracy was $0.5°$ in the roll and pitch directions and $1°$ in the yaw direction. The linear velocity of the robot was provided by the encoder. A standard camera was also mounted on the top of the robot with an output of 640×480 images at 30 fps. Moreover, a standard commercial GPS module was integrated onboard to provide only an initial estimated position for the robot. (Note that this is not a must in the proposed approach, and an alternative method could be considered as long as the initial position is available for the robot.) The sampling period for all experiments was 0.1 s. In all experiments, the robot moved at a speed of less than 3 m/s and sent a request for a local map with a radius of 200 m when it traveled up to 100 m. Three outdoor scenarios were selected near the Shenzhen University Town for experimental validation. All the experiments were run in real-time using the wireless network. Two localization methods were used to do comparison with the discussed method such as the GPS-only method and a traditional particle-filter-based method incorporating GPS and inertial sensors without using a cloud service (refer to "Particle filter with GPS/INS" throughout this whole section).

Scenario #1: An outdoor environment with an area of $400 \text{ m} \times 200 \text{ m}$ was used for performance evaluation, as Figure 9.4a shows ($R1 \rightarrow R2 \rightarrow R3 \rightarrow R4$). The performance of localization is first tested in this scenario. The initial position error could be more than 10 m with the GPS. Thus, a series of experiments were conducted with different initial errors from 5 to 20 m to evaluate the robustness of the proposed method in terms of different initial position errors. A few artificial markers with the same interval (20 m) were labeled along the road. Then, the positions of those markers were calculated individually from the road network map as references. Moreover, network disconnections between the robot and the cloud were occasionally observed. The system performance under this situation was evaluated in this scenario as well.

Scenario #2: The experimental area spans approximately $700 \text{ m} \times 500 \text{ m}$, as Figure 9.4b shows. The robot traversed 1.8 km from the points P1 to P8 covering several different types of roads such as minor arterial, service ways and urban canyons. The experiments conducted in Scenario 2 were used to demonstrate that the cloud-based technique is applicable to trips with complex road types.

Scenario #3: The third experimental area was about $2500 \text{ m} \times 6700 \text{ m}$. The robot traversed more than 13 km on nearly all kinds of road types, including urban expressway, primary arterial, minor arterial, service way, urban canyons, tunnels. This experiment was used to demonstrate the performance of the cloud-based architecture on more general large-scale outdoor environments.

Figure 9.4 Pictures of experimental areas, (a) Scenario #1 and (b) Scenario #2.

9.4.2 Results and Discussion

Scenario #1: The road networks of the selected area were extracted from Google Earth and sent to the cloud server before the localization task started. Comparing with the road network database saved previously (Figure 9.5a), it was found that Roads #1 and #2 on the current road networks were new (Figure 9.5b). Therefore, the latest road network information was updated in the cloud.

When the robot started to move on the road, the initial GPS position estimation $E1$ was transmitted to the cloud. The roads within an area of radius δ centered at point $E1$ were obtained, as Figure 9.5b shows. The initial position estimation may not be on the road due to the drift of GPS. In such cases, the nearest road point from $E1$ was chosen as the starting point of the RTI model. Then, a local RTI model starting from this road point along the pre-planned path was computed in the cloud and sent back to the mobile robot. Finally, localization can be achieved on the robot by applying the particle filter algorithm in Section 9.3.2.2

(a)

(b)

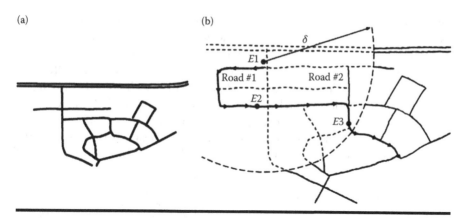

Figure 9.5 Road networks of navigation area, (a) previously existing road network and (b) updated road network (the road with arrows represents the planned robot path).

(Tables 9.1 and 9.2). When the robot travelled on road segments with a constant distance (200 m), the estimated robot position at the end of each segment (*E2* and *E3* in Figure 9.5b) was sent to the cloud again, and the above procedures repeated continuously. Twenty five discrete reference positions were used in this scenario.

Figure 9.6 shows the position estimation errors with different initial errors that were used to simulate different resolutions of GPS. The position estimation error *Δd* was defined as the 3D Euclidean distance between the estimated position and the reference position. Figure 9.6a and b show the localization performance without and with using sensor resetting, respectively. For the case of without sensor resetting, it can be seen that the performance was acceptable only when the initial error provided by GPS was less than 5 m, but the error diverged away when the initial errors were

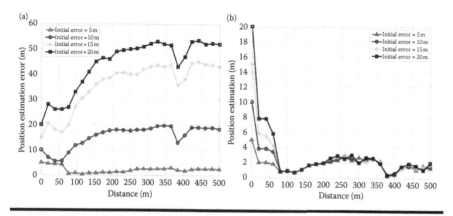

Figure 9.6 Position estimation errors with different initial errors, (a) without sensor resetting and (b) with sensor resetting.

larger than 5 m. Conversely, with sensor resetting in our algorithm, the position-estimation error was reduced quickly even with an initial error of 20 m. Hence, the cloud-based method presented in this chapter is robust to large initial position errors.

Figure 9.7 depicts the position estimation of the robot using CLAOR (solid line) compared with GPS-only (dots), and particle filter with GPS/INS (triangles) and the reference positions (circles). Position estimation by CLAOR is much closer to the references. Area #1 (reference points $R1{\rightarrow}R2$) and Area #2 ($R3{\rightarrow}R4$) were surrounded by tall buildings and the resolution of GPS signals was instable. The same phenomena were also observed in Figure 9.8, which shows a comparison of

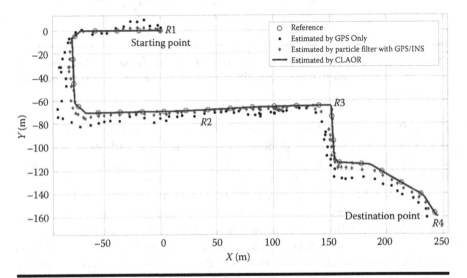

Figure 9.7 Comparison of position estimation (Scenario #1).

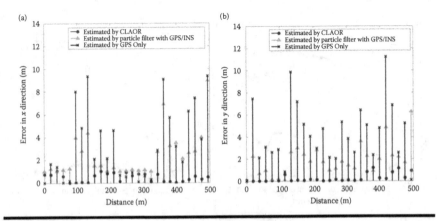

Figure 9.8 Comparison of position estimation errors in Cartesian coordinates (Scenario #1), (a) x direction and (b) y direction.

the position-estimation errors using CLAOR and the counterparts in the Cartesian coordinates. The estimation error at the travelling distance of 360 m was up to (9, 6 m) and (6, 2.3 m) using GPS only and particle filter with GPS/INS, respectively, because GPS was partially blocked around this area. It was already somewhere off-road. In contrast, the estimation error using CLAOR was only (0.2, 0.3 m), which was consistent with the real situation.

The influence of network connection loss was also evaluated in Scenario #1. The robot will invoke a request for new local road information to the cloud only when the robot travels out of a constant circular area, i.e., a radius of 200 m. Thus, if the robot is moving within such area, the disconnection of the network would not greatly influence the localization performance because terrain-based localization algorithms still work without the vision-based supplement. When the robot moves out of the area, dead reckoning is used to estimate the position with the IMU and encoder module on the robot. Because of vibrations and sensor drift, the position-estimation error of dead reckoning increases with time (Figure 9.9). Once the robot reconnects to the cloud, the robot sends the previous estimated position to the cloud. Then the cloud responds to the robot with the nearby road network information. The position-estimation error caused by network disconnection could be treated as the initial error. According to the previous analysis, our presented algorithm is robust to large initial errors. Hence, a short period of network loss would not affect the performance of the whole system.

Scenario 2: Figure 9.10 shows the comparison of position estimation with CLAOR (solid line), GPS-only (dotted line), and particle filter with GPS/INS (solid line) in a larger outdoor environment (Scenario #2). The robot traversed on several types of roads where the GPS signals were not always good. It can be seen that

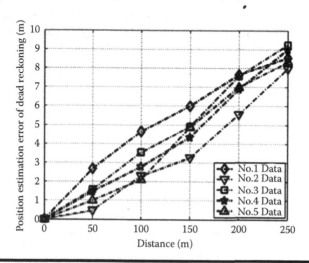

Figure 9.9 Position estimation errors of dead reckoning with network disconnection (the five lines represent five different records).

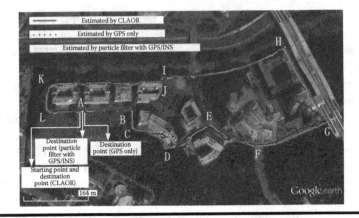

Figure 9.10 Comparison of position estimation in a large outdoor environment (Scenario #2).

when the robot traversed on service ways (C to D, 100 m) and urban canyons (G to H, 230 m), localization results deviated far away from the references on the road because the GPS signal was seriously blocked by the tall buildings. The position-estimation error by GPS in these two road segments was more than 30 m while the maximum position error using CLAOR was about 2 m. It is also observed that the destination point estimated by CLAOR was very close (0.5 m) to the expected location, while the estimation by GPS-only and particle filter with GPS/INS was about 8 and 4 m away from the real destination, respectively.

It was found that when the robot moves along a relatively long, straight, and flat service way that has few terrain variations, the particles may tend to scatter away because of accumulated localization error. This resulted in the estimated position falling behind the real position. However, this phenomenon could be eliminated efficiently with the vision-based supplement (Figure 9.11). According

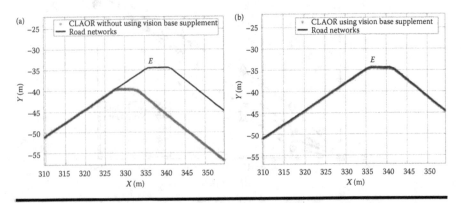

Figure 9.11 Position estimation, (a) without vision-based supplement in turning point *E* in Figure 9.11 and (b) with vision-based supplement.

to Figure 9.11b, the estimation errors around the turning point E were efficiently decreased with the combination of vision-aided supplement in CLAOR compared with Figure 9.11a.

Image-matching performance is evaluated in this scenario as well. For a typical outdoor environment, illumination/shadow conditions varied randomly due to different weathers. For instance, the left image in Figure 9.12a is the reference image taken in a cloudy day, whereas the right image was taken by the robot in a sunny day. Figure 9.12b shows the matching result of two images where the small circles in different colors are the feature points and the lines connect the matched feature points. According to Figure 9.12b, the matching result is closely related to the building part where most of the reliable matches generated. The illumination changes caused by different weather have a relatively small impact on the variation of the gradient of the buildings in the image. Therefore, the SURF-based matching was not influenced under most conditions except when special colorful lights shine in some particular angle to the building, causing obvious variations of the gradients

(a)

(b)

Figure 9.12 **Image matching with changing illumination conditions, (a) reference image taken in a cloudy day (left) and image taken by the robot in a sunny day (right) and (b) matching result.**

between two images. Figure 9.13 shows a case of the reference image (Figure 9.13a, left) with a stage on the ground and other decorations on the building while the stage and decorations have been removed in the image taken by the robot (Figure 9.13a, right) in real time. Figure 9.13b shows the matching result. Since the main features of the building where most reliable matches generated are not changed between the two images, this kind of change did not influence the matching result, according to Figure 9.13b. However, in some uncommon situations when objects (a car parked at roadside or people around) block the main features in the image, the matching process would fail. Nevertheless, if the matching fails, then the current reference image will be abandoned, and the result will not be sent back to the robot. A small number of failures would not produce any side effects to localization performance.

The camera mounting position and elevation angle on the robot were not strictly constrained except that it should point to the lateral side of the road in our experiments. Figure 9.14 shows the images taken with different mounting positions and elevation angles. Figure 9.14a is the reference image. Figure 9.14b and c are taken at a height of 0.5 m with different elevation angles. Figure 9.14d and e are taken at a height of 1.2 m with different elevation angles. All four images could match the

Figure 9.13 Image matching with changing objects in the images, (a) reference image (left) and image taken by the robot (right) and (b) matching result.

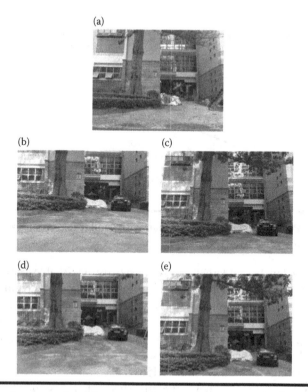

Figure 9.14 **An example of images where (a) is the reference image, and (b–e) were taken with different camera mounting positions and elevation angles.**

reference image successfully with our presented method because the main features of the building are not changed due to variations of the camera mounting position and elevation angles.

Although most wrong matches could be avoided due to the strict definition of a successful match, in some special situations, such as two exactly-the-same buildings or objects at different places, wrong matches might still happen. Under these circumstances, the framework we presented here has additional strategies to handle the problem. First, only the images within the area of the local road network are searched in the reference image database and matched with the real-time image. Second, if there is a candidate match nearby, the backup IMU and encoder data would help recall the location of robot where it took that image and compare it to the location tagged with the reference image. If two locations are much different, a wrong match is detected and the result of the wrong match will not be sent back to the robot. The matching process will restart without any influence on the localization process.

On the other hand, when the robot is moving in an environment with extremely similar texture, e.g., a road with only trees and other plants by the side, the image

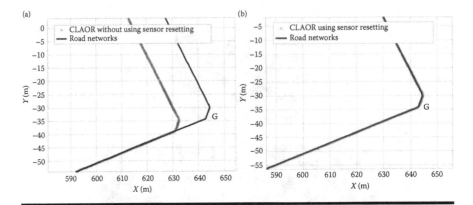

Figure 9.15 **Position estimation on a road with similar texture, (a) without sensor setting and (b) with sensor setting.**

matching may fail because there are too few distinguishable features. In such scenarios, sensor resetting could be used to solve the problem. Figure 9.15 shows comparison of the localization results with and without sensor resetting when the robot arrived close to the road turning point G in Figure 9.11. Note that the error becomes huge when the robot approaches the turning point because of the image-matching failure. However, with the sensor-resetting technique, the error could be recovered from failure quickly, Figure 9.15b.

Scenario 3: Figure 9.16 shows the estimated robot positions by CLAOR in a more general large-scale outdoor environment. The whole distance of this scenario is 13.1 km and covers several areas where GPS signals are severely blocked. In Figure 9.16, the road segment S1 is a long corridor covered by the library with a 230 m length that can be treated as an urban canyon because the GPS has deviated far away from the reference on the road. Another two road segments, S2 and S3, are long tunnels with 250 and 450 m length where GPS signals are completely blocked. S4 and S5 are service ways where the GPS signal is blocked severely by the trees beside the road. Figure 9.17 shows the estimated position of three segments S1, S3, and S4 where triangle marks represent the estimated position by GPS-only, asterisks represent the estimated position by particle filter with GPS/INS, the squares represent the estimated position by CLAOR, and points represent the reference points. The reference points are the road network points extracted in the offline phase. The mobile robot took 3 h and 8 min to finish the whole trip with an average speed of 1.21 m/s. And no crash of the system happened. The position-estimation errors for the whole journey are shown in Figure 9.18. The error is defined as the Euclidean distance between the estimated point and the reference road network point extracted in the offline phase. The accuracies of those reference points depend on the GIS system and the error for the reference point was always less than 1 m in our experiments. It is concluded according to Figure 9.18 that the system performance was pretty stable within reasonable estimation errors even in a large-scale

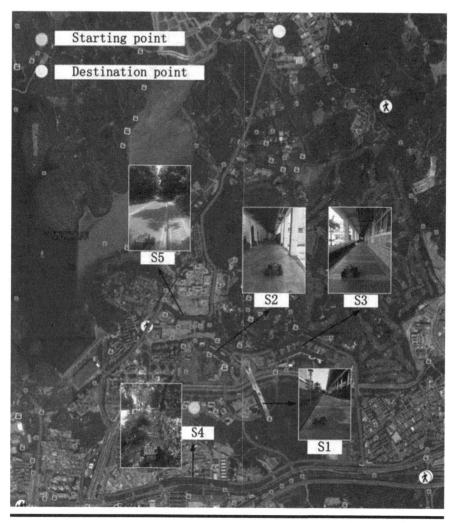

Figure 9.16   Position estimation in a large-scale outdoor environment.

complex outdoor environment. It is worth noticing that the radius change of the earth would affect localization error when the robot moves in the longitudinal direction over quite a long distance (over 10 or 100 km) because the Cartesian coordinates are used for localization here. In such circumstances, a second initial position would be set to the current location once the robot moves over 10 km longitudinally.

Experimental evaluations in this scenario can also illustrate the real-time properties of the cloud framework we present in this chapter as compared with the traditional method of running all algorithms onboard. According to the area of this scenario (about 2500 m × 6700 m), 1 GB storage space is needed for the road

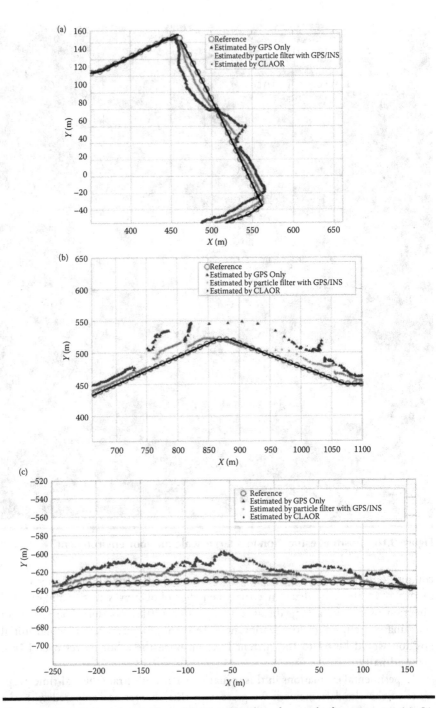

Figure 9.17 Comparison of position estimation for typical segments, (a) S1, (b) S3, and (c) S4.

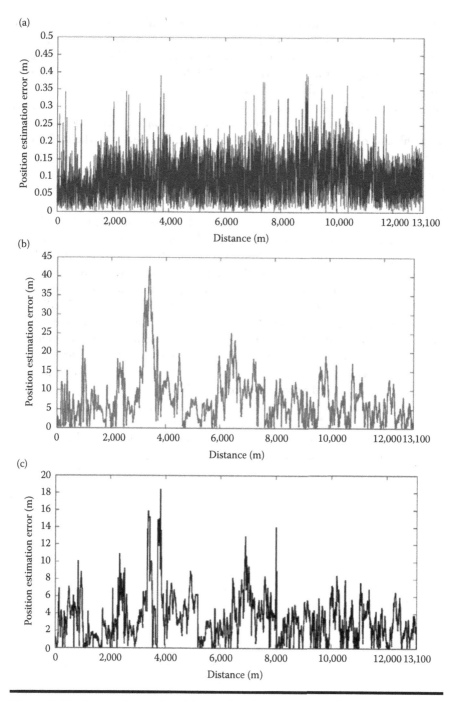

Figure 9.18 Comparison of position estimation errors, (a) the CLAOR, (b) GPS only, and (c) particle filter with GPS/INS.

network with 1.087 million records and another 4 GB for the reference image database. The computation load could be divided into two main parts such as the RTI model part and the vision-based supplement part. The RTI model part consists of searching for the local road network information and the calculation of the RTI model. It took about 1 ms to search for local road network information on the cloud server (with MySQL), whereas it would take the smartphone-level onboard processor (with SQLite) more than 11 s to complete searching if it is running onboard rather than on the cloud server. The calculation of the RTI model on the cloud service took less than 20 ms, whereas it would take about 3.5 s for the onboard processor. Similarly, image matching in the vision-based supplement part consumed less than 450 ms and no more than 1.5 s with network delay in our cloud-based framework. But it would take about 6 s for the low-cost smartphone-level onboard processor. Apparently, in order to meet the requirements for real-time performance, traditional frameworks need onboard processors to be much more demanding and expensive as travelling areas become larger and larger. Instead, the cloud-based framework presented in this chapter has more potential to handle even larger areas (e.g., a city) without greatly leveraging requirement of the robots.

In summary, this chapter introduced a cloud-based outsourcing localization architecture for a mobile robot in a large-scale outdoor environment. It takes advantage of existing outsourced road network maps and reference images without relying on GPS. Computational and memory loads are mostly distributed on the cloud and network delay is compensated. This cloud-based framework makes it possible to achieve accurate localization performance without leveraging requirements of the robot platform as the environment becomes larger and larger. Comprehensive experiments were conducted to evaluate how different factors affect the performance of this method. Experimental results show that the cloud-based architecture can be applied to more complex large-scale circumstances.

References

1. George A. Bekey, *Autonomous Robots: From Biological Inspiration to Implementation and Control*, MIT Press, Cambridge, MA, 2005.
2. Richard Welch, Daniel Limonadi, and Robert Manning, Systems engineering the Curiosity rover: A retrospective, in *International Conference on System of Systems Engineering*, Maui, HI, June 2–6, 2013, pp. 70–75.
3. Thomas Hellström, Autonomous navigation for forest machines, A project pre-study in the Department of Computer Science, Umea University, Umeå, Sweden, 2002.
4. Kerry Hill, How are we going to log all our steeper slopes?—The "Kelly" harvesting machine, *New Zealand Journal of Forestry*, vol. 55, p. 3, 2010.
5. David Wooden, Matthew Malchano, Kevin Blankespoor, Andrew Howardy, Alfred A. Rizzi, and Marc Raibert, Autonomous navigation for BigDog, in *Proceedings of 2010 IEEE International Conference on Robotics and Automation*, Anchorage, AK, May 3–7, 2010, pp. 4736–4741.
6. Evan Ackerman, BigDog throws cinder blocks with huge robotic face-arm, IEEE Spectrum, New York, March 1, 2013.
7. Jueyao Wang, Xiaorui Zhu, Fude Tie, Tao Zhao, and Xu Xu, Design of a modular robotic system for archaeological exploration, in *Proceedings of 2009 IEEE International Conference on Robotics and Automation*, Kobe, Japan, May 12–17, 2009, pp. 1435–1440.
8. Jennifer Casper and Robin Roberson Murphy, Human-robot interactions during the robot-assisted urban search and rescue response at the World Trade Center, *IEEE Transactions on Systems Man and Cybernetics Part B Cybernetics A Publication of the IEEE Systems Man and Cybernetics Society*, vol. 33, pp. 367–385, 2003.
9. Hitoshi Kimura, Keisuke Shimizu, and Shigeo Hirose, Development of Genbu: Active-wheel passive-joint snake-like mobile robot, *Journal of Robotics and Mechatronics*, vol. 16, pp. 293–303, 2004.
10. http://tdworld.com/transmission/drones-power-line-inspections#slide-2-field_images-61661.
11. Fucheng Deng, Xiaorui Zhu, Xiaochun Li, and Meng Li, 3D digitisation of large-scale unstructured great wall heritage sites by a small unmanned helicopter, *Remote Sensing*, vol. 9, p. 423, 2017.
12. Chris Urmson, Joshua Anhalt, Drew Bagnell, Christopher Baker, Robert Bittner, M. N. Clark et al., Autonomous driving in urban environments: Boss and the urban challenge, *Journal of Field Robotics*, vol. 25, pp. 425–466, 2009.

13. Massimo Bertozzi, Alberto Broggi, Alessandro Coati, and Rean Isabella Fedriga, A 13,000 km intercontinental trip with driverless vehicles: The VIAC experiment, *IEEE Intelligent Transportation Systems Magazine*, vol. 5, pp. 28–41, 2013.

14. https://en.wikipedia.org/wiki/Waymo#/media/File:Google%27s_Lexus_RX_450h_Self-Driving_Car.jpg.

15. https://www.clearpathrobotics.com/husky-unmanned-ground-vehicle-robot/.

16. http://www.mobilerobots.com/ResearchRobots/P3AT.aspx.

17. http://www.robotnik.eu/mobile-robots/summit-xl-steel/.

18. Roland Siegwart, Illah R. Nourbakhsh, and Davide Scaramuzza, *Introduction to Autonomous Mobile Robots*, 2nd edition, MIT Press, Cambridge, MA, vol. 2, pp. 645–649, 2011.

19. Mieczyslaw G. Bekker, Vehicle with flexible frame, United States Patent 3,235,020, 1962.

20. Paul L. Spanski, Flexible frame vehicle, United States Patent 3,550,710, 1970.

21. Johann Borenstein, Control and kinematic design of multi-degree-of-freedom mobile robots with compliant linkage, *IEEE Transactions on Robotics and Automation*, vol. 11, pp. 21–35, 1995.

22. A. Kemurdjian, V. Gromov, V. Mishkinyuk, V. Kucherenko, and P. Sologub, Small Marsokhod configuration, in *Proceedings of 1992 IEEE International Conference on Robotics and Automation*, Nice, France, May 12–14, 1992, pp. 165–168.

23. Kenneth J. Waldron and Christopher J. Hubert, Control of contact forces in wheeled and legged off-road vehicles, in *Proceedings of Sixth International Symposium on Experimental Robotics*, Sydney, NSW, March 26–28, 1999, pp. 205–14.

24. Shigeo Hirose, Biologically inspired robots: Snake-like locomotors and manipulators, *Applied Mechanics Reviews*, vol. 48, p. B27, 1995.

25. Mark Yim, Kimon Roufas, David Duff, and Ying Zhang, Modular reconfigurable robots in space applications, *Autonomous Robots*, vol. 14, pp. 225–237, 2003.

26. Andres Castano and Peter Will, Representing and discovering the configuration of Conro robots, in *Proceedings of 2001 IEEE International Conference on Robotics and Automation*, vol. 4, Seoul, South Korea, May 21–26, 2001, pp. 3503–3509.

27. Makoto Mori and Shigeo Hirose, Three-dimensional serpentine motion and lateral rolling by active cord mechanism ACM-R3, in *Proceedings of 2002 IEEE/RSJ International Conference on Intelligent Robots and Systems*, Lausanne, Switzerland, September 30–October 4, 2002, pp. 829–834.

28. Tetsushi Kamegawa, Tatsuhiro Yamasaki, Hiroki Igarashi, and Fumitoshi Matsuno, Development of the snake-like rescue robot KOHGA, in *Proceedings of 2004 IEEE International Conference on Robotics and Automation*, New Orleans, LA, April 26–May 1, 2004, pp. 5081–5086.

29. Bernhard Klaassen and Karl L. Paap, GMD-SNAKE2: A snake-like robot driven by wheels and a method for motion control, in *Proceedings of 1999 IEEE International Conference on Robotics and Automation*, Detroit, MI, May 10–15, 1999, vol. 4, pp. 3014–3019.

30. Keith D. Kotay and Daniela L. Rus, Task-reconfigurable robots: Navigators and manipulators, in *Proceedings of 1997 IEEE/RSJ International Conference on Intelligent Robots and Systems*, New York, 1997, pp. 1081–1089.

31. Shinichi Kimura, Shigeru Tsuchiya, Shinichiro Nishida, and Tomoki Takegai, A module type manipulator for remote inspection in space, in *Proceedings of 1999 IEEE*

International Conference on Systems, Man, and Cybernetics, Tokyo, Japan, October 12–15, 1999, pp. 819–824.

32. Yuri L. Sarkissyan, Armen G. Kharatyan, Karo M. Egishyan, and Tigran F. Parikyan, Synthesis of mechanisms with variable structure and geometry for reconfigurable manipulation systems, in *Proceedings of 2009 ASME/IFTOMM International Conference on Reconfigurable Mechanisms and Robots*, London, UK, June 22–24, 2009, pp. 195–199.

33. Matteo-Claudio Palpacelli, Luca Carbonari, Giacomo Palmieri, and Massimo Callegari, Analysis and design of a reconfigurable 3-DoF parallel manipulator for multimodal tasks, *IEEE/ASME Transactions on Mechatronics*, vol. 20, pp. 1975–1985, 2015.

34. Simon Kalouche, David Rollinson, and Howie Choset, Modularity for maximum mobility and manipulation: Control of a reconfigurable legged robot with series-elastic actuators, in *Proceedings of 2015 IEEE International Symposium on Safety, Security, and Rescue Robotics*, October 18–20, 2015, pp. 1–8.

35. Amit Pamecha and Gregory Chirikjian, A useful metric for modular robot motion planning, in *Proceedings of 1996 IEEE International Conference on Robotics Automation*, Minneapolis, MN, April 22–28, 1996, pp. 442–447.

36. Satoshi Murata, Haruhisa Kurokawa, and Shigeru Kokaji, Self-assembling machine, in *Proceedings of 1994 IEEE International Conference on Robotics and Automation*, San Diego, CA, May 8–13, 1994, pp. 441–448.

37. Keith D. Kotay and Daniela L. Rus, Algorithms for self-reconfiguring molecule motion planning, in *Proceedings of 2000 IEEE/RSJ International Conference on Intelligent Robots and Systems*, Takamatsu, Japan, October 31–November 5, 2000, pp. 2184–2193.

38. Luenin Barrios, Thomas Collins, Robert Kovac, and Wei-Min Shen, Autonomous 6D-docking and manipulation with non-stationary-base using self-reconfigurable modular robots, in *Proceedings of 2016 IEEE/RSJ International Conference on Intelligent Robots and Systems*, Daejeon, South Korea, October 9–14, 2016, pp. 2913–2919.

39. Wenqiang Wu, Yisheng Guan, Yufeng Yang, and Biyun Dong, Multi-objective configuration optimization of assembly-level reconfigurable modular robots, in *Proceedings of 2016 IEEE International Conference on Information and Automation*, Ningbo, China, August 1–3, 2016, pp. 528–533.

40. Jie Huang, Weimin Ge, Xiaofeng Wang, and Jun Liu, Structure design and dynamic modelling of a novel modular self-reconfigurable robot, in *Proceedings of 2016 IEEE International Conference on Mechatronics and Automation*, Harbin, China, August 7–10, 2016, pp. 2284–2289.

41. Robert O. Ambrose, Martin P. Aalund, and Delbert Tesar, Designing modular robots for a spectrum of space applications, in *Proceedings of the SPIE*, Boston, MA, November 16–18, 1992, vol. 1829, pp. 371–381.

42. Egor Paul Popov, *Mechanics of Materials*, 2nd edition, Prentice-Hall, Englewood Cliffs, NJ, 1976.

43. Javier Urruzola, Juan Tomas Celigueta, and Javier Garcia de Jalon, Generalization of foreshortening through new reduced geometrically nonlinear structural formulation, *Journal of Guidance, Control, and Dynamics*, vol. 23, pp. 673–682, 2000.

44. Sungyong Park and Mark A. Minor, Modelling and dynamic control of compliant framed wheeled modular mobile robots, in *Proceedings of 2004 IEEE International*

Conference on Robotics and Automation, New Orleans, LA, April 26–May 1, 2004, pp. 3937–3943.

45. Roger W. Brockett, Asymptotic stability and feedback stabilization, in R. W. Brockett, R. S. Millman, and H. J. Sussmann, editors, *Differential Geometric Control Theory*, vol. 27 of Progress in Mathematics, Birkhauser, Boston, MA, 1983, pp. 181–191.

46. Alessandro Astolfi, On the stabilization of nonholonomic systems, in *Proceedings of 1994 IEEE Conference on Decision and Control*, vol. 4, New York, 1994, pp. 3481–3486.

47. Brian W. Albiston and Mark A. Minor, Curvature based point stabilization for compliant framed wheeled modular mobile robots, in *Proceedings of 2003 IEEE International Conference on Robotics and Automation*, Taipei, Taiwan, 2003, pp. 81–89.

48. Brian W. Albiston, Curvature Based Point Stabilization and Path Following for Compliant Framed Wheeled Modular Mobile Robots, Masters Thesis, Mechanical Engineering, University of Utah, Salt Lake City, UT, 2003.

49. Egbert Bakker, Lars Nyborg, and Hans B. Pacejka, Tyre modelling for use in vehicle dynamics studies, in SAE Technical Paper Series, Paper No. 870421, ed SAE, Detroit, MI, 1987, p. 15.

50. Sally Shoop, B. Young, R. Alger, and Julian Davis, Winter traction testing, *Automotive Engineering (Warrendale, Pennsylvania)*, vol. 102, pp. 75–78, 1994.

51. Cynthia Rawlins Vechinski, Clarence E. Johnson, and Randy L. Raper, Evaluation of an empirical traction equation for forestry tires, *Journal of Terramechanics*, vol. 35, pp. 55–67, 1998.

52. Rafael Fierro and Frank. L. Lewis, Control of a nonholonomic mobile robot: Backstepping kinematics into dynamics, *Journal of Robotic Systems*, vol. 14, pp. 149–163, 1997.

53. Jung Min Yang and Jong Hwan Kim, Sliding mode motion control of nonholonomic mobile robots, *IEEE Control Systems*, vol. 19, pp. 15–23, 1999.

54. Chin Pei Tang, Rajankumar Bhatt, and Venkat Krovi, Decentralized kinematic control of payload by a system of mobile manipulators, in *Proceedings of 2004 IEEE International Conference on Robotics and Automation*, New Orleans, LA, April 26–May 1, 2004, pp. 2462–2467.

55. Yasuhisa Hirata, Youhei Kume, Takuro Sawada, Zhi-Dong Wang, and Kazuhiro Kosuge, Handling of an object by multiple mobile manipulators in coordination based on caster-like dynamics, in *Proceedings of 2004 IEEE International Conference on Robotics and Automation*, New Orleans, LA, April 26–May 1, 2004, pp. 807–812.

56. Alejandro Rodriguez-Angeles and Henk Nijmeijer, Mutual synchronization of robots via estimated state feedback: A cooperative approach, *IEEE Transactions on Control Systems Technology*, vol. 12, pp. 542–554, 2004.

57. Arthur G. O. Mutambara and Hugh F. Durrant-Whyte, Estimation and control for a modular wheeled mobile robot, *IEEE Transactions on Control Systems Technology*, vol. 8, pp. 35–46, 2000.

58. Herbert G. Tanner, Savvas G. Loizou, and Kostas J. Kyriakopoulos, Nonholonomic navigation and control of cooperating mobile manipulators, *IEEE Transactions on Robotics and Automation*, vol. 19, pp. 53–64, 2003.

59. Kazuhiro Kosuge and Manabu Sato, Transportation of a single object by multiple decentralized-controlled nonholonomic mobile robots, in *Proceedings of 1999 IEEE/RSJ International Conference on Intelligent Robots and Systems: Human and Environment Friendly Robots with High Intelligence and Emotional Quotients*, Gyeongju, South Korea, October 17–21, 1999, pp. 1681–1686.

60. Hitoshi Kimura, Shigeo Hirose, and Keisuke Shimizu, Stuck evasion control for active-wheel passive-joint snake-like mobile robot 'Genbu', in *Proceedings of 2004 IEEE International Conference on Robotics and Automation*, New Orleans, LA, April 26–May 1, 2004, pp. 5087–5092.

61. Todd D. Murphey and Joel W. Burdick, The power dissipation method and kinematic reducibility of multiple-model robotic systems, *IEEE Transactions on Robotics*, vol. 22, pp. 694–710, 2006.

62. Mark A. Minor, Brian Albiston, and Cory Schwensen, Simplified motion control of a two axle compliant framed wheeled mobile robot, *IEEE Transactions on Robotics*, vol. 22, pp. 491–506, 2006.

63. Youngshik Kim and Mark A. Minor, Decentralized kinematic motion control for multiple axle compliant framed modular wheeled mobile robots, in *Proceedings of 2006 IEEE/RSJ International Conference on Intelligent Robots and Systems*, Beijing, China, October 9–15, 2006, pp. 392–397.

64. Xiaorui Zhu, Youngshik Kim, and Mark A. Minor, Cooperative distributed robust control of modular mobile robots with bounded curvature and velocity, in *Proceedings of 2005 IEEE/ASME International Conference on Advanced Intelligent Mechatronics*, Monterey, CA, July 24–28, 2005, pp. 1151–1157.

65. Mark A. Minor and Roy Merrell, Instrumentation and algorithms for posture estimation in compliant framed modular mobile robots, *International Journal of Robotics Research*, vol. 26, pp. 491–512, 2007.

66. Xiaorui Zhu and Mark A. Minor, Distributed robust control of compliant framed wheeled modular mobile robots, *Journal of Dynamic Systems Measurement and Control*, vol. 128, pp. 489–498, 2006.

67. Xiaorui Zhu, Roy Merrell, and Mark A. Minor, Motion control and sensing strategy for a two-axle compliant framed wheeled modular mobile robot, in *Proceedings of 2006 IEEE International Conference on Robotics and Automation*, Orlando, FL, May 15–19, 2006, pp. 3526–3531.

68. Xiaorui Zhu, Youngshik Kim, R. Merrell, and M. A. Minor, Cooperative motion control and sensing architecture in compliant framed modular mobile robots, *IEEE Transactions on Robotics*, vol. 23, pp. 1095–1101, 2007.

69. Youngshik Kim and Mark A. Minor, Path manifold-based kinematic control of wheeled mobile robot considering physical constraints, *International Journal of Robotics Research*, vol. 26, pp. 955–975, 2007.

70. Giuseppe Oriolo, Alessandro De Luca, and Marilena Vendittelli, WMR control via dynamic feedback linearization: Design, implementation, and experimental validation, *IEEE Transactions on Control Systems Technology*, vol. 10, pp. 835–852, 2002.

71. Michele Aicardi, Giuseppe Casalino, Antonio Bicchi, and Aldo Balestrino, Closed loop steering of unicycle like vehicles via Lyapunov techniques, *IEEE Robotics and Automation Magazine*, vol. 2, pp. 27–35, 1995.

72. Youngshik Kim and Mark A. Minor, Bounded smooth time invariant motion control of unicycle kinematic models, in *Proceedings of IEEE International Conference on Robotics and Automation*, Barcelona, Spain, April 18–22, 2005, pp. 3687–3692.

73. Abdelhamid Tayebi and Ahmed Rachid, A unified discontinuous state feedback controller for the path-following and the point-stabilization problems of a unicycle-like mobile robot, in *Proceedings of International Conference on Control Applications*, New York, October 5–7, 1997, pp. 31–35.

74. Claude Samson, Time-varying feedback stabilization of car-like wheeled mobile robots, *International Journal of Robotics Research*, vol. 12, pp. 55–64, 1993.

75. Claude Samson, Control of chained systems application to path following and time-varying point-stabilization of mobile robots, *IEEE Transactions on Automatic Control*, vol. 40, pp. 64–77, 1995.

76. Abdelhamid Tayebi, Mohamed Tadjine, and Ahmed Rachid, Path-following and point-stabilization control laws for a wheeled mobile robot, in *Proceedings of UKACC International Conference on Control*, Exeter, UK, 2–5 September, 1996, pp. 878–883.

77. Jean-Michel Coron and Brigitte D'Andrea-Novel, Smooth stabilizing time-varying control laws for a class of nonlinear systems. Application to mobile robots, in *Proceedings of 1992 IFAC Symposium Nonlinear Control Systems Design*, Bordeaux, France, June 24–26, 1993, pp. 413–418.

78. Pascal Morin and Claude Samson, Control of nonlinear chained systems: From the Routh-Hurwitz stability criterion to time-varying exponential stabilizers, *IEEE Transactions on Automatic Control*, vol. 45, pp. 141–146, 2000.

79. Carlos Canudas De Wit and Ole Jakob Sørdalen, Exponential stabilization of mobile robots with nonholonomic constraints, *IEEE Transactions on Automatic Control*, vol. 37, pp. 1791–1797, 1992.

80. Essameddin Badreddin and M. Mansour, Fuzzy-tuned state-feedback control of a non-holonomic mobile robot, in *Proceedings of the 12th Triennial World Congress of IFAC*, Sydney, NSW, July 18–23, 1993, pp. 769–772.

81. Alessandro Astolfi, Exponential stabilization of a wheeled mobile robot via discontinuous control, *Transactions of the ASME: Journal of Dynamic Systems, Measurement and Control*, vol. 121, pp. 121–127, 1999.

82. Jurgen Sellen, Planning paths of minimal curvature, in *Proceedings of IEEE International Conference on Robotics and Automation*, Nagoya, Japan, May 21–27, 1995, pp. 1976–1982.

83. Andrei M. Shkel and Vladimir J. Lumelsky, Curvature-constrained motion within a limited workspace, in *Proceedings of IEEE International Conference on Robotics and Automation*, Albuquerque, NM, October 5–7, 1997, pp. 1394–1399.

84. Ti-Chung Lee, Kai-Tai Song, Ching-Hung Lee, and Ching-Cheng Teng, Tracking control of unicycle-modeled mobile robots using a saturation feedback controller, *IEEE Transactions on Control Systems Technology*, vol. 9, pp. 305–318, 2001.

85. Giovanni Indiveri, Kinematic time-invariant control of a 2D nonholonomic vehicle, in *Proceedings of IEEE International Conference on Decision and Control*, Phoenix, AZ, December 7–10, 1999, pp. 2112–2117.

86. Christfried Webers and Uwe R. Zimmer, Practical trade-offs in robust target following, in *Proceedings of International Congress on Intelligent Systems and Applications, International Symposium on Industrial Systems*, University of Wollongong, NSW, December 12–15, 2000.

87. Roland Siegwart and Illah R. Nourbakhsh, *Introduction to Autonomous Mobile Robots*, MIT Press, Cambridge, MA, 2004.

88. Gianluca Antonelli, Stefano Chiaverini, and Giuseppe Fusco, Real-time path tracking for unicycle-like mobile robots under velocity and acceleration constraints, in *Proceedings of American Control Conference*, Arlington, VA, June 25–27, 2001, pp. 119–124.

89. Dieter Foxt, Wolfram Burgardt, and Sebastian Thrunft, The dynamic window approach to collision avoidance, *IEEE Robotics and Automation Magazine*, vol. 4, pp. 23–33, 1997.

90. Oliver Brock and Oussama Khatib, High-speed navigation using the global dynamic window approach, in *Proceedings of IEEE International Conference on Robotics and Automation*, Detroit, MI, May 10–15, 1999, pp. 341–346.

91. Matthew Spenko, Yoji Kuroda, Steven Dubowsky, and Karl Iagnemma, Hazard avoidance for high-speed mobile robots in rough terrain, *Journal of Field Robotics*, vol. 23, pp. 311–331, 2006.

92. Dongkyoung Chwa, Sliding-mode tracking control of nonholonomic wheeled mobile robots in polar coordinates, *IEEE Transactions on Control Systems Technology*, vol. 12, pp. 637–644, 2004.

93. Jurgen Guldner and Vadim I. Utkin, Sliding mode control for an obstacle avoidance strategy based on an harmonic potential field, in *Proceedings of IEEE Conference on Decision and Control*, San Antonio, TX, December 15–17, 1993, pp. 424–429.

94. Andrea Bacciotti, *Local Stabilizability of Nonlinear Control Systems*, vol. 8, World Scientific, Singapore, 1991.

95. Tae Ho Jang and Youngshik Kim, Effects of the sampling time in motion controller implementation for mobile robots, *Journal of Korea Industrial and Systems Engineering*, vol. 37, pp. 154–161, 2014.

96. Tae Ho Jang, Youngshik Kim, and Hyeontae Kim, Comparison of PID controllers by using linear and nonlinear models for control of mobile robot driving system, *Journal of the Korean Society for Precision Engineering*, vol. 33, pp. 183–190, 2016.

97. Yoshihiko Nakamura, Hideaki Ezaki, Yuegang Tan, and Woojin Chung, Design of steering mechanism and control of nonholonomic trailer systems, *IEEE Transactions on Robotics and Automation*, vol. 17, pp. 367–374, 2001.

98. Stamatis Manesis, Gregory Davrazos, and Nick T. Koussoulas, Controller design for off-tracking elimination in multi-articulated vehicles, in *15th IFAC World Congress*, Barcelona, Spain, July 21–26, 2002, pp. 379–384.

99. Claudio Altafini, Path following with reduced off-tracking for multibody wheeled vehicles, *IEEE Transactions on Control Systems Technology*, vol. 11, pp. 598–605, 2003.

100. Jinyan Shao, Guangming Xie, Junzhi Yu, and Long Wang, Leader-following formation control of multiple mobile robots, in *2005 IEEE International Symposium on Intelligent Control and 13th Mediterranean Conference on Control and Automation*, Limassol, Cyprus, June 27–29, 2005, pp. 808–813.

101. Atsushi Fujimori, Takeshi Fujimoto, and Gabor Bohatcs, Distributed leader-follower navigation of mobile robots, in *International Conference on Control and Automation*, Budapest, Hungary, June 26–29, 2005, pp. 960–965.

102. Michel Abou-Samah, Chin Pei Tang, Rajankumar Bhatt, and Venkat Krovi, A kinematically compatible framework for cooperative payload transport by nonholonomic mobile manipulators, *Autonomous Robots*, vol. 21, pp. 227–242, 2006.

103. Thomas Sugar and Vijay Kumar, Decentralized control of cooperating mobile manipulators, in *Proceedings of 1998 IEEE International Conference on Robotics and Automation*, Leuven, Belgium, May 16–20, 1998, pp. 2916–2921.

104. Masafumi Hashimoto, Fuminori Oba, and Satoru Zenitani, Coordinative object-transportation by multiple industrial mobile robots using coupler with mechanical compliance, in *Proceedings of International Conference on Industrial Electronics, Control, and Instrumentation*, Maui, HI, November 15–19, 1993, pp. 1577–1582.

105. Johann Borenstein, The OmniMate: A guidewire- and beacon-free AGV for highly reconfigurable applications, *International Journal of Production Research*, vol. 38, pp. 1993–2010, 2000.

106. Hassan K. Khalil, *Nonlinear Systems*, 3rd edition, Prentice Hall, Upper Saddle River, NJ, 2002.

107. James Alexander Reeds III and Lawrence A. Shepp, Optimal paths for a car that goes both forwards and backwards, *Pacific Journal of Mathematics*, vol. 145, no. 2, pp. 367–393, 1990.

108. Johann Borenstein, Experimental results from internal odometry error correction with the OmniMate mobile robot, *IEEE Transactions on Robotics and Automation*, vol. 14, pp. 963–969, 1998.

109. Takashi Maeno, Shinichi Hiromitsu, and Takashi Kawai, Control of grasping force by detecting stick/slip distribution at the curved surface of an elastic finger, in *Proceedings of 2000 IEEE International Conference on Robotics and Automation*, San Francisco, CA, April 24–28, 2000, pp. 3895–3900.

110. Antonino S. Fiorillo, A piezoresistive tactile sensor, *IEEE Transactions on Instrumentation and Measurement*, vol. 46, pp. 15–17, 1997.

111. Kouji Murakami and Tsutomu Hasegawa, Novel fingertip equipped with soft skin and hard nail for dexterous multi-fingered robotic manipulation, in *Proceedings of 2003 IEEE International Conference on Robotics and Automation*, Taipei, Taiwan, September 14–19, 2003, pp. 708–713.

112. Akio Namiki, Yoshiro Imai, Masatoshi Ishikawa, and Makoto Kaneko, Development of a high-speed multifingered hand system and its application to catching, in *Proceedings of 2003 IEEE/RSJ International Conference on Intelligent Robots and Systems*, Las Vegas, NV, October 27–31, 2003, pp. 2666–2671.

113. Farshad Khorrami and Shihua Zheng, Vibration control of flexible-link manipulators, in *American Control Conference*, San Diego, CA, May 23–25, 1990, pp. 175–180.

114. J. Carusone, K. S. Buchan, and G. M. T. D'Eleuterio, Experiments in end-effector tracking control for structurally flexible space manipulators, *IEEE Transactions on Robotics and Automation*, vol. 9, pp. 553–560, 1993.

115. Jean-Claude Piedboeuf and Sharon J. Miller, Estimation of endpoint position and orientation of a flexible link using strain gauges, *IFAC Proceedings Volumes*, vol. 27, pp. 675–680, 1994.

116. Constantinos Mavroidis, P. Rowe, and Steven Dubowsky, Inferred end-point control of long reach manipulators, in *Proceedings of 1995 IEEE/RSJ International Conference on Intelligent Robots and Systems*, Pittsburgh, PA, August 5–9, 1995, pp. 2071–2071.

117. Constantinos Mavroidis and Steven Dubowsky, Optimal sensor location in motion control of flexibly supported long reach manipulators, *Journal of Dynamic Systems Measurement and Control*, vol. 119, pp. 726–726, 1999.

118. Dieter Vischer and Oussama Khatib, Design and development of high-performance torque-controlled joints, *IEEE Transactions on Robotics and Automation*, vol. 11, pp. 537–544, 1995.

119. Xiaoping Zhang, Wenwei Xu, Satish S. Nair, and Vijay Sekhar Chellaboina, PDE modeling and control of a flexible two-link manipulator, *IEEE Transactions on Control Systems Technology*, vol. 13, pp. 301–312, 2005.

120. Paul T. Kotnik, Stephen Yurkovich, and Umit Ozguner, Acceleration feedback control for a flexible manipulator arm, in *Proceedings of 1988 IEEE International Conference on Robotics and Automation*, Philadelphia, PA, April 24–29, 1988, pp. 181–196.

121. Yoshiyuki Sakawa, Fumitoshi Matsuno, Yoshiki Ohsawa, Makoto Kiyohara, and Toshihisa Abe, Modelling and vibration control of a flexible manipulator with three axes by using accelerometers, *Advanced Robotics*, vol. 4, pp. 42–51, 1989.

122. Farshad Khorrami and Shihua Zheng, An inner/outer loop controller for rigid-flexible manipulators, *Journal of Dynamic Systems Measurement and Control*, vol. 114, pp. 580–588, 1992.

123. Kourosh Parsa, Jorge Angeles, and Arun Misra, Estimation of the flexural states of a macro-micro manipulator using acceleration data, in *Proceedings of 2003 IEEE International Conference on Robotics and Automation*, Taipei, Taiwan, September 14–19, 2003, pp. 3120–3125.

124. Kenneth L. Hillsley and Stephen Yurkovich, Vibration control of a two-link flexible robot arm, in *Proceedings of 1991 IEEE International Conference on Robotics and Automation*, Sacramento, CA, April 9–11, 1991, pp. 261–280.

125. Kourosh Parsa, Jorge Angeles, and Arun Misra, Estimation of the flexural states of a macro–micro manipulator using point-acceleration data, *IEEE Transactions on Robotics*, vol. 21, pp. 565–573, 2005.

126. Roy Merrell and Mark A. Minor, Internal posture sensing for a flexible frame modular mobile robot, in *Proceedings of 2003 IEEE International Conference on Robotics and Automation*, Taipei, Taiwan, September 14–19, 2003, pp. 452–457.

127. Fumitoshi Matsuno, Eigclian Kim, and Yoshiyuki Sakawa, Dynamic hybrid position/force control of a flexible manipulator which has two degrees of freedom and flexible second link, in *Proceedings of 1991 International Conference on Industrial Electronics, Control and Instrumentation*, Kobe, Japan, October 28–November 1, 1991, pp. 1031–1036.

128. Kyungsang Cho, Nouriyuki Hori, and Jorge Angeles, On the controllability and observability of flexible beams under rigid-body motion, in *Proceedings of 1991 International Conference on Industrial Electronics, Control and Instrumentation*, Kobe, Japan, October 28–November 1, 1991, pp. 455–460.

129. Alessandro De Luca and Bruno Siciliano, Closed-form dynamic model of planar multilink lightweight robots, *IEEE Transactions on Systems Man and Cybernetics*, vol. 21, pp. 826–839, 1991.

130. Mark Whalen and H. J. Sommer III, Modal analysis and mode shape selection for modelling an experimental two-link flexible manipulator, *Robotics Research-1990, ASME Dynamics Systems Control Division*, vol. 26, pp. 47–52, 1990.

131. Toyoshiroh Inamura, Yoshitaka Morimoto, and Kenji Mizoguchi, Dynamic control of a flexible robot arm by using experimental modal analysis, *Transactions of the Japan Society of Mechanical Engineers*, vol. 33, pp. 634–640, 1990.

132. Vicente Feliu Batlle, Jose A. Somolinos, Andres J. Garcia, and Luis Sánchez, Robustness comparative study of two control schemes for 3-DOF flexible manipulators, *Journal of Intelligent and Robotic Systems*, vol. 34, pp. 467–488, 2002.

133. Clarence W. De Silva, *Mechatronics: An Integrated Approach*, CRC Press, Boca Raton, FL, 2004.

134. Omar A. A. Orqueda and Rafael Fierro, A vision-based nonlinear decentralized controller for unmanned vehicles, in *Proceedings of 2006 IEEE International Conference on Robotics and Automation*, Orlando, FL, May 15–19, 2006, pp. 1–6.

135. Zhiguang Zhong, Jianqiang Yi, Dongbin Zhao, and Yiping Hong, Novel approach for mobile robot localization using monocular vision, *Proceedings of SPIE*, vol. 5286, pp. 159–162, 2003.

136. Seung-Yong Kim, Kim Jeehong, and Chang-goo Lee, Calculating distance by wireless ethernet signal strength for global positioning method, in *Proceedings of SPIE*, Chongqing, China, September 20–23, 2005, pp. 60412H. 1–60412H. 6.

137. Kevin J. Krizman, Thomas E. Biedka, and Theodore S. Rappaportt, Wireless position location: Fundamentals, implementation strategies, and sources of error, in *Proceedings of IEEE 47th Vehicular Technology Conference*, Phoenix, AZ, May 4–7, 1997, pp. 919–923.

138. Simon J. Julier and Jeffrey K. Uhlmann, A non-divergent estimation algorithm in the presence of unknown correlations, in *Proceedings of 1997 American Control Conference*, Albuquerque, NM, June 4–6, 1997, pp. 2369–2373.

139. Pablo O. Arambel, Constantino Rago, and Raman K. Mehra, Covariance intersection algorithm for distributed spacecraft state estimation, in *American Control Conference*, Arlington, VA, June 25–27, 2001, pp. 4398–4403.

140. Thomas Dall Larsen, Karsten Lentfer Hansen, Nils A. Andersen, and Ole Ravn, Design of Kalman filters for mobile robots; evaluation of the kinematic and odometric approach, in *Proceedings of 1999 IEEE International Conference on Control Applications*, Kohala Coast, HI, August 22–27, 1999, pp. 1021–1026.

141. Johann Borenstein, Internal correction of dead-reckoning errors with a dual-drive compliant linkage mobile robot, *Journal of Field Robotics*, vol. 12, pp. 257–273, 1995.

142. Egor Paul Popov, *Engineering Mechanics of Solids*, Prentice Hall, Upper Saddle River, NJ, 1990.

143. Joono Cheong, Kyun Chung Wan, and Youngil Youm, PID composite controller and its tuning for flexible link robots, in *Proceedings of IEEE/RSJ International Conference on Intelligent Robots and Systems*, Lausanne, Switzerland, September 30–October 4, 2002, pp. 2122–2127.

144. Xiaoyun Wang and James K. Mills, A FEM model for active vibration control of flexible linkages, in *Proceedings of 2004 IEEE International Conference on Robotics and Automation*, New Orleans, LA, April 26–May 1, 2004, pp. 189–192.

145. Abdelhamid Tayebi, Mohamed Tadjine, and Ahmed Rachid, Invariant manifold approach for the stabilization of nonholonomic systems in chained form: Application to a car-like mobile robot, in *Proceedings of the 36th IEEE Conference on Decision and Control, 1997*, San Diego, CA, December 10–12, 1997, pp. 235–251.

146. Rafael Fierro and Frank L. Lewis, Control of a nonholonomic mobile robot: Backstepping kinematics into dynamics, in *Proceedings of the 34th IEEE Conference on Decision and Control*, New Orleans, LA, December 13–15, 1995, pp. 149–163.

147. Sheng Lin and A. Goldenberg, Robust damping control of wheeled mobile robots, in *Proceedings of 2000 IEEE International Conference on Robotics and Automation*, San Francisco, CA, April 24–28, 2000, pp. 2919–2924.

148. Z. P. Wang, Shuzhi Sam Ge, and Tong H. Lee, Robust motion/force control of uncertain holonomic/nonholonomic mechanical systems, *IEEE/ASME Transactions on Mechatronics*, vol. 9, pp. 118–123, 2004.

149. David G. Wilson and Rush D. Robinett, Robust adaptive backstepping control for a nonholonomic mobile robot, in *IEEE International Conference on Systems, Man, and Cybernetics*, Tucson, AZ, October 7–10, 2001, pp. 3241–3245.

150. Min-Soeng Kim, Jin-Ho Shin, and Ju-Jang Lee, Design of a robust adaptive controller for a mobile robot, in *Proceedings of 2000 IEEE/RSJ International Conference on Intelligent Robots and Systems*, Takamatsu, Japan, October 31–November 5, 2000, pp. 1816–1821.

151. Rafael Fierro and Frank L. Lewis, Control of a nonholonomic mobile robot using neural networks, *IEEE Transactions on Neural Networks*, vol. 9, pp. 589–600, 1998.

152. Rafael Fierro and Frank L. Lewis, Practical point stabilization of a nonholonomic mobile robot using neural networks, in *Proceedings of the 35th IEEE Conference on Decision and Control*, Kobe, Japan, December 11–13, 1996, pp. 1722–1727.

153. Yutake Kanayama, Yoshihiko Kimura, Fumio Miyazaki, and Tetsuo Noguchi, A stable tracking control method for an autonomous mobile robot, in *Proceedings of 1990 IEEE International Conference on Robotics and Automation*, Cincinnati, OH, May 13–18, 1990, pp. 384–389.

154. Sebastian Thrun, Wolfram Burgard, and Dieter Fox, *Probabilistic Robotics*, MIT Press, Cambridge, MA, 2005.

155. Hartmut Surmann, Andreas Nüchter, and Joachim Hertzberg, An autonomous mobile robot with a 3D laser range finder for 3D exploration and digitalization of indoor environments, *Robotics and Autonomous Systems*, vol. 45, pp. 181–198, 2003.

156. Zhuang Yan, Wang Wei, Wang Ke, and Xu Xiao-Dong, Mobile robot indoor simultaneous localization and mapping using laser range finder and monocular vision, *Acta Automatica Sinica*, vol. 31, pp. 925–933, 2005.

157. Christian Brenneke, Oliver Wuif, and Bernard Wagner, Using 3D laser range data for SLAM in outdoor environments, in *Proceedings of 2003 IEEE/RSJ International Conference on Intelligent Robots and Systems*, Las Vegas, NV, October 27–31, 2003, pp. 188–193.

158. Keiji Nagatani, Hiroshi Ishida, Satoshi Yamanaka, and Yutaka Tanaka, Three-dimensional localization and mapping for mobile robot in disaster environments, in *Proceedings of 2003 IEEE/RSJ International Conference on Intelligent Robots and Systems*, Las Vegas, NV, October 27–31, 2003, pp. 3112–3117.

159. Darius Burschka and Gregory D. Hager, V-GPS(SLAM): Vision-based inertial system for mobile robots, in *Proceedings of 2004 IEEE International Conference on Robotics and Automation*, New Orleans, LA, April 26–May 1, 2004, pp. 409–415.

160. Aldo Cumani, Sandra Denasi, Antonio Guiducci, and Giorgio Quaglia, Integrating monocular vision and odometry for SLAM, *WSEAS Transactions on Computers*, vol. 3, pp. 625–630, 2004.

161. Stefano Panzieri, Federica Pascucci, I. Santinelli, and Giovanni Ulivi, Merging topological data into Kalman based slam, in *Proceedings of 2004 World Automation Congress*, Seville, Spain, June 28–July 1, 2004, pp. 57–62.

162. Albert Diosi and Lindsay Kleeman, Advanced sonar and laser range finder fusion for simultaneous localization and mapping, in *Proceedings of 2004 IEEE/RSJ International Conference on Intelligent Robots and Systems*, Sendai, Japan, September 28–October 2, 2004, pp. 1854–1859.

163. Yong-Ju Lee and Jae-Bok Song, Three-dimensional iterative closest point-based outdoor SLAM using terrain classification, *Intelligent Service Robotics*, vol. 4, pp. 147–158, 2011.

164. Paul J. Besl and Neil D. Mckay, Method for registration of 3-D shapes, *IEEE Transactions on Pattern Analysis and Machine Intelligence*, vol. 14, pp. 239–256, 1992.

165. Andreas Nuchter, Hartmut Surmann, Kai Lingemann, Joachim Hertzberg, and Sebastian Thrun, 6D SLAM with an application in autonomous mine mapping, in *Proceedings of 2004 IEEE International Conference on Robotics and Automation*, New Orleans, LA, April 26–May 1, 2004, pp. 1998–2003.

166. Rainer Kümmerle, Rudolph Triebel, Patrick Pfaff, and Wolfram Burgard, Monte Carlo localization in outdoor terrains using multilevel surface maps, *Journal of Field Robotics*, vol. 25, pp. 346–359, 2008.

167. Patrick Pfaff, Rudolph Triebel, and Wolfram Burgard, An efficient extension to elevation maps for outdoor terrain mapping and loop closing, *International Journal of Robotics Research*, vol. 26, pp. 217–230, 2007.

168. Andreas Nüchter, Kai Lingemann, Joachim Hertzberg, and Hartmut Surmann, 6D SLAM with approximate data association, in *Proceedings of 2005 International Conference on Advanced Robotics*, Seattle, WA, July 18–20, 2005, pp. 242–249.

169. Andreas Nüchter, Kai Lingemann, Joachim Hertzberg, and Hartmut Surmann, 6D SLAM—3D mapping outdoor environments, *Journal of Field Robotics*, vol. 24, pp. 699–722, 2007.

170. Janusz Bedkowski and Andrzej Maslowski, On-line data registration in outdoor environment, in *Proceedings of 2011 International Conference on Methods and Models in Automation and Robotics*, Miedzyzdroje, Poland, August 22–25, 2011, pp. 266–271.

171. Xiaorui Zhu and Mark A. Minor, Terrain feature localization for mobile robots in outdoor environments, in *Proceedings of 2009 International Conference on Information and Automation*, Zhuhai, Macau, China, June 22–24, 2009, pp. 1074–1080.

172. Huan-huan Chen, Xing Li, and Wen-xiu Ding, Twelve kinds of gridding methods of surfer 8.0 in isoline drawing, *Chinese Journal of Engineering Geophysics*, vol. 4, pp. 52–57, 2007.

173. Frank Dellaert, Dieter Fox, Wolfram Burgard, and Sebastian Thrun, Monte Carlo localization for mobile robots, in *Proceedings of 1999 IEEE International Conference on Robotics and Automation*, Detroit, MI, May 10–15, 1999, pp. 1322–1328.

174. Christian Mandel and Tim Laue, Particle filter-based position estimation in road networks using digital elevation models, in *Proceedings of 2010 IEEE/RSJ International Conference on Intelligent Robots and Systems*, Taipei, Taiwan, October 18–22, 2010, pp. 5744–5749.

175. Zhengbin He and Yongrui Tian, Filtering algorithm for non-ground point from airborne laser scanner data, *Journal of Geodesy and Geodynamics*, vol. 29, pp. 97–101, 2009.

176. Szymon Rusinkiewicz and Maic Levoy, Efficient variants of the ICP algorithm, in *Proceedings of 2001 IEEE International Conference on 3-D Digital Imaging and Modeling*, Quebec City, QC, May 28–June 1, 2001, pp. 145–152.

177. Nabil M. Drawil, Haitham M. Amar, and Otman A. Basir, GPS localization accuracy classification: A context-based approach, *IEEE Transactions on Intelligent Transportation Systems*, vol. 14, pp. 262–273, 2013.

178. Philippe Bonnifait, Pascal Bouron, Paul Crubillé, and Dominique Meizel, Data fusion of four ABS sensors and GPS for an enhanced localization of car-like vehicles, in *Proceedings of 2001 IEEE International Conference on Robotics and Automation*, Seoul, South Korea, May 21–26, 2001, pp. 1597–1602.

179. Miguel Cazorla and Boyan Bonev, Large scale environment partitioning in mobile robotics recognition tasks, *Journal of Physical Agents*, vol. 4, pp. 11–18, 2010.

180. Xiaorui Zhu, Chunxin Qiu, and Mark A. Minor, Terrain inclination aided three-dimensional localization and mapping for an outdoor mobile robot, *International Journal of Advanced Robotic Systems*, vol. 10, pp. 257–271, 2013.

181. Xiaorui Zhu, Chunxin Qiu, and Mark A. Minor, Terrain-inclination based three-dimensional localization for mobile robots in outdoor environments, *Journal of Field Robotics*, vol. 31, pp. 477–492, 2014.

182. Danfei Xu, Hernan Badino, and Daniel Huber, Topometric localization on a road network, in *Proceedings of 2014 IEEE/RSJ International Conference on Intelligent Robots and Systems*, Chicago, IL, September 14–18, 2014, pp. 3448–3455.

183. András L. Majdik, Damiano Verda, Yves Albers-Schoenberg, and Davide Scaramuzza, Air-ground matching: Appearance-based GPS-denied urban localization of micro aerial vehicles, *Journal of Field Robotics*, vol. 32, pp. 1015–1039, 2015.

184. Benjamin Kuipers and Yung Tai Byun, A robot exploration and mapping strategy based on a semantic hierarchy of spatial representations, *Robotics and Autonomous Systems*, vol. 8, pp. 47–63, 1991.

185. Nicolas Vandapel, Raghavendra Donamukkala, and Martial Hebert, Experimental results in using aerial LADAR data for mobile robot navigation, in S. Yuta, H. Asama, E. Prassler, T. Tsubouchi, and S. Thrun, editors, *Springer Tracts in Advanced Robotics*, Springer, Berlin, Heidelberg, pp. 103–112, 2013.

186. Sebastian Thrun, Mike Montemerlo, Hendrik Dahlkamp, David Stavens, Andrei Aron, James Diebel et al., Stanley: The robot that won the DARPA Grand Challenge, *Journal of Field Robotics*, vol. 23, pp. 1–43, 2004.

187. Axel Lankenau and Thomas Rofer, Mobile robot self-localization in large-scale environments, in *Proceedings of 2002 International Conference on Robotics and Automation*, Washington, DC, May 11–15, 2002, pp. 1359–1364.

188. David M. Bradley, Rashmi Patel, Nicolas Vandapel, and Scott M. Thayer, Real-time image-based topological localization in large outdoor environments, in *Proceedings of 2005 IEEE/RSJ International Conference on Intelligent Robots and Systems*, Edmonton, AB, August 2–6, 2005, pp. 3670–3677.

189. Christoffer Valgren and Achim J. Lilienthal, SIFT, SURF and seasons: Long-term outdoor localization using local features, in *Proceedings of 2007 European Conference on Mobile Robots*, Freiburg, Germany, September 19–21, 2007.

190. Jianping Xie, Fawzi Nashashibi, Michel Parent, and Olivier Garcia Favrot, A real-time robust global localization for autonomous mobile robots in large environments, in *Proceedings of 2010 International Conference on Control Automation Robotics and Vision*, Singapore, December 7–10, 2010, pp. 1397–1402.

191. Ken Goldberg and Ben Kehoe, Cloud robotics and automation: A survey of related work, EECS Department, University of California, Berkeley, Technical Report. UCB/EECS-2013-5, 2013.

192. James Kuffner, Cloud-enabled robots, in *IEEE RAS International Conference on Humanoid Robotics*, Nashville, TN, December 6–8, 2010.

193. Rajesh Arumugam, Vikas Reddy Enti, Liu Bingbing, Wu Xiaojun, Krishnamoorthy Baskaran, Foong Foo Kong et al., DAvinCi: A cloud computing framework for service robots, in *Proceedings of 2010 IEEE International Conference on Robotics and Automation*, Anchorage, AK, May 3–7, 2010, pp. 3084–3089.

194. Luis Riazuelo, Javier Civera, and J. M. Martínez Montiel, C² TAM: A cloud framework for cooperative tracking and mapping, *Robotics and Autonomous Systems*, vol. 62, pp. 401–413, 2014.

195. Ben Kehoe, Akihiro Matsukawa, Sal Candido, James Kuffner, and Ken Goldberg, Cloud-based robot grasping with the google object recognition engine, in *Proceedings of 2013 IEEE International Conference on Robotics and Automation*, Karlsruhe, Germany, May 6–10, 2013, pp. 4263–4270.

196. Kevin Lai and Dieter Fox, Object recognition in 3D point clouds using web data and domain adaptation, *International Journal of Robotics Research*, vol. 29, pp. 1019–1037, 2010.

197. Guoqiang Hu, Wee Peng Tay, and Yonggang Wen, Cloud robotics: Architecture, challenges and applications, *IEEE Network*, vol. 26, pp. 21–28, 2012.

198. Lujia Wang, Ming Liu, and Max Q. -H. Meng, Towards cloud robotic system: A case study of online co-localization for fair resource competence, in *Proceedings of IEEE International Conference on Robotics and Biomimetics*, Guangzhou, China, December 11–14, 2012, pp. 2132–2137.

199. Herbert Bay, Andreas Ess, Tinne Tuytelaars, and Luc Van Gool, Speeded-up robust features, *Computer Vision and Image Understanding*, vol. 110, pp. 404–417, 2008.

200. Sean P. Engelson and Drew V. Mcdermott, Error correction in mobile robot map learning, in *Proceedings of 1992 IEEE International Conference on Robotics and Automation*, Nice, France, May 12–14, 1992, pp. 2555–2560.

201. Scott Lenser and Manuela Veloso, Sensor resetting localization for poorly modelled mobile robots, in *Proceedings of 2000 International Conference on Robotics and Automation*, San Francisco, CA, April 24–28, 2000, pp. 1225–1232.

Index

Printed in the United States
by Baker & Taylor Publisher Services